GIACOMO PUCCINI

GIACOMO PUCCINI
A youthful portrait

GIACOMO PUCCINI

THE MAN HIS LIFE HIS WORK

BY

RICHARD SPECHT *1870-1932*

TRANSLATED BY

CATHERINE ALISON
PHILLIPS

WITH SIXTEEN PAGES
OF ILLUSTRATIONS

GREENWOOD PRESS, PUBLISHERS
WESTPORT, CONNECTICUT

The Library of Congress cataloged this book as follows:

Specht, Richard, 1870–1932.
　　Giacomo Puccini; the man, his life, his work.　Translated by Catherine Alison Phillips.　Westport, Conn., Greenwood Press [1970]

　　　xvi, 256 p.　illus., facsims., ports.　23 cm.

　　　Reprint of the 1933 ed.
　　　Includes bibliographical references.

　　　1. Puccini, Giacomo, 1858–1924.

ML410.P89S61　1970　　　　782.1'0924　[B]　　　　72–100844
ISBN 0–8371–4030–7　　　　　　　　　　　　　　　　　　　MARC
Library of Congress　　　　　　　71 [7]　　　　　　　　　　MN

C.2

Originally published in 1933 by Alfred A. Knopf, New York

Reprinted in 1970 by Greenwood Press, Inc.,
51 Riverside Avenue, Westport, Conn. 06880

Library of Congress catalog card number 72-100844
ISBN 0-8371-4030-7

Printed in the United States of America

10 9 8 7 6 5 4 3 2

TO

ALMA MAHLER

INCOMPARABLE AS BOTH WOMAN AND FRIEND

THIS BOOK

IS AFFECTIONATELY AND ADMIRINGLY DEDICATED

'Small things, too, have power to charm us.'

HUGO WOLF, *Italian Song Book*.

TRANSLATOR'S NOTE

THE translator wishes to acknowledge the kind assistance of Miss Agnes Bedford and her great indebtedness to Mr. Eric Blom for his generous help. She also desires to thank Messrs. G. Ricordi and Co. for their courtesy in allowing her access to the vocal and other scores published by them, for their kind permission to quote the English libretti, of which they hold the copyright, and for leave to reproduce a facsimile of the MS. score of *La Bohème* from Arnaldo Fraccaroli's *Vita di Giacomo Puccini*, published by them.

INTRODUCTORY NOTE

THIS book represents an admission of error on the part of its author, and is, as such, an act of atonement and expiation.

For more than twenty years past my mind has been at work upon the problem presented by Giacomo Puccini, and all the contradictions and misunderstandings with which it is invariably accompanied, especially in countries of other than Latin [1] culture. For his own part, Puccini never regarded himself as a composer on the grand scale; he knew his own powers and their limitations to a nicety. 'I love small things,' he said repeatedly, 'and the only music I can or will make is that of small things . . . so long as they are true and full of passion and humanity, and touch the heart.' Yet often, even in his own country, and more especially in Germany—not only the Germany of years that are gone, either—he has been represented as the great corruptor, the very negation of an artist, a merely theatrical composer striving after nothing but effectiveness, and the incarnation of modern degeneracy and insincerity; and, to my shame be it spoken, I must confess that for a long time I, too, thought and spoke of him in exactly the same way, for it seemed to me impossible to reconcile the shameless theatricality of his libretti with artistic probity and purity, though these are so often to be found in his music. At last, however, it became evident to me that the cause of this strange

[1] TRANSLATOR'S NOTE.—The original text has 'lands of German culture' (*in deutschen Landen*). In this passage and a few similar ones, in which the author's remarks about the German public are also applicable to that of other countries in both northern Europe and North America, the translator has taken the liberty of substituting 'non-Latin', or some equivalent expression, for 'German'.

lack of focus in our views with regard to the composer and his work was an error of vision, due to a racial difference, which was therefore responsible for the imperfect, and often distorted conception that we had formed of his essential qualities as an artist. The Italian approaches the scenic element in an opera from a point of view totally different from that of the non-Latin peoples, who regard many things in Puccini's work as the crudest theatricality and a revolting sensationalism appealing to the lowest instincts. To a native of southern Europe all these things are never more than mere make-believe, the pretext for an outpouring of music of a passionate, poignant, elementally emotional and almost exhibitionist order. If it were not for this, what we are about to demonstrate in the following pages would have been an impossibility: the fact, that is, that Puccini, who, for all his apparent subtlety, remained throughout his whole life no more than a great child, could accept even such libretti as those of *Tosca* and *The Girl of the Golden West* as humanly and convincingly true, nay more, as appealing directly to both the soul and the temperament. He was a thorough Italian, and, in consequence, thoroughly naive and candid, and it is precisely to this cause that so many of the contradictory elements in his nature may be attributed. The task of finding a common denominator for all the factors going to make up this artistic unity, even though they may appear mutually destructive, or, at the very least, highly contradictory, attracted me quite as much as that of drawing a portrait of Puccini as an artist. Nor need I disguise the fact that mingling with these reasons was a certain curiosity, that prompted the author to determine exactly what were the reasons that, in the course of the last ten years, had modified his attitude towards the problem of Puccini and his estimate of that composer.

In addition to the criticisms that I am sure to incur on the score of certain quite intentional repetitions, due to what I may call the musical and symphonic construction of the present work, and on account of the unscientific character of the exposition—not to speak of the accusation of 'journalism', which no writer born and working in Vienna can hope to escape—I am further prepared for the accusation of lack of character and of denying my former principles, though what I am abjuring in this book is not a principle, but only a judgment that has become untenable. But I cannot believe that it is necessarily frivolous and superficial to strive for liveliness, colour, and attractiveness of form, or that it is better to be so dignified as to bore one's readers; nor do I believe that it is a sign of character to persist pig-headedly in a view that one has recognized to be false. On the contrary, I believe it to be a better proof of character to recognize one's error, and, so far as possible, make reparation for it.

Among the many people who have kindly lent me their assistance in the preparation of this book I have first of all to express my gratitude to the Master's children: Donna Fosca Leonardi-Puccini, who has helped me by informing me of a number of personal traits and episodes in the life of Puccini, and Signor Antonio Puccini, who has shown the greatest possible courtesy in kindly granting me access to the original drafts of the scores, as well as to letters, manuscripts, newspaper cuttings, and notes, together with his private collection of photographs and caricatures, and put himself to an amount of trouble that I cannot sufficiently acknowledge in assisting me to obtain illustrations. I have also to thank my father-in-law Ferdinand Pagin, till recently resident in Florence, for procuring me published material on the subject of Puccini that is obtainable only in Italy. And, in addition to the Universal Publishing Company of Vienna and its director Emil Hertzka, to whom I am indebted for the text and music of *La Rondine*. Last, but not least, I wish to thank the house of G. Ricordi and Co., which published the Master's works, and its director, Carlo Clausetti of Milan, Puccini's intimate friend, to whom I am indebted not only for communicating to me personally a number of biographical details, especially with regard to Puccini's last days, during the fatal illness that ended in his death, but also for placing at my disposal the conductor's scores and piano scores of Puccini's operas, giving me permission to consult the manuscript scores of these works, and also communicating to me publications to which it was difficult for me to have access. They have all had a share in the production of a book the writing of which has given me great pleasure. It will have achieved its object if it succeeds in communicating only a part of this pleasure to its readers, in bringing the figure of Giacomo Puccini nearer to them, and in awakening a real affection for him, born sometimes of admiration and sometimes of touched sympathy for his human qualities, his work as an artist and the vicissitudes of his life.

R. S.

Vienna,
       Summer 1931.

LIST OF WORKS CONSULTED

APART from a number of details personally communicated to me by word of mouth, my chief sources have been Puccini's works and their libretti, and, next to these, his letters, published under the title of *Epistolario*, by Giuseppe Adami (A. Mondadori, Milan, 1928), with admirable introductions; English translation by E. Makin, 1931; and *Giacomo Puccini intimo*, by his friends Guido Marotti and Ferruccio Pagni (Vallecchi, Florence, 1926). I have also made use of the following:

GINO MONALDI. *Giacomo Puccini e la sua opera* (Libreria editrice Mantegazza di Pietro Cremonese, Rome).

ARNALDO BONAVENTURA. *Giacomo Puccini. L'uomo—l'artista* (Raffaello Giusti, Leghorn).

VITTORIO GUI. *Giacomo Puccini*, article in *Il Pianoforte*.

ADOLF WEISSMANN. *Giacomo Puccini* (Drei Masken-Verlag, 1922).

OSCAR BIE. *Die Oper* (S. Fischer, Berlin, 1913).

JULIUS KORNGOLD. *Die romanische Oper der Gegenwart* (Rikola-Verlag, Vienna, 1922).

GEORG CAPELLEN. *Ein neuer exotischer Musikstil* (Verlag Carl Grüninger, Klett and Hartmann, Stuttgart).

Turandot. Published by the La Scala Opera-house on the occasion of the first performance of the work.

Also a large number of articles in Italian and foreign periodicals, which space does not permit me to enumerate.

R. S.

TABLE OF CONTENTS

LIST OF ILLUSTRATIONS

CHAPTER I

THERE is no success without a good reason. As Richard Strauss once said—in effect, if not in so many words: 'There are two kinds of work that make their way whatever happens: the creations of the very greatest masters, and utter trash (*absoluter Schund*)'. And for this reason, he maintained, there is no need to plead the cause of such music as falls under these categories, but rather of that composed by 'good masters' of the second rank, who are otherwise pushed aside. Yet, though Puccini's work has advanced on its career with such overwhelming force, it is neither that of a really great master, nor such as one may make bold to characterize as 'trash'—though some have been found to do even that. It is the work of a minor master of the first rank, a creator of delicate musical miniatures, melodies of a passionate melancholy, subtle harmonies with an individual distinction, and orchestration with a subtle and unerring magic, possessed, moreover, of a robust dramatic sense. It has qualities of quite a special order, which, however, are certainly not for the masses: it uses a dramatic musical method by which masses of colour and high lights are subtly touched in against a groundwork of *Leitmotive*, enhanced by a kaleidoscopic treatment of melody and a power of spontaneous thematic and melodic development, with a suggestion of improvisation which, when others attempt it, ends in blank failure. It produces its effects not by any irresistible unity between words and music, or any unambiguous characterization of the characters and their setting—for, granted the necessary changes in the words, many passages in *La Bohème*

B   I

(Bohemian Life), *Tosca*, *La Fanciulla del West* (The Girl of the Golden West), *Il Tabarro* (The Cloak), or *La Rondine* (The Swallow)—and by no means the worst of them, either—might easily be interchanged with one another and would suit the different dramatic situation equally well, or equally badly; so small is the extent to which this music is differentiated by any variety in the action or characters, or in the destinies of the latter. None but *Manon Lescaut*, *Madama Butterfly*, and the masterly *Turandot* are pervaded by something of the colour of their period and country, and even in these it is, as it were, illustrative, rather than an integral part of the picture. Seductively though it insinuates itself into the soul with its almost poignant sweetness and sensuousness, Puccini's melody has neither the mighty impact and plenitude of Verdi's music nor that clear, plastic, declamatory quality of which both Wagner and Strauss possessed the secret. His subject-matter has neither the legendary power, drawn from the depths of the national character, that makes it possible to represent on the stage things transcending ordinary life, nor the lofty, peculiarly noble poetic quality that characterizes the true work of art, bringing ravishment and release to the spirit and sending the hearer away with a sense of exaltation. Hence it is comprehensible that some should have been of the opinion that he appeals solely to the evil instincts of the masses, to those who find satisfaction in the sensationalism of the film, the 'shocker', and the popular melodrama, for whom his music merely provides another stimulus —at times, indeed, an over-stimulus—not due to any constructive or well-articulated quality, for it is, as it were, merely illustrative and exclamatory, though constantly reinforced by inspired melody. But this judgment is neutralized by the circumstance that musicians of serious standing have a respect for him; his essential qualities, his subtle touch, his wayward, insinuating, yet distinguished tone-colour, the poignantly sweet fragrance of his amorous *cantilena*, with its rush of soaring ardour, its subtle cruelty, and its power to sting the nerves. But not only do they esteem him, they also imitate him. Talents which from the first displayed such power as that of Eugen d'Albert fell entirely under his influence, masters of comedy possessing such a delicate constructive faculty as Ermanno Wolf-Ferrari abjured Rossini to become his disciples, and even musicians and artists of high seriousness, with aspirations quite out of the ordinary, such as Max von Schillings, and distinguished talents of a rich and elemental fullness such as that of Erich Wolfgang Korngold, have not succeeded in entirely resisting his seductive poison. Whence, we may ask, comes his prodigious, world-wide, irresistible, unique success, to which no other is comparable, for it surpasses them all, even that of Johann Strauss, and has lasted unimpaired for close upon forty years—a fact which is conclusive? Is it the strongly 'theatrical' element in Puccini's operas that produces such an overwhelming effect? It is certainly not that alone; for his music is equally triumphant in the concert-hall. Or is it due to the level of this infatuating music? Not exclusively so, certainly, strong as are the stimulants that are peculiarly its own. Perhaps we may succeed in discovering the factors that determine the curve of this universal success. We may, at any rate, make the attempt.

In the first place, though it has achieved success, this is only a qualified one. People, and even serious people, are fond of Puccini, but they do not profess allegiance to him, as they do to Wagner or Mahler or Richard Strauss. When men of merit confess their liking for his music, they always do so with a touch of embarrassment, just as they may be ardent readers of Eugène Sue or Conan Doyle without quite liking to admit it. So, too, where Puccini is concerned, they have to add a saving clause to the effect that, apart from his artful faculty of nervous titillation, what they value in him is the subtle, strange savour of those accessory elements which are not essential to his main purpose, but in which he proves the fastidiousness of his taste, so that, 'in spite of all', he is an artist. Though he produces his effects by crudities of the most brutal sort, he is none the less a highly subtle, cultured type with over-sensitive nerves, an epicure in melody of a positively sadic voluptuousness; nor is he at all robust in his music, even in such passages as those which give expression to tortures worthy of Red Indians; his are the frenzy of weakness goaded to exasperation, the brutality of an over-subtle brain, the crudity of a perverted sensibility. He assaults the nerves by jets of music charged with violent excitement, while at the same time caressing the revolting ganglia with every sort of anaesthetic, the result being to produce a sinfully voluptuous sense of gratification. Moreover, our personal impression is that he himself is absolutely unconscious of it all. He is thoroughly sincere and convinced that what he is transmuting into music are the simple human emotions, not the artful effects of the Grand Guignol; so that even amid his extremest refinements of exasperated excitation, he still remains artistically in a state of grace. He offers us film drama in its frankest and most uncompromising form, yet justifies it by the subtle eroticism of his music, the perfumed atmosphere of his harmonization, the almost unbearably exciting effect of his insistent motives, which produce a sort of *perpetuum mobile*, and the strange, sophisticated charm of his orchestral colour. This is poster art of the most blatant description, but painted with the most delicate water-colour technique, and often with genuine heart's blood. It is like some booth at a fair with Verlaine or Arthur Schnitzler acting as salesman—an impossible combination of qualities, but in this very fact lies the secret of his unexampled effectiveness. At times he stirs up the plebeian element in us, with which he deals like the aristocrat that he really is at heart. There is never anything coarse, vulgar, or offensively banal in his approach, but always a noble and fastidious delicacy, the quintessence, so to speak, of exquisite music; yet, easy of approach though his melody may be, it has nothing ostentatiously inviting about it, with the result that the touch of the plebeian in us has the irresistible gratification of feeling itself transformed by being drawn into the circle of what is distinguished and exclusive. Hence his world-wide fame. He flatters all our bad instincts, while at the same

time appeasing our conscience. This is his spell, from which
there is no escaping. He satisfies our need for sensation and
excitement, our perverted craving for the torturing and voluptuous, which finds its true atmosphere in the mingled fumes of
reeking blood and incense, our longing for primitive drama
and what is directly comprehensible, and he goads and hammers
upon our jaded nerves like a musical Scarpia and Cavaradossi
in one. He is at once the torturer and the tortured, and
evidently derives from this state a sublime ecstasy of over-
excitement. But at the same time he calms the uneasiness of
his listeners, whose most secret desires he thus gratifies; for
their snobbery will not allow them to feel this pleasing, yet
tormenting excitation to be quite legitimate, since it is not
seemly to give way to the primitive, cannibalistic impulses of
human nature, besides which they have, after all, been taught
that such subjects are highly crude and inartistic. But he
soothes their conscience by himself remaining refined and
exempt from banality, for he is as lavish of music as of blood,
and presents what is hideous under the most charming guise,
expressing the shrieks of the tortured creature with a crude
power that never fails to turn the cruel curiosity of the sensation-
loving public into genuine pity; for amid his most enchanting
blooms of melody there lurks a nameless dread, a sense of
ineluctable, ineffable pain. But, above all, he sets their minds
at rest, because, in spite of everything, his ideas are full of an
inimitable elegance, a quivering grace, and a sure feeling for
artistic tact and taste, which colours even the smallest phrase
with his personality; because he has his own peculiar, unforgettable note, and further, a bitter-sweet, gently irritating aroma
that is all his own, not only in his orchestration, but also in pure
tone and harmony, though this may often seem to have become
a mannerism, and though its ingredients may not be altogether
unobjectionable, suggesting as they do a blend of heliotrope,
stramonium, holy water, Spanish flies, and vitriol. In a word:
he wins favour because he is, after all, an artist in music and a
master of it, though he often composes music that is inartistic.

All this is, of course, abominable; but it is none the less irresistible, and we need not attempt to deny it.

The question we have to answer, then, is the following: whether this contradictory juxtaposition of eroticism, sadism, sentimentality, nerve-torture, and unbridled theatricality with a music that is persuasive, penetratingly melodious, and compounded of the most subtle poisons and burning love-philtres, is the cause of the unprecedented effect of these operas, which have triumphed over the whole world.   One thing seems certain: that for his own part, Puccini had to lash himself into a state of excitement through scenes of torment before he could become productive; that if he was to bring his most primitive and essential qualities to the surface, he had to rouse himself to a fearful, pitying horror at the sufferings of the figures he had created, and sympathize with them to such a point as himself to feel an almost physical and unendurable pain; that the sufferings of the characters in his dramas produced a shudder of perverted emotion in himself as well, which may well astonish us, as pointing to yet another contradiction in his healthy, thoroughly Italian nature, at home in the Tuscan country-side and with the type of humanity to be found there—all those things among which he constantly sought a refuge from town life.   But in the over-cultivated, spiritually anaemic, luxurious dwellers in great cities this emotion has nothing barbaric about it, but is a cruelly subtle nuance of voluptuous self-indulgence.   It is strange, and indeed puzzling, that even such a great, simple child as Puccini was, and remained throughout his whole life, should seem to have required a sadic stimulus to set his nerves vibrating and enable him to arrive at that note of sensuous exaltation and passionate sadness that is peculiarly his own, and penetrates the senses with such persuasive insistence, for ever crying out as in a voice choked with hot tears, and injecting into the soul, with a subtle stab, the opiate that lulls and yet inflames.   It is equally indubitable that he fails when he has to dispense with the stimulus of such a subject, as is evident in *La Rondine*. On the other hand, again, it is by no means certain that we are not here faced with a double self-deception, on the part of both composer and public, in supposing that Puccini really required to resort to such nerve-racking and flagellatory expedients. It remains the fact that *La Bohème*, with its simple, lovable figures, human and akin to ourselves, in which Mimi's death has nothing repellent even to the most sensitive, and does not offend our taste any more than, for instance, the corresponding scene in *La Traviata*, still remains the favourite among his works, and is likely to appeal to posterity more strongly than any of them. At any rate, it is clear that his attraction towards the horrible was not an indispensable element in Puccini's work; though it is certainly hard to decide whether his world-wide reputation would have suffered or been enhanced had this not been so. If we consider the eternal craving of the masses for excitement, we are drawn towards the former supposition, but we incline toward the latter when we consider that, had this dash of the melodramatic been absent from his work, the troubadour element in Puccini, whose most lasting and beautiful creations were in the form of feminine self-sacrifice and long-suffering love, would perhaps have won an even more heartfelt affection, aroused an even purer and more intimate emotion, in those feminine circles that were the predestined partisans of his music and the human characters he created. However that may be, there seems no question that Puccini's still growing influence in all five continents of the globe, which has gone on unchecked for decades past, and is, in many ways, still on the increase, rests far more upon all that is intimate, tenderly melancholy, heart-stirring, and poignant in his music than upon those explosive attacks which may carry one away with far greater vehemence and power at the moment, but whose effect usually subsides with equal rapidity. Only a slight impression of them lingers on the mind, and nothing but a questionable after-taste remains to remind us of all that is painful—not the quivering after-vibrations set up by a destiny into whose experiences we have ourselves been projected, but at most a few bars of one of those wildly convulsive, feverishly ardent, hysterically sweet melodies, that capture the ear with such uncontrollable violence and cling to it so insinuatingly, but seldom penetrate any further than the ear; whereas the former class of his melodies weave their ineluctable spells till they penetrate to the very soul, sometimes with a childlike trustfulness and a shy hesitation; after which, detaching themselves from the fate of the characters who sing them, they ensconce themselves in the memory and linger on in the listener's mind with a life of their own. In view of all these considera-tions, it will be no easy matter to make up our minds whether the dazzling, triumphant progress of Puccini's operas is to be attributed to their own rare qualities, to the spell cast by his personality as an artist and the elusive magic of his inspired 'music of small things', or to the coarse-fibred quality of his subjects, with their situations worthy of the film, the stifled shrieks that he turns to song, and the gratification, without any dangerous reactions, of the blood-lust common to humanity, which, from the beginning of its days, has always found the same secret pleasure in tortures, and in gloating over the writhings of helpless victims. Possibly it is to be attributed to both.

But the time has come to respond to the demands of honesty, and raise the question whether all that we have said above is really true. It is certainly true for the non-Latin peoples only. German-speaking countries cannot be satisfied with an operatic composer, even one with the most powerful talent, if he confines himself solely to what is obvious, directly comprehensible, and eloquent in music, together with the scenic element, without pressing forward into the regions of the mind, however strikingly attractive and delightful the music, and however thrilling and breathlessly exciting the dramatic action may be. An Italian musician, and, what is more, a Tuscan, deeply rooted in the rich soil of his home-land, would feel the utmost astonishment if confronted with all these distinctions. The Teuton suffers with the figures in a drama, even if they are mere puppets; he cries out at the torture of Cavaradossi, he feels round his own neck the rope that is to throttle the noble brigand

Ramerrez, he shares poor Mimi's fever, and heaves a sigh of relief at the murder of Scarpia. But to Italians all this is mere make-believe; they murder for sport and threaten torture as a pastime, and do not feel these things to be realities. From ancient days they have been addicted to the pleasures of the eye and ear, and the old traditions of comedy imply a sane conception of these as entirely unreal, as a mere dramatic recreation, a heightening of vital enjoyment by what is only fiction; in fact, the more furious and frightful the action, the better. But above all, the story, whether veristic or fantastic, is the pretext for music; the points to which the Italians attach importance are brilliance of invention, enthralling melody, and the finish of the singer's performance, and not even the most powerful plot or the most convincing performance will save either the composer or the singers from being hissed if the music is felt to be hackneyed or lacking in beauty, or if the singer has sung a note flat. No Italian ever lost his appetite through seeing *Tosca*; whereas in Germany it is striking to observe how empty the buffet always is after the second act. The difference here is a racial one, bound up with the whole attitude of different countries towards the theatre, and this has to be recognized. My own belief is in salvation through the Wagnerian gospel of art; but I no longer believe it to be the only way of salvation. It was in Italy that I first learnt to modify my exaggeratedly German attitude towards modern opera, and to revise many ideas that I had supposed to be firmly established. It was there, too, that I first learnt to take another, and, as I believe, a fairer view of the phenomenon of Puccini, and to form a juster estimate of him.

CHAPTER II

Oh com' è dura
la vita mia!
eppur a molti
sembro felice.
Ma i miei successi?
Passano . . . e resta
ben poca cosa.
Son cose effimere:
La vita corre,
va verso il baratro. . . .[1]

GIACOMO PUCCINI (1923).

IT was about the beginning of the twenties, in 1921 or 1923
—I cannot recall which—in the resplendently illuminated hall
of one of the great hotels on the Ringstrasse, Vienna. A
brilliant gathering had assembled, and intellectual Vienna was
present to a man, especially all which that city contains in the
way of musicians and singers.   (With one exception, however;
Richard Strauss was absent.)   They had all come to do honour
to the Maestro, Giacomo Puccini, who had arrived for the first
performance of his *Trittico* (Triptych), consisting of *Il Tabarro*,
Suor Angelica (Sister Angelica), and *Gianni Schicchi*, and had
also in view a performance of his *Tosca*, with Maria Jeritza in the
title role.   He was now resting in an arm-chair, a little weary,
with a happy sparkle in his fine, dark eyes, veiled from time to
time by their heavy lids, and with a pleasant smile on his
fastidious mouth, often drawn into an expression of melancholy

---

[1] Ah! How hard is my life! And yet to many I seem happy.   But my
successes? They pass away, and there remains but little. They are ephemeral
things. Life slips away and descends swiftly towards the abyss.

10

irony, and scarcely concealed by the soft, full moustache. The Master had constantly, however, to rise from his comfortable seat, for everybody there desired to be presented to him, to speak a word of gratitude and affection, shake hands with him, or carry away a few words from him on some such subject as his musical impressions of Vienna, or his next opera. On this occasion I, too, was permitted to hold his slender, powerful hand in mine and listen to his cordial voice, observing from its slightly veiled tones that on good days it was a *voce bruna* (deep voice), a cheerful, ringing baritone, though capable on occasion of a harsh abruptness. Even during an animated conversation, however, its full, healthy ring was damped by a huskiness foreshadowing the insidious disease that, within so terribly short a time, was to snatch him, all unaware, from his equally unsuspecting friends. It may be observed in passing that his finely shaped, thoroughly manly hand, with its long, musical fingers, though very well kept, was not altogether irreproachable, but suggested the suspicion that, like so many of his fellow-musicians, he bit his nails during moments of nervous impatience or tormenting doubt while meditating over his composition—a surmise in which I was correct. Any one who desires to call up the image of a striking personality at some subsequent time knows that such a handclasp, together with the characteristic timbre of the voice, however irrelevant the words uttered by it, bring one closer to the magic of the living being, and, without any rational explanation, throw more light upon the secret of his work, than all critical analysis or the fullest accounts of him derived from hearsay. Such a statement admits of no proof; but, not for the first time, I felt the indisputable truth of it as I listened to Puccini's voice and was able to look into his frank, noble countenance, only occasionally clouded by a distressing languor, with the vigorous chin and bold brow round which clustered the thick brown hair slightly touched with grey. It was a face that need not necessarily have belonged to an artist, though it was unquestionably that of a man of breeding, with an active brain, easily kindled

sensibilities, and an eager receptivity, at once shy and conscious
of his own worth, full of strong vitality, sensuous curiosity, and
an instinctive repugnance for all that is vulgar; a man, too, in
whom primitive, popular elements were combined with a subtle
culture, an unconstrained *naïveté* with the acquired exterior of
a man of the world and a dash of eternal youthfulness that made
an enchanting mixture.

On the occasion to which I have referred, after the tumultuous
cordiality with which his new work had been received, and amid
a throng of radiant women and a crush of fashionable enthusiasm
—which, next to a primitive existence amid the solitudes of
nature, was what appealed most to the Maestro, perhaps by
very reason of the contrast, though, at the same time, he always
felt it disturbing and irksome—Puccini talked in the most
animated and interesting way on every conceivable subject, for
the most part in French, and, whenever possible, in his native
Italian of Tuscany; for his store of German did not go far
beyond such phrases as *Auf Wiedersehen! Guten Tag*, and
Kotelette mit Kartoffeln [1] (Cutlet with potatoes), and his English
was, if anything, even more defective, if such a thing can be
imagined. He spoke courteously and with extreme animation,
yet often as though with a slight constraint, quite comprehensible
to those who knew his love of the open air and his passion for
sport, his repugnance for all stiff formality, and his robust
delight in strong language, though it may, too, have been due
to his limitations as a linguist. When Puccini had to hunt
for a word too long, he had a way of snapping his fingers
irritably, with a comical gesture as though he were trying to
catch a fly. He was correspondingly polite in acknowledging
any assistance, after which he would continue the conversation
with heightened animation. He expressed his extreme gratification at the performance of his *Trittico* and the reception with
which it had met—which, from such a severe critic, who was

[1] TRANSLATOR'S NOTE.—*Kotelette mit Kartoffeln.* Fraccaroli (*Vita di G. P.*)
relates that this was the only dish on the menu that Puccini could understand
during his first visit to Vienna, so that he lived on cutlets with potato all the time.

scarcely ever satisfied, must certainly have meant something. He spoke enthusiastically of Madame Jeritza, who had been magnificent, he said, in *Il Tabarro*, but most of all as Tosca, and had little need to fear a rival; yet even here he could not entirely silence the ever-vigilant voice of his rigorous artistic conscience, which was never quite appeased. In spite of all he found to praise in her performance, he had the same objection to make to this Tosca as Hans Sachs makes to Walther: that is, that she was 'a little free with the melody',[1] and that, in her prayer-scene in particular, she had at times sacrificed pure singing to her dramatic rendering—though this was unjust, for on a subsequent occasion the irritable composer managed to find fault with her for sacrificing dramatic expression to over-correct singing. As a matter of fact Puccini was a peculiarly inexorable, and not always a very amiable judge of his conductors and singers, and his exaggerated demands and unmitigated candour often made the rehearsals an ordeal dreaded by everybody. He may often have had cause to regret such remarks as I have quoted, when he let them fall outside the theatre and his own particular sphere of work, for they were possibly repeated in an exaggerated and distorted form. On that evening, indeed, he seemed to have felt that his uncompromising expression of his objections, in spite of the fact that they were subjectively justified, was rather ungracious and hypercritical; for he excused himself with a laugh for his insuperable tendency to speak his mind, which had sometimes led to the most comical situations. And he related—with more complacence than regret, it must be confessed—how, after rather a deplorable performance of *Tosca*, he had had to shake hands with the conductor for the sake of form. The good man, who knew about as much Italian as Puccini did German, bowed with a flattered expression after every word, quite unaware that the Maestro, smiling grimly, was accompanying each handshake with the words: 'Rogue! Beast! Bandit! Murderer! Executioner! Cur!' and

---

[1] TRANSLATOR'S NOTE.—*Die Meistersinger*, Act iii, sc. 1: 'nur mit der Melodei seid ihr ein wenig frei'.

finally dismissed him with the winning assurance that 'If only
we were in Italy, I would have you shot in place of Cavaradossi!'
Yet on the following day the worthy conductor could not stop
talking about the enthusiastic eulogies showered upon him by
the delighted Master. When an indiscreet inquirer asked
whether this incident had not taken place in Vienna, the mis-
chievous musician merely responded with a delightfully sly and
knowing wink; so that, from a supposition, it became almost a
certainty that the hero of the incident was the same doughty
wielder of the baton who had once, in all seriousness, given me
his word of honour that he was a first-class conductor, and, on
another occasion, assured me that he would be capable of
achievements at least equal to those of Toscanini, if only he
could be given the same opportunities for rehearsal—an incredible piece of self-sufficiency, which quite ignored the fact
that the power of a great personality, and the qualities that make
it what it is, are shown precisely by insisting upon these opportunities, whereas the impotence of the smaller man lies precisely
in the fact that he is unable to obtain them. But we can well
imagine the sufferings of a composer with such over-acute
sensibilities as Puccini, who had exactly calculated and weighed
every accent, the value of every note and every nuance of timbre,
when his work was handed over to the elementary musical
capacities and unholy stupidity of such a conductor, as wooden
as a second-rate bandmaster, eaten up with his own importance
and utterly incapable of any of the subtler and more exquisite
shades of interpretation.

On that same evening it was plainly evident to every one
not already aware of Puccini's keen interest in the compositions
of the day that, for all his unbounded admiration of Beethoven
and Wagner, he felt a lively curiosity with regard to present-
day musicians. He spoke with a natural shrewdness, in his
unaffected fashion, about Stravinsky and Debussy, who, as he
always freely acknowledged, had exerted a decisive influence on
his own harmonic and melodic style, though this was cast in a
new and personal mould. He took the most vigilant interest

in both of them, but not so much in Richard Strauss, though
this feeling was mutual. He was most anxious to acquaint
himself more thoroughly with Arnold Schönberg's work, and
asked to be informed where, during his visit to Vienna, he
could hear something by this composer, who had provoked so
much controversy by his abrupt departure from the musical
traditions of the day. On receiving the answer, 'Nowhere',
he somewhat testily expressed his regret at having visited Vienna
at such an inauspicious time; but in this he was mistaken, for
he could never have come to Vienna at any but an inauspicious
moment where Schönberg was concerned—and this is still true
to-day. Among the musicians of the rising generation young
Erich Korngold seemed to him the most attractive figure; which
would tend to confirm the authenticity of the remark that he is
reported to have made after a performance of Korngold's *Die
tote Stadt*: 'The fellow has so much talent that he could safely
give some of it to the others and still have enough left for himself'; while the positively affectionate regard that Puccini felt
for Franz Lehár—which, in spite of the different intellectual planes
on which the two artists existed, may have been based upon an
undeniable affinity between their natures, expressed in the melancholy, sensuous aroma of their music, and the amorous sweetness
of their seductively worldly and somewhat luscious melody—
was almost touchingly apparent when the two most successful
composers of our day for the theatre were together, like two
sovereigns doing the honours to each other with modest dignity.

Those who saw Puccini on that evening, at a time when death
had already sealed him as its own, carried away an impression
of a highly luxurious dweller in great cities, inordinately spoilt
by the ladies, somewhat capricious, and rather indifferent to
his own fame, though not in the least blasé, who associated on
the same easy footing with kings and peasants, and had long
since lost the power of being astonished, whether at the marvels
of life or at those of nature. Even when young he had never
had the sun-clear, seeing eye for these, in spite of his passion
for sport and the fact that he simply could not bear to live

anywhere but in the country.   Any one seeing him on that
evening could not but say to himself that he could hardly have
imagined the creator of *Manon Lescaut*, *La Bohème*, *Tosca*, and
Butterfly as being otherwise.   Yet this impression, though just,
is none the less deceptive.   For that occasion was not such as
to reveal the fundamental traits of Puccini's nature, but only
the product of the conditions inevitably surrounding a much-
fêted operatic composer, who is expected to be familiar with
the usages and manners of society and to possess a certain
intellectual aristocracy, yet who has also to maintain an attitude
of superiority in his struggle with the preposterous material
conditions of the theatre, the intrigues of the green-room and
the rivalries of the theatrical world, as childish as it is cunning,
whose conspiracies with the press have, moreover, a certain
danger.   This superior attitude was hardly to be acquired by
associating with peasants and shepherds, or even with jolly
painters and prudent revenue officers; yet in spite of this,
throughout the whole of the Master's life it was such society
as this that he always preferred and found most congenial.   He
was never fond of society; shy to the core and essentially helpless
as he was, he always felt constrained and ill at ease among the
bourgeoisie, and even in artistic circles in the town.   In particular when he had to appear at a banquet, and especially when
he had to make an after-dinner speech—which he found the
greatest difficulty in stammering out, even when he had notes,
jotted down with the utmost brevity—his annoyance and despair
knew no bounds.   He loved to mix with his friends and with
simple men in an atmosphere of unpretentious jollity, and in
such company he could feel quite at his ease.   Here, among the
uncultured residents of Torre del Lago and Viareggio, his two
beloved retreats, he was the best and most care-free of companions, for he had escaped from the 'great Puccini', the part
that he had to play outside in the world—though, as a matter
of fact, he did not do so.   Here he took part in every prank,
nor did these spare even his own person; he smoked like a
chimney, indulged in strong language to his heart's content,

helped the needy, and felt quite at home. Yet amid all this fraternal simplicity and easy jollity he was alone, thanks to his insuperable melancholy and the artist's life that isolated him; but it was only here that he could breathe, and only here that he could create. Life in the great artistic centres would have been the ruin of him; here, among his intimates, either shooting water-fowl, a sport for which he had what almost amounted to a monomania, or fishing or making excursions in his motorboat, he was entirely himself, and managed to endure even those periods which he execrated so furiously, when the lack of a suitable libretto condemned him to enforced and despairing inaction. He insisted that his friends, whom he formed into a 'La Bohème Club' at Torre del Lago and a 'Gianni Schicchi Club' at Viareggio, should appear at his house every evening, there to smoke, drink, and play cards. Curiously enough these hours were his favourite time for work. He did not feel the presence of his friends in the least disturbing; on the contrary, it was a stimulus to him, and if by chance they suddenly became aware that he was in a creative mood, and fell into an awed silence, hanging upon some chord struck by the Master on the little cottage piano, he would fly into a rage, hurl some vigorous epithet at them, and ask them to go on arguing and talking, without bothering about him; 'otherwise,' he would say, 'I feel as if you were listening to me, and that makes me ill!' Whereupon the squabble over politics or a game of cards that had got into a muddle would be resumed, and those engaged in it would once more disappear amid heavy clouds of tobacco. Puccini had, moreover, a curious habit: in spite of his unusually thick hair, he almost always kept his hat on, even in the house, and while working at the piano or his writing-table. One might almost have thought that he went to bed in his favourite felt hat, whose dented form is now gradually fading into oblivion: but I feel sure that during those hours when he was committing to paper the heart-rending orchestral epilogue to *La Bohème* or the ominous strains that accompany the execution in the third act of *Tosca*, he bared his head.

c

As a matter of fact, he had a thoroughly primitive nature, and it is this very quality, combined with his fastidious artistic taste, his sensitive touch, his refined sense of the dramatic, and the delicacy of his meticulous miniaturist's art, that lends his figure its attractively contradictory stamp. If we read the *Epistolario*, containing his collected letters, and pass in review the imposing accumulation of anecdotes about him that have been handed down by word of mouth or in writing, setting apart the fact that the letters are to a large extent concerned with performances of his operas, and business arrangements connected with them, we are struck by their unintellectual quality, and even commonness of expression, not to speak of a cheap, or at best, free-and-easy delight in horse-play, worthier of the president of a skittle-club than of the master of a highly individual art, far removed from all that is plebeian and hack-neyed. Nor can this side of his nature be explained as due merely to an incapacity for precise and clearly-formulated language, or to his dread of betraying the innermost thoughts of his soul. Only rarely can we detect in them the voice of an artist's hopes or despondencies, a passing expression of proud confidence or anxious doubt while a new work is coming into being, or a burst of despairing objurgations provoked by his dependence upon his accursed librettists, whom he was con-stantly coaxing or goading into activity, yet who were always too slow and never produced as much as he required. Even those entirely pleasing traits that are vouched for, such as his simplicity, sincerity, and good-heartedness, his often very blunt straightforwardness, his good humour and fits of gloom, the charity which he practised in secret—even the mad pranks and youthful jests into which he entered up to the last—do not seem the inevitable attributes of a man to whom, in his mature years, we owe a work of the scintillating intensity, uncanny, fantastic glamour, and compelling mastery of *Turandot*. He may, in fact, be one of those who, though hearing the dictates of the creative faculty, and lavishly endowed at the supreme moment with the gifts that come from the Unconscious, none the less spend their hours of conscious human life in an existence that is divorced from their artistic functions, and have neither the desire nor the capacity to ascend into their own, or any other intellectual sphere during their everyday life, or to range through the world of ideas, eager both to give and take, thus heightening their own powers, and not leaving the maturing of their creative faculties in the hands of nature alone. Possibly he is one of those whose instinctive vital impulses condition his productivity, yet at the same time bar his way into the sphere of intellect. This assertion is easily made, yet it does not quite meet the case. In this connexion we are bound to recall the fact that Puccini wrote verses full of genuine feeling, such as those quoted at the beginning of this chapter, touching verses, which express in affecting terms his consciousness of the vanity of outward life, his contempt for fame and his lasting and insuperable melancholy. We cannot but recall that, after the completion of *Manon Lescaut*, this very composer, who is reproached for his unscrupulous theatricality, worthy of the cinema, wished to compose music for a tragedy on the subject of Buddha; and that this same notorious striver after effectiveness made every possible effort to rid himself of the professional librettists, and to induce poets of outstanding merit to collaborate with him in his operas. D'Annunzio, Maeterlinck, Émile Zola, Verga, and Alphonse Daudet were only a few of those approached by Puccini, unfortunately without success, in his unending, but always unsatisfied quest for really poetical operatic texts. Yet in spite of this, he did not content himself with the clumsy journeyman work and commonplace style of the ordinary run of librettists; nay more, he might often himself claim credit for the choice of a subject, the main lines of the dramatic situations, and the grouping of the scenes; often, too, as in *The Girl of the Golden West*, for devising and constructing a whole act, and, further, for a leading share in the shaping of the text. With the daemonic energy and virtuosity of Luigi Illica, that practised writer for the theatre, he associated the more tender vein of the dramatist Giuseppe Giacosa; while in shaping the drafts of his operas he subsequently adopted as literary collaborators a few clever, subtle, and unspoilt literary brains, foremost among them Giuseppe Adami, who had a clear appreciation of his own capacity and was not lacking in imagination. Those who know what an active part Puccini took in perfecting the words for his operas, and how he harassed the compilers of his opera-books, constantly finding fault, encouraging, stimulating, and urging them on till they reached the utmost attainable conciseness, power, and logical connexion between the scenes, and wringing from them the greatest possible perfection in this type of text, cannot but admit that, in this respect, the *Trittico* and *Turandot* are like metal refined in the fire and possess a noble maturity that would have been quite unattainable to an artist of an unintellectual order.

If we next proceed to inquire to what extent and in what fashion all these human contradictions have found expression in Puccini's music, the answer to this question will at first cause us some embarrassment; for at first sight it would seem as though the Puccini of every day and Puccini the musician lived separate lives, each going his own way, and having no essential features in common. In his highly cultivated music, blended of the finest essences from a witches' kitchen that is at once exquisite and abominable, it would be hard to find the Tuscan, born of a good, strong, healthy stock, but with no over-refined grace of body, who in ordinary life was a good-hearted companion, always ready for a jest, and ready, too, to help, though sometimes far from tolerant, and who, even in his later years, when discovered on some illicit adventure, whether sporting or amorous, had something of the defiant but embarrassed school-boy about him. We must still try to distinguish every characteristic, whether positive or negative, of his personality as a man if we are to succeed in establishing that connexion between the creative artist and the Puccini of real life, without which a genuine and permanent work of art remains unthinkable.

First and foremost it must be laid down that there was not a single trace of the revolutionary in Puccini, in which he stood

in great contrast with most of his fellow-countrymen, and
especially the artists among them, and in complete contrast
with Verdi, in particular, who was incomparably the greater and
more productive genius of the two, with his elemental force
and red-hot blaze of passion, and a revolutionary even in his
subjects, as well as in his flaming choruses with their tocsin-like
ring, and the blood-red colour of his glowing melodies, with
the result that the performance of his works was prohibited over
and over again; both in his youth and his maturity they suggest
the flapping of flags and the wild, fiery, rousing dithyrambs of
liberty that arose from a rejuvenated Italy. He is the Garibaldi
of music. Puccini stood entirely apart from politics, being a
convinced supporter of the legitimate monarchy; but the affairs
of political and public life left him quite unmoved. All he
wanted was to discover good texts for operas, and, in the
tranquil seclusion of Torre del Lago, to live for the work that
he loved so passionately. Not even his *Inno a Roma*, the Hymn
that he addressed to Rome in its character as the Eternal City,
the great symbol, and not as the actual Italian capital, which
he could not endure—not even this hymn had a trace of revolt
or of Latin liberty in its composition. Its themes suggest
neither the red shirt nor the black. On one occasion he even
had an interview with Mussolini, a figure who had a powerful
fascination for him, and with whom he desired to shake hands;
but the conversation was confined exclusively to the subject
of a grandiose reform of the theatrical and operatic system.
He attached no importance to orders and decorations, and, while
still quite a young man, he made merry over the Cavaliere's
cross that he had just received. Again, though his nomination
as a senator, which took place a few weeks before his death,
caused him sincere pleasure, he preferred a few days later to
sign himself 'Suonatore del Regno' rather than 'Senatore'—
the chosen musician of the Kingdom of Italy rather than its
chosen senator. Nor had Puccini anything anarchical about
him as a musician, though he kept a vigilant look-out for every
sign of a new tendency in his art, and made an interesting and

piquant application of many daring experiments in harmony, rhythm, and tone-colour, as well as of other and more essential and intimate modes of expression, by adapting them to his own individual musical idiom. But in all this there was nothing revolutionary, and in music he always remained an evolutionist.

There is no denying that a trace of cruelty lurked in some secret corner of his soul. His mania for sport would alone bear witness to this, and so would his tendency to treat crude subjects and scenes of torture. I have already drawn attention to the fertilizing effects of the commotion set up in his sensitive nervous system by scenes such as that of the double torture, the murder of Scarpia and the execution in *Tosca*, the last of which, though ostensibly a sham, is really such a grim reality, or the scene of threatened torture and the game of poker played with a man's life as the stake in *The Girl of the Golden West*, or Butterfly's *hara-kiri*, the severed heads in *Turandot*, or the scene of the strangling in *Il Tabarro*, and pleasing events of that sort; and I have suggested that this sadic stimulus may obviously be interpreted as the reaction upon his music of a corresponding element in his nature, and that he positively required such flagellatory and pathological sexual stimulation in order to rise to the act of creation. Even when he tried to tear himself entirely away from tragic horror, and abandon himself to the most exuberant mirth, as in *Gianni Schicchi*, that sparkling masterpiece of modern *buffo* art, there must be some buffoonery over a corpse, if no more, to act as the occasion for his most wayward and witty humour. And if it be objected that all this is only preliminary by-play, intended to set the action of the drama going, we are forced to answer that an operatic composer's choice of a subject is not merely an expression of his will, for which he is responsible, but also a fateful and predestined decision from which it is permissible to draw conclusions in interpreting his personality, which cannot be separated from the characters he creates and their experiences; for these go beyond mere dream, being closely connected with the possibilities of his own real nature, so that in them he may

see, often with a shudder of horror, the reflection of his most
secret and mysterious promptings, and perhaps, too, a release
from his dark impulses through embodying them in the artistic
image.   There can be no doubt that, in this sense, it is almost
possible to draw conclusions with the illuminating precision of
a horoscope with regard to the character of a dramatist or a
dramatic composer as a man.

But in this particular instance such a conclusion would be open
to objection as being not only one-sided, but apt to mislead us
so far that the image we form of him will be a false one, unless
we study the whole complex from a diametrically opposite point
of view as well.   And at this point we have first to consider
whether the process by which Puccini was enabled to produce
his work is really to be sought exclusively in the reaction upon
an over-cultured nervous system produced by the brutality of a
drama consisting mainly in effective situations, and having none
of the effect of deliverance and relaxation of tension produced
by the great writers of tragedy, but having as its only result
to enervate the spectator, whose nervous resistance is beaten
down by an accumulation of horrors; or whether it is not rather
based upon an emotional appeal, a poignant sympathy for all
that is defenceless, frail, suffering, and sickly, for pathetic
creatures sacrificed to unscrupulous greed and inhuman on-
slaughts of violence, for graceful weakness that is unable to
cope with the brutalities of life and succumbs to them, as well
as for self-abnegating devotion defending itself in vain against
the blows of ruthless power and its myrmidons, and seeking
refuge in death rather than resign itself to the infamous abuses
of arrogant officialdom.   Needless to say, these are usually
feminine figures, forced to recognize the futility of revolt against
blind, inexorable destiny and human violence; though Des
Grieux, Rodolfo and Cavaradossi fall under this category as
well.   But above all, it is the childish and fragile, the brave and
patient, those who, though willing to struggle, are none the less
laid low, as well as the purely passive feminine figures, frivolous
and tender, such as Mimi or Cho-Cho-San, Tosca or Suor

Angelica, Manon, or even Minnie—though she does triumph in the end—who cry out most loudly for help against the baseness of the social order and its consequences, against their helplessness in the face of selfish, irresponsible cowardice and the vengeful, lustful attacks of man, who sets up as their judge and executioner. It is not till *Turandot* that a change is apparent: here the high-spirited, intellectually superior man, inspired by the purest love, and preferring to die rather than renounce a pure consummation of it, is faced by the icy, cunning cruelty of the woman with her unfeeling hardness—a cruelty, moreover, that is shown to be no more than perverted desire and love. It must be confessed that Puccini's most irresistible power is to be found in this very point: in the shriek of the tortured creature, the sense of paralysing dread before the approach of a horror as yet concealed, but creeping nearer and nearer with an ominous certainty, and the way in which the silent threat of disaster gradually makes itself heard in the music, already casting its shadow over hours of apparently unmenaced happiness, and people as yet blissfully unconscious of its approach. In such situations as these his music has a paralysing insistence from which we cannot escape. It consists in his gift, which almost defies analysis, for suggesting the cloud that hangs over love's innocent dalliance and sunshiny brightness, and from which the lightning is soon to leap forth; or, to change the metaphor, the grim clenching of an iron fist that is to crush all the bloom and splendour without mercy. The power of musical tone to suggest this ambiguous atmosphere has seldom been so clearly displayed as in Puccini's music, though it is entirely of this world and devoid of all that is transcendental, allegorical, or symbolic. Within the blossom of his melodies there lurks a canker-worm; even in his sweetest cantilena there is a note of quivering anguish, a sense of pain, that weighs upon the heart of the listener with a heavy oppression—and doubly so when the characters are still standing 'up there in the light' and have not the slightest inkling of the horror that is fated soon to fall upon them. In this art of quivering suspense (of which

he himself was hardly conscious), of stirring up an almost unbearable sense of sympathy and indignation, and allowing us
to divine in advance the fate of tormented human beings; or
again, in their outbursts of agonized sobbing, and the contrast
between these and the brutal calm and cold passion of their
tormentors, Puccini is unique, and it is possible that the enduring effect and permanent value of his operas lies even more
in this than in the melody that is his most personal secret.

It is true, however, that he would never have been able to
create all these touching, and often, in my opinion, sentimental
feminine figures, with their striking ardour and animation, had
he not himself been the lover and slave of feminine fascination
throughout his whole life. He was the type of the *homme à
femmes*, and in some ways surpassed the type. He never lost
himself in adventures; but he always sought them and found
them. To quote his own avowal: 'Sono sempre innamorato (I
am always in love)', and once, when he was taken to task for his
love of the chase, he answered calmly: 'Yes, I am a passionate
hunter of water-fowl, good libretti, and women'. He was a
perfect troubadour, and that not only in his music; he was a
women's composer, in a sense in which few others have been,
and they all loved him, from the needy little seamstress in her
garret to the proud duchess in her princely palace, not to mention the princesses of the Italian ruling house; they all fell under
the charm of his song, and no less of his personality. It is
small wonder that an artist with his winning, manly exterior
and aureole of world-wide fame—which he wore, be it said, as
unconcernedly as he did his inevitable felt hat—and with a
melancholy reserve and noble bearing that promised a still
further attraction, and who was, moreover, a lover of beauty
with inflammable passions, should have had feminine favours
showered upon him without any effort on his part. It is not
surprising that he hardly ever had to waste much time in wooing
a woman whom he desired, and that he accepted without any
serious qualms of self-reproach every tribute paid, equally
unrepentantly, by feminine charm to this operatic composer

accustomed to love and raised to eminence by success—the 'male siren (*Sirenerich*)' as Alfred Kerr [1] has called him. Nor is it any wonder that Donna Elvira, his chosen companion, did not have an easy life with such an inflammable person, who regarded the slightest constraint as a wrong. She had to preserve her own dignity and that of her home, and in spite of all her loving indulgence, she had to overcome much vexation and jealousy as a result of the escapades of the man whom she loved; nor did she always do so in silence. Perhaps, indeed, she did not always go the right way to work to attach 'Monsieur Butterfly' to his home for good, and suffered bitterly in consequence; though perhaps she made him suffer, too, for forcing her to play Donna Elvira, whose name she bore, to his Don Juan. Yet, in spite of all, she loved him as no other woman did in his life, filled though it was with all that was rich and exquisite.

No! Giacomo Puccini's nature was not a simple one, and the fact that, in spite of all the complexity and contradictions of his character, it remained consistently natural, still further complicates the problem. He is a singular phenomenon, if only for the reason that his work was merely a partial reflection of himself and his experience, and not of their most individual features at that; besides which, it is far from representing that common denominator to which it is generally possible to reduce all the qualities of a creative genius occupying a rank all his own, and possessed of thoroughly personal idiosyncrasies—we need only instance Mozart, Beethoven, Wagner, Verdi, Brahms, or Schumann. The fact that the same thing is possible even with Mahler and Richard Strauss proves that nearness or remoteness in time need have nothing to do with the matter. For the present—and I make this reservation advisedly—*La Bohème* is the only one of Puccini's works in which it is possible to establish the existence of a reciprocal action of his life upon his work and vice versa. Nor does it make much difference that

[1] TRANSLATOR'S NOTE.—Alfred Kerr of the *Berliner Tageblatt*.

reality and dream often become confused in his mind, that he was often in love with his Mimi or his Cho-Cho-San, and even with his Turandot, in exactly the same way as with some living woman, and shed hot tears while he was clothing the death of his little grisette and his charming geisha in the splendour of his immortal and heart-rending music. Yet perhaps, after all, he is too near to us for it to be possible to arrive at a right attitude towards him. Possibly we must adopt a different point of view, on a plane from which it may be possible to discern the true relation between the man and his works. But even if the results at which we arrive prove identical, it cannot but be profitable to review the whole course of his life, with all its troubles and successes, its happinesses and conflicts. And perhaps, to venture a last conjecture, it may be that he was simply too shy to make a show of his violent and most intimate emotions in his art, which is one that should be devoid of all reserve. However this may be, nothing but his life, with its anxieties and crises—though, as a matter of fact, there was little in it that was dramatic—can reveal the roots of his creative work; though in minds of the highest order, we may add, it is the contrary that holds good.

CHAPTER III

THE LAST HEIR TO A MUSICAL TRADITION

Was einem angehört, wird man nicht los, und wenn man es wegwürfe.[1]—GOETHE

THE organ peals out in the cathedral at Lucca, not for divine worship, for the church is empty, and even one absorbed in solitary prayer might well cast a glance of astonishment up at the organ-loft, for the jerky and disconnected sounds that float down from above have little about them that suggests a sacred melody. But he would be still more surprised at the picture that would meet his eyes if he were to mount the steps to the choir and examine into the origin of these sudden noises. For on the organist's bench, side by side with a dignified gentleman of fifty, sits a little fellow aged five at the outside, fumbling with his tiny hands at the manuals, on the keys of which his father has laid some coins. Every time his fingers reach out to collect the pieces of money, the organ-pipes begin to boom, to the ecstatic delight of the little boy, who goes on pressing down the keys even when all the *soldi* have gone, rejoicing immoderately in the noises that he manages to draw from the mighty instrument. Such was the means devised by Michele Puccini, organist, composer, and director of the Lucca Conservatorio, for inspiring his little boy Giacomo with a desire to play the organ, and familiarizing him at an early age with the complicated apparatus of manuals and registers, pedals and couplers; for the little fellow was already intended to be an organist, and in point of fact became one. Perhaps he would even have continued to pursue this career, had he not, while still a lad,

[1] One could not get rid of what really pertains to one, even if one were to throw it away.

been drawn by a vague longing into walking one day from Lucca to Pisa to hear Verdi's *Aida*.

From the very day of Giacomo Puccini's birth, on 22nd December 1858, it was irrevocably decided that he was to become a musician.   Nor was this surprising, since for generations past the Puccinis, like the Bach family in Germany, had been accredited servants of St. Cecilia, beginning with Giacomo Puccini, the great-great-grandfather of our Maestro, who was an illustrious musician and *primo maestro* (master of the music) to the Republic of Lucca, his adopted home, for the sake of which he had abandoned for good his native town of Gello di Pescaglia. The status occupied by artists in the seventeenth century, in spite of all the external marks of honour granted them by the authorities who controlled these matters, is shown by the delightful fact that the 'general music-director' to the state ranked for purposes of salary in the same grade as the executioner, who may well, indeed, have been the more important person in the eyes of the rulers.   The authorities were, however, gentlemen of discrimination: when the ancestor of the Puccinis, that family of musicians, lodged a complaint with regard to the status assigned him, he was granted a rise, amounting to a small loaf, in his monthly salary in order to make plain to the eyes of all that, formally at least, the composer took precedence of the executioner.

His son Antonio succeeded him in all his honourable functions in Lucca, and apparently inherited his talents too, as is testified by a number of Masses and no less than thirteen dramatic works.   But Antonio's son Domenico succeeded in shedding even greater lustre upon the name of Puccini; he died so suddenly and at such an early age—for he had barely reached his forty-fourth year—that many people persisted stubbornly in believing that a friend and rival had given him poison in a fruit ice of which he had partaken on the previous day at the table of a rich patron.   In the archives of Torre del Lago is to be found an obituary notice of Giacomo's grandfather written by Pacini, in which may be read a prophetic passage that is all the more remarkable because this Domenico Puccini died forty-three years before the birth of his grandson, and so, though he may have had a presentiment of his future existence, can have had no knowledge of him: 'Ad un garzoncello, solo superstite ed erede di quella gloria, che i suoi antenati ben si meritarono nell' arte armonica, e che forse potrà egli rivivare un giorno (To a boy, sole survivor and heir to that fame so justly merited by his forefathers in the art of harmony, which he will perhaps be able to revive one day)'. Of his three children, Michele proved to be the one marked out to carry on the family tradition: and he, too, took an important step forward, for he gained a wide reputation as a composer of church music of merit, besides two operas, and an even wider one, perhaps, as a teacher, having among his pupils a number of musicians who afterwards won a considerable reputation. Among these was Fortunato Magi, afterwards appointed director of the world-famous Liceo Benedetto Marcello in Venice, and Alberto Franchetti, whose operas *Asrael* and *Germania* attracted attention far beyond the borders of Italy. By a curious coincidence it was Franchetti, of all people, who in after years tried to acquire Illica's libretto for *La Tosca*, based on Sardou's drama, for the purpose of setting it to music, and Giacomo Puccini, the much-fêted son of his former master, who managed to get it away from him by all sorts of petty tricks.

A curious similarity may be noted in the course followed by the genealogies of distinguished families, which generally show the same steadily rising zigzag line, in which the specifically creative gift emerges more and more clearly, culminating in the brilliant phenomenon of the predestined heir, in whom all the isolated capacities of his forefathers are concentrated in a supreme and unique manifestation of maximum intensity; after which comes an abrupt break, as though the accumulated talent of generations had been saving itself up for the purpose of producing its purest bloom in this single scion, forming an epitome of all its ancestors, yet, in doing so, had exhausted itself so completely that no productive faculty was left for the generation immediately succeeding it. In the exceptional cases of Bach and Wagner alone do we find the survival of a capacity for artistic production in the sons, very much weakened, it is true, but still with a personal quality. This has not been so with Giacomo Puccini. Tonio, the Maestro's son, insists that he has never felt the slightest signs of musicianship. As a child, it is true, he was urged to learn the violin as a delightful surprise for his father; but legend records neither surprise nor delight on the Master's part when his work was interrupted by wails, squeaks, and shrill scraping sounds of unknown origin, floating down from an upper story. It does, however, relate how one day Giacomo Puccini, who had in the meantime heard of his little son's secret practising, called the boy to him and asked him to play something. Unkind rumour has it that, after the very first bars, the Maestro rushed out of the room stopping his ears; but this much is vouched for, that half an hour later the fiddle, gaily decked with streamers, was floating on the lake off Torre del Lago, and that Tonio Puccini never touched either it or any other instrument again.

It would appear that the same thing very nearly happened to young Giacomo Puccini: at the very age when love of music and musical capacity usually show the most decisive signs of their presence he hated music and all pertaining to it like poison. I have not been able to ascertain whether little Giacomo was one of those typically Tuscan, wild, untractable boys—who may equally well develop into very boring dignitaries or into fiery artists—or whether, like many musicians, he was a shy, introspective, rather inert and dreamy child. But such information as we have about him at that age would rather point towards the latter conclusion, though from time to time he would emerge from his hothouse atmosphere of *dolce far niente* and be ready for all sorts of boyish mischief. But there is good evidence that he could only be driven to practise his music unwillingly and listlessly, and that the opinion generally prevailing in Lucca, to the effect that he was sure to become a great *maestro*, was a matter of complete indifference to him. Arnaldo Fraccaroli,

Puccini's friend and biographer, relates that the training of his boyish alto voice at the singing lessons given him by his mother's brother, 'Uncle Magi', was peculiarly trying to him, not only because these lessons meant an unwelcome interruption of his dreamy indolence, but also because every note he sang out of tune was marked by a sharp kick on the shins, so that even long afterwards the sound of a false note is said to have set up a reflex action in him, sending his foot up into the air with a jerk.   It can well be understood that this drastic method was scarcely calculated to awaken a genuine love of vocalises and other boring musical exercises in a self-willed, dreamy lad who showed little eagerness to learn anything else, while his inward voices were ready to sing him a sweeter and happier music of quite a different kind.

This did not prevent him from being actively engaged at quite an early age in playing the organ in every church in Lucca, or, like young Johannes Brahms, having to play dance music on pianos that were more or less out of tune.   He did so with a growing pleasure in his work, though also under the spur of necessity.   At the age of six he had lost his father, and his prudent, hard-working mother, Albina Puccini-Magi, whose love knew no bounds, was burdened with the care of seven young children, so that by the time he was fourteen it became Giacomo's duty to assist his careworn mother and relieve her at least of the burden of his own support.   At school he had failed in his examinations every year in the consistent fashion that was characteristic of him; but at the Pacini Institute of Music his abilities seem to have developed so astoundingly that this half-grown boy could already be entrusted with the most responsible musical functions at the services of the Church. It is true that neither young Giacomo nor those of his little friends who took turns at blowing the organ, out of enthusiasm for the organist whom they admired, always displayed the pious reverence they should have done for the sanctity of the house of God.   At any rate, the story goes that one day they stole some of the tin organ-pipes in order to buy cigarettes and

ELVIRA PUCCINI
The composer's wife

FOSCA LEONARDI-PUCCINI
The composer's daughter

sweets with the proceeds, and that the next time Giacomo seated himself before the manuals, their own fresh boys' voices did duty for the missing notes of the pipes they had abstracted for this evil purpose; though the fact that neither the congregation nor the pious canons noticed any difference would seem to indicate that they had not a very fine ear for music; and so would another occurrence related by Carlo Paladini, Giacomo's teacher, and recorded by Fraccaroli, who is my authority for most of these stories of Giacomo's youth. During a solemn service in the oratory of the Benedictine Nuns, the boy was seated at the organ, and sending its music pealing through the brilliantly lighted edifice. Suddenly a thrill of rapture ran through the congregation, the pale faces of the nuns were covered with a delicate blush, and bright, shy glances were turned on high; for the strains that were now streaming down to them no longer had any of the solemn austerity of sacred music, but were sweet, appealing and full of a sensuous charm, their enchanting melody being no more nor less than love translated into music. It was frankly based upon themes from an opera that Giacomo had heard a little time before, upon which he was composing variations, fughettas and free, melodious improvisations, giving free rein to his fancy, till he suddenly came to himself, realized with astonishment where he was, and, in a flurry of alarm, fell after a modulation into the austere severity of a Gregorian chorale, which accordingly restored the threatened dignity of the sacred edifice in all its ascetic austerity. Yet this time, again, the priestly servants of God do not seem to have noticed any sign of this unseemly impiety, otherwise the absent-minded organist would immediately have been relieved of his duties.

There is a curious parallel to this in the life of young Johann Strauss, to whom it also happened on one occasion that, while he was playing the organ in a church in Vienna, he suddenly and quite unintentionally glided into a highly profane and lively polka, to the consternation of the faithful congregation, though possibly to the secret delight of the less pious.

D

The birth of the composer in Giacomo Puccini dates from this period, when church music was in the ascendant in his life. It is an irony of fate that this 'atrociously theatrical' composer should have started his career under such non-secular auspices, exclusively devoted to the service of the Church militant, whose requirements he met by countless chants, motets, and Masses; and it is doubly an irony that Puccini, as a composer of church music, should have reached his proud consummation not through these still somewhat impersonal and artless works, but in the ill-famed and thoroughly irreligious sphere of the theatre: the subtle music accompanying the solemn church ceremonies in the finale of the first act of *Tosca*, the innocent, ecstatic chants of the nuns and the tender exaltation of the music, painted, as it were, against a background of gold, that accompany the miracle in *Suor Angelica*, bear most emphatic witness to the heights that he would have been capable of attaining had he remained faithful to sacred music, and, above all, had he never made that pilgrimage to Pisa on which he heard *Aïda*. Little seems to have survived of the sacred compositions of Puccini's youth, not even the motet performed in the church of San Paolino at Lucca on the name-day of its patron saint, which marked the first considerable success of the twenty-year-old musician, and which is not the only thing for which we have to thank St. Paulinus, who was the first Bishop of Lucca, and, in addition to this, the inventor of bells. Those who remember the scene in the church to which we have referred above in *Tosca*, and the strangely blended tone of the various kinds of bell-instrument in *Turandot*, and the intervals sounded on them, will be able to measure how great is Puccini's debt of gratitude to that saintly man.

One work, at least, among his compositions of that first period, has, however, been preserved from destruction, and enables us to draw conclusions with regard to the quality of the young composer's talent at that time; for it was not till later that it reached such a dazzling development. In the little museum which Tonio Puccini has arranged with such fine filial piety in his father's study at Torre del Lago, there is, among other things, the manuscript of a vocal Mass with orchestral obbligato, which is, moreover, written in a remarkably neat, somewhat stiff script, without a trace of the nervously dashed off, almost illegible notation of his later scores, which were the terror of all copyists, as he well knew, for now and then, when a page was in a particularly abominable mess, he would throw in a 'Scusi! (Pardon!)' for the benefit of the unfortunate person who had to copy it. In the manuscript of this Mass can already be seen plainly the as yet unemancipated, chrysalis stage of the young artist, confusedly seeking his way, yet already, as it were, sure of himself, and, though still immature and entirely dependent upon his models, yet none the less pressing resolutely forward towards his own individual mode of expression. Similarly, the work itself in many ways resembles the honest production of a worthy and competent choirmaster (*Regens chori*) in a little provincial town—an Italian one, naturally, having none of his German counterpart's pedagogical ambitions towards displaying his erudite contrapuntal and polyphonic skill in stiff double fugues, 'mirror' canons, and choral variations to the glory and boredom of God, but preferring to infuse the life-blood of melody into everything, endeavouring to adapt the operatic *preghiera* and the simple hymn to a stricter style, and striving not so much after correct polyphony as after rich effects of harmony, remaining all the while more akin to this fair earth than to a remote heaven. Yet it is almost touching to see how, amid all that is impersonal and thoroughly schematic, some sweet, shy little phrase raises its flower-like head here and there, like a promise of the highly secular operatic composer of the future, together with many touches of a surprising sureness, having that unique, tenderly appealing, caressing tone to which the whole world was to surrender ten years later. One is seized with a strange emotion as one turns the pages of this score dating from the year 1880, and already yellowing a little, and feels the first slight stir of the wings that would have loved to soar into the free air, away from the constraints of this four-part Mass in A flat, only to be frightened back into them over and over again. The broad melody of the exultant, almost dance-like *Gloria* in two-four time, following a gently animated *Kyrie*, already anticipates the finale of the first act of *Tosca*, some of the phrases being almost note for note the same; again, the majestic advance of the 'Quoniam' phrase in the *Gratias*, written in the ancient notation with square signs for the long notes, is operatic in its character, and the light touch of the young musician is again heard in a regular fugue, still hampered, however, by a certain constraint; while in the *Agnus Dei* can be heard the madrigal from *Manon Lescaut*, with hardly a change, but here used as a tranquil, devotional song of praise to the Lamb of God, forming a curiously amorous end to a pious work, in which the voice of the world can, however, be detected here and there in a way that has almost a symbolic significance. Nothing can be more touchingly illuminating than such a retrospective examination. When subjected to it, this work, which was probably rejected as being too modern and difficult for performance at the time when it was written, is seen to be mere routine work, talented, if hardly sufficiently so to justify its existence, yet already betraying such symptoms of a vocation as may at first have provoked a certain antipathy to the new musician. Only those looking back at these in the light of subsequent events can recognize them as the distinctive marks of a man and artist of an individual type, gradually throwing off his outer shell and pushing forward hesitatingly, yet irresistibly, into the light.

One lesson Giacomo Puccini had to learn, like everybody else, that in the evolution of an artist nothing can be forced, for it has to proceed step by step, and that sudden success, obtained at a bound, is usually followed by an ominous reaction. One of these facts he experienced in his own person, and the other was exemplified in his friend and fellow-artist Pietro Mascagni's strangely tragic fate. Perhaps it was fortunate for Puccini that, unlike the composer of *Cavalleria Rusticana*, he never met with any success in those prize competitions for which he

entered with youthful impatience, after a brief period during
which he was brought into prominence and raised upon an
exalted pedestal.   His first opera *Le Villi* (The Witch-Dancers),
which was passed over in the competition for a one-act piece
initiated by the musical publishing house of Sonzogno, would
hardly have obtained as much success in its original form as it
did when rewritten in two acts.   Moreover, it was a fortunate
dispensation of Providence that this very failure should have
brought him into touch with Giulio Ricordi, Verdi's mag-
nanimous publisher and friend, who was at the same time
Sonzogno's principal rival, and to whose encouragement, advice,
and patronage the young composer owed his steady progress
more than to those of all others.   Puccini had already been
unsuccessful in an earlier prize competition in connexion with
a hymn with which the municipality of Lucca had had the idea
of opening an art exhibition.   But this, again, proved fortunate, for otherwise he might possibly have remained in his
native town, winning premature admiration as a local celebrity,
and continuing to play the organ.   But Puccini was too much
stirred by all the elements of growth and spring-like freshness
in the world surrounding him, filled as it then was with impatient questionings and disturbing doubts of all that was
traditional, to find satisfaction within the bounds of an easy,
philistine artistic existence.   It was his wild longings and his
instinctive consciousness that he had a. personal aim, of a
different order from any to be found in Lucca, that first drove
him forth on that tramp to Pisa to hear the performance of
Aïda, which roused a storm within him like a raging gale and
first revealed to him his true vocation.   They, too, shortly
afterwards inspired him with an inflexible determination to
leave his native city and go to Milan, where he felt, with clair-
voyant certainty, that everything of which he still stood in need
in the way of teaching, inspiration, artistic companionship and
spontaneous awakening of his powers must be awaiting him.
There, and there alone, in the city of Verdi, the Scala opera
house and the famous Conservatorio, at which masters such as

Bazzini and Amilcare Ponchielli were teaching, must be the starting-point of the path marked out for him by the powers of destiny.   And with an indomitable, imperturbable energy, almost amounting to a monomania, and marked by a decision and sternness wonderful in a young man of twenty, he achieved his clearly-defined purpose in the teeth of all obstacles and all objections based merely upon what was reasonable.

Yet had it not been for the insight and help of his mother, a woman with a wonderful capacity for silent sacrifice, he would scarcely have succeeded in gaining his ends; for the obstacles were mainly of a material order.   Signora Puccini would have found it impossible to support her Giacomo in Milan in addition to providing him with the wherewithal to pursue his studies; for the burden of maintaining her band of children at home was already almost more than she could bear.   She managed, however, to think of an expedient: the Countess Pallavicini,[1] a lady-in-waiting to Queen Margherita, was kindly disposed towards her, and succeeded in persuading the queen to grant young Puccini a monthly allowance of a hundred lire for the period of a year.   Great was his rejoicing.   But the first period, during which Giacomo swaggered about puffed up with pride and feeling a perfect Croesus, soon gave place to a helpless sense of want.   Even at that time a hundred lire a month was none too much for a young man like Puccini, living away from home, with a stomach that was always hungry and a mania for smoking endless cigarettes, not to speak of an occasional desire to offer a few flowers to some nice young girl and treat her to a *gelato* (ice) now and then in the Galleria at Milan.   With such tastes as these he would have found it hard to become a capitalist. But not only had Giacomo to live on this legendary hundred lire, but his brother Michele had to share them, not to speak of a poor cousin, and since the postal official whose duty it was to deliver the monthly instalments of his allowance to the future genius was also the landlord of the little room shared by the three young men, and had the unkind habit of keeping back

[1] TRANSLATOR'S NOTE.—The *Epistolario* says it was the Marchesa Viola-Marina.

thirty lire for the rent as soon as the remittance arrived, in order to be on the safe side, none of the poor young fellows received much more than twenty lire each after the deduction of this heavy sum—that is, about two-thirds of a lira a day; so they evidently cannot have drunk very much champagne in those days.   Puccini often went very hungry at that period, and since his stomach revolted with the utmost determination against its compulsory emptiness, he loaded it with such quantities of watery broth and beans, that in after days the very sight of a *minestra* (broth with vegetables, rice, Italian paste, etc.), or a dish of beans made him, to quote his own words, 'feel violently ill'.   As a rule he wrote reassuringly to his mother of his well-being and the good progress of his studies, but we can see from the touching involuntary revelations in his letters to her, in which he denied that he was in need of anything, in how sad and pitiable a case this musical student was, for the very reason that his vigorous and healthy temperament rebelled against all privations.   Once, however, a little request slipped timidly and insinuatingly into his usual dry reports of facts, which, though it says but little in words, throws a flood of light upon his poverty in those days.   He simply asked for a tin (*cassettina*) of olive-oil, which he could not afford to buy in the great city; but, he said, he could not bear the linseed oil in which he had to cook his few beans.   He reproached himself all the while for his presumption, for he knew that his mother, too, had little money to spare for such luxuries; but he was delighted when he really got what he had longed for so much.   How glorious is the strength of youth, which knows that it has time before it, feels all its powers growing day by day, and rushes towards its goal, undaunted by bad luck and enforced priva-tion; for not only is it steeled against disappointment and care by its wonderful, imperturbable confidence and firm belief in the future, but it is capable of laughing away all these cramping conditions and enduring them with undismayed cheerfulness. To-morrow, thinks the young man, will come the great piece of luck, and by next year, when fame, success and wealth have

arrived, he feels quite surprised to think that life could ever
have been really hard and full of anxiety!

But what we should like to know is whether, living as he did
from the first under the shadow of melancholy and doubt,
Giacomo Puccini really passed through this period with such
light-hearted faith and high spirits. We cannot really say, for
the scanty remarks in his letters tell us nothing definite, but he
may well have had many hours of grievous weariness and
depression, when he was all alone and could throw aside his
usual mask of self-advertising magniloquence. What is certain
is that, if he was ever overtaken by moods of this sort, they never
lasted long; but he, and his brother and cousin too, faced life
in an unconcerned, easy-going spirit, or, at worst, in a rather
devil-may-care mood, and neglected no opportunity of wheedling
some of her gifts out of Fortune. Perhaps the reason why *La
Bohème* rings truer than all his works, and is filled with the
warmest humanity, as well as with the most vigorous vitality,
is that it represents his own personal experience as none of his
other works do, for he was himself at once Rodolfo and Marcello,
Schaunard and Colline, and had had the same opportunities of
experiencing and reciprocating the charming loves, at once
flighty and constant, of just such winning young girls as those
with whom they mixed, who, though knowing life, had a goodness of heart that prevented them from being spoilt by it.
There are scenes in his life that might have come out of the
first act of *La Bohème*. On one occasion, for instance, the landlady had forbidden the young men to do any cooking in their
wretched little room, on the ground that the polish on the
furniture—which was, however, quite innocent of any such
thing as french polish—might possibly end by suffering some
damage from the fire in the stove or the flames of the spirit-
lamp. But since they were not prepared either to freeze with
cold or to go hungry, Giacomo devised an ingenious idea that
saved the situation. First he pretended to be going on a visit
to the country, and went off with a small, empty bag; but he
returned again almost at once, told the landlady, with many

objurgations, some story about missing a train, and then, having locked the door, produced three eggs and some butter from his coat pockets and some wood and coal from the bag, sat down to the piano and began to thunder away at it with much brilliance and many crashing chords, in order to drown the clatter of lighting the stove and the noise of sputtering butter, while outside the door the postman's wife wiped tears of emotion from her eyes at the unexampled industry of this young musician and his pathetic lot. It may even have been motives from *La Bohème* that were already welling up beneath his fingers with such exuberant brilliance and unbridled merriment. As we shall see shortly, these had already begun to shape themselves in his mind, and were pressing tumultuously towards the light.

It is not quite easy to make out exactly how hard Giacomo worked at this time. The legend is current that he showed up the same fugue some dozen times, each time in a different key, to the kindly, absent-minded Maestro Amilcare Ponchielli, who taught him counterpoint and loved him like a father, and that the composer of *La Gioconda* never noticed it. The masterly ability and conscientious technical workmanship, the exquisite nobility and personal stamp of the harmonies, and the blend of instrumental timbre in Puccini's works are no proof of diligent theoretical studies during his period of instruction. Creative minds of his strongly individual type do not as a rule get very much out of what they can learn from others, or what the schools have to offer them. However that may be, he himself over and over again speaks of his diligence in executing his tasks, and the way in which he distributed his hours of study, for his days were almost entirely filled with music; but we shall hardly be wronging him if we assume that he devoted far more time to his own secret work of composition, the thorough study of important operatic scores, and improvisation at the piano, than to dry technical exercises. If this were so, then he was acting in the right, and only possible way; for otherwise his own individuality would not have made its way to the light so rapidly and with such tempestuous force, and his first decisive step towards independence would not have met with such astonishing success as was achieved by his *Capriccio sinfonico*, which attracted so much attention, and in which he provided, as it were, his own diploma as master on leaving the Conservatorio.

Among the professors at the Milan school of music Ponchielli and Bazzini were the two who felt the greatest affection for the young composer, who had obviously received the stigmata of art; but for that very reason it may be questioned whether they imposed severe enough tests upon him. This would hardly have been necessary, however, for Puccini never chose the easy way when working on his own account, however carelessly he might sweep aside all that was irrelevant to himself and his real nature. Besides which, he never liked to be beholden to others for anything, whether for their affection or, still less, for their patronage, but preferred to owe everything to his own strength and ability. When his ever prudent and obsequious friends tried to recommend him to call upon some all-powerful person or another before the examinations and solicit his recommendation and influence, he wrote home indignantly: 'Voi altri a Lucca l'avete sempre colle raccomandazioni: maledetto a chi le ha inventate (You people at Lucca are always bothering about introductions; curses on the man who invented them)'. And he had every reason for this proud sense of independence and self-confidence. He now knew his own worth, and of what he was capable, and he meant to prove it.

He sincerely reciprocated the affection of his two chief professors, though, it would seem, in a varying degree. He nick-named that clear-sighted, yet indulgent old gentleman Bazzini 'il Padre Eterno', the Eternal Father, and his attitude towards him was obviously one of good-humoured youthful superiority, with its smile of understanding and indulgent rejection of the circumscribed wisdom of the mature, and its preference for trusting to its own tempestuous and uncertain career. But he was genuinely proud of Ponchielli's friendship, and appreciated his boundless warm-heartedness and entire absence of envy. He would escort him home every day, when he was allowed to listen to his fiery discourses on art. And he might well be proud of this friendship, for it proved itself in the most noble and unselfish fashion long after his student days were at an end. We may here anticipate a little, and state at once that it was Ponchielli, the much-fêted composer of operas, who positively forced young Puccini to compose for the stage, thereby creating himself a rival of a dangerous and outstanding order, before whom both he himself and all the accredited masters of the Italian operatic stage were soon to be forced to abdicate. He further endeavoured to interest Arrigo Boito in the eager young aspirant, but Boito preferred to remain his own librettist and that of the glorious old master Verdi. Next, in spite of this failure, he was untiring in his efforts to find his protégé an operatic libretto, and succeeded in obtaining as the author of this longed-for book the poet Ferdinando Fontana, who had made a reputation that is not altogether easy to explain. This success may, however, almost be said to have been regrettable, when we think of the unspeakably poor and inadequate words of Puccini's two earliest operas. And when *Le Villi* was finished, Ponchielli still never wearied in his assistance. He promoted the first performance of it at the Teatro dal Verme, Milan, and introduced the inexperienced composer to his own publisher, Giulio Ricordi, the most experienced, far-sighted, and helpful of men, who now caused a general shaking of heads by abandoning the meteor Mascagni and harnessing the fixed star Puccini to his own career. Even after this Ponchielli's kind solicitude still did not flag: he approached Ghislanzoni, who had written the book for *Aïda*, and tried to associate him with Puccini as a collaborator. This time, however, he was unsuccessful. In all this Ponchielli showed himself a model of the unselfishness of the true artist, who knows nothing of ill-will, self-love, or vanity, and to whom nothing is of importance save the cause of the art he loves; who stepped modestly aside into the shade, in order that the full light might fall upon him whose rise was the joy of his old age, though he extinguished his own glory.

Again, by an odd freak of an ironic destiny, it must needs be through Giacomo Puccini, who owed him the greatest gratitude, that Ponchielli's most prominent work, *La Gioconda*, was finally deposed from its predominant position. Only those of my own generation can still recall the German performance of this opera, and the daemonic passion of Pauline Lucca,[1] thanks to whose talent the life of this work, belonging to a period of transition, was prolonged on the German stage, by grace of the devil. The success of *Tosca* meant the end for *La Gioconda*, and that in a double sense. Puccini himself certainly never observed that his lovely cantatrice Floria was the natural daughter of the highly unnatural Gioconda, but the parallel between the two subjects is unmistakable: in the one we have a prima donna, and in the other a street singer, each of whom is subjected to brutal violence in order to force her to save her lover, whose person and life are threatened by the law and its torturers, by surrendering herself to the monster who has at his command the whole power of the police. The only difference is that Tosca preserves her honour by murdering her tormentor, and La Gioconda by suicide. But even the sham execution is common to both operas, and nothing can be more instructive than a comparison of the two scores, in which the dramatic action is inspired by so many similar motives. They belong to two different worlds, and are separated by an abyss which is not merely that dividing one generation from the next: it is the abyss between two ages, severed from each other by a turning-point in intellectual history. There are undoubtedly fine qualities in *La Gioconda*: the *cantabile* is on a high plane, the arias have a melodic line that is often noble in its earnest emotion, and there are portions of the work that show real inspiration; but how dead most of it is, how dragging and arid even in its impassioned moments, how hackneyed in their phrasing are the recitatives and the dialogue in the declamatory passages, how rigid in their traditional form and almost

[1] TRANSLATOR'S NOTE.—Pauline Lucca, a famous prima donna at the Vienna Opera.

sculptural articulation are the vocal parts, in spite of their finely projected line; and their impassioned pathos is too often lacking in elasticity. That which had the power to carry away an audience fifty years ago like an elemental outburst of frenzied agony and impotent despair now reveals itself as being largely artificial in construction, scientifically concocted, or the mere echo of a great tradition that has lost its vitality. It is hardly necessary to compare Puccini's delicately animated, supple, finely, if often slightly articulated melody with that of his predecessor very closely, to see in what the novel element in him consists. There is scarcely any ground of comparison between the two; as little, indeed, as there is between a rather conventional academic study and an enchantingly subtle, brilliant water-colour, full of colour and life down to the smallest detail. Equally incomparable is Puccini's prodigious economy, which reduces everything to its most concise expression, avoiding all *longueurs*, however insignificant, and insisting upon the utmost concentration in dramatic composition. There is scarcely any display of mere solo virtuosity, and hardly ever is there any check in the action or break in the relation between the music and the dramatic situation on the stage for the sake of rounding off the musical form or prolonging a fine melodic idea. This shows a self-denial on the part of the composer as a musician for the benefit of the dramatic development, which neither Mozart nor Wagner, Verdi nor Richard Strauss was capable of practising with such consistent self-abnegation; for in them the musician over and over again gains the upper hand to the detriment of the dramatist. But if we wish to obtain a full impression of Puccini's essential modernity and of what it is that lends his intensified mode of expression its peculiar quality, we shall find it in the imperceptible touches, as impalpable as a breath, of his dialogues in recitative, with their economy of both words and music, even more than in his cantilena and the softly piquant aroma of his highly-seasoned (*pfefferstäubend*) harmonies. In these passages of dialogue we find delicacy, simplicity, and naturalness without a trace of exaggerated pathos, and a genuinely human note in the music, coming straight from the heart, from which even Massenet, who has been proclaimed so often, and with so little justification, as Puccini's true ancestor, is worlds away, if only by reason of the anaemic, poverty-stricken quality of his invention, the lack of variety, not to say monotony, of his modes of expression, and, above all, the insincerity of his perfumed elegance. Puccini's intimate quality was the revelation of a new world. The *recitativo secco* (declamatory recitative), with its intolerable monotony, has given place to a *recitativo limpido*, *tenero*, and *piangendo* —of a limpid, tender, and plaintive type. The supple cadence of this musical, everyday speech can be sprightly, tender, and tearful by turns, and is capable of expressing modest endurance and silent suffering as they become imperceptibly articulate— feats of which the stiff, psalmodizing *recitativo secco* was always incapable. It is not surprising that it was the entire absence of rhetorical declamation and exalted pathos, and the avoidance of heroic gesticulation characteristic of Puccini's treatment of recitative, combined with its abandonment of conventional forms and its more supple, nervous handling of the melody, that showed the hollowness and stilted movement of *opera seria* to be an impossibility. The fact that on this account, and not only by virtue of his more sensitive and modern musical setting of a similar subject, he could not help eclipsing the famous work of his dearly loved master for ever, without being in the least aware that he was doing so, remains one of the unkind jests of those incomprehensible powers which delight in making sport of the wretched creatures of earth.

Giacomo Puccini owed his first year's study in Milan to the generosity of Queen Margherita (though we may say in passing that this was none too handsome). In the second year his great-uncle, Dr. Cerù, a physician at Lucca, came forward in the role of Maecenas, but we find no record that his *La Bohème*-like existence became any more opulent in consequence. But it was now time to show what use he had made of his time. The young composer was now equipped for his career.

Kind old Ponchielli never ceased shaking his head during those days. Countless times during his experience it had happened that, on approaching the close of their lessons, his pupils had submitted to him neatly copied-out compositions as a final test of proficiency, sometimes, too, in the form of an independent composition, to which their revered master was expected to set his signature as confirmation of his pupil's arrival at maturity. What now met his eye, however, was rather a novel experience in its naively confident formlessness and impatience. He now realized that, during all those years for which he had gone on existing complacently in a fictitious world, a new type of musician had grown up, independent, caring nothing for bourgeois propriety, and possessed by a frenzied determination to find self-expression. And now came this devil of a Puccini, this worthless fellow of whom he was so fond—but no, he was anything but worthless, though his master had almost lost patience with him during the last few weeks, so absent-minded, so unsettled and full of capricious whims had he been, at one moment in despair, an hour later full of megalomania, and then, again, ready to buy a rope and hang himself for good. Every morning the youngster would arrive with a handful of bits and ends of paper, margins torn off newspapers, or old letters with a blank page at the back of them; and wherever there was any sort of blank space, it was filled with a jumble of musical hieroglyphs jotted down on staves that rose and fell like the waves of the sea.   All this had to be deciphered, arranged in order and finally even played!   The old *maestro* was quite perturbed at the sight of this almost illegible script, peppered with blots, in which every line encroached on the next, so that it was impossible to disentangle them. What a way to compose! he thought.   Surely no well-ordered piece could possible come into being in such a disorderly fashion! It was hardly possible; and yet a disappointment would be so painful.   The best thing to do was simply not to look at the stuff, but to comfort the poor fellow with all sorts of encouraging speeches, however feverishly he might beg with pleading eyes for advice and an opinion.

But this was no disappointment, and it became evident that the young man stood in no need of either advice or encouragement. The pile of pages to which this extraordinary collection of slips, looking as if they had come out of the dustbin, had swelled by degrees, was gradually arranged in due sequence and written out in a normal score, and, as this process went on, it proved to be a brilliant symphonic *Capriccio*, bubbling over with temperament and caprice, which, when performed at the students' concert which closed the session at the Conservatorio, caused a sensation that was not confined to those connected with the institution. Franco Faccio, the much-fêted conductor, offered to repeat this brilliant piece at a concert at the Scala opera house, while a leading critic, Filippo Filippi, devoted an exhaustive article to it, in which he referred to it as one of the abiding and most gratifying impressions of the musical year and said that it had aroused a storm of enthusiasm.[1] This little work, which had been, as it were, wafted to the young composer by dream voices and written down as though at the dictation of some external force, during a trance-like state in which his own will had seemed suspended, at once drew the attention of all musical Italy to a rising talent. It was now known that such a person as Giacomo Puccini existed, and was full of promise. It was that fateful moment which leads a man to discover his real self, and it came at the right time, or perhaps even a little too late. Puccini had never been a prodigy, though Lucca had been quite prepared to treat him as one; and he was now twenty-five years of age. The danger that a talent may be bottled up till it is too late is more frequent than is supposed, and it is not impossible that even Puccini had been threatened by it. But after a long period of hibernation, the glittering butterfly had at last emerged from the chrysalis stage to reflect not only the splendours of the day but also the ecstasies of night. . . .

---

[1] Translator's Note.—But the critic's actual words, as quoted in Fraccaroli (*Vita di Giacomo Puccini*), were: 'rimarrà come una delle migliori impressioni dei saggi di quest' anno'. In passages where the author paraphrases freely, the Italian text is appended in footnotes.

FIRST PAGE OF THE *Capriccio sinfonico* (reduced facsimile)

Even to-day, when viewed not merely as a subject for retrospective criticism by those seeking the early traces of nascent talent, the *Capriccio sinfonico* remains a fine work, full of youth, life, and wayward caprice, often with a clever touch of the bizarre that is original in the best sense of the word, and proclaims the advent of a new composer and a new type of music that can no longer be ignored.   It is a piece in three sections: an introduction, a principal section, and an epilogue.   After a trill swelling to a vehement crescendo on the cellos and kettle-drums, a grave, stately theme is given out at the beginning on the brass, advancing proudly above a weighty, chromatically descending series of octaves in the bass parts, with rolling kettle-drums and rushing *tremoli* on the strings, after which it is developed with a clearly-defined and strongly rhythmical line.   The final section takes it up once more, develops it further, and leads it towards a spirited close.   The whole is tersely vigorous, confident, and well constructed, and is written with a sure touch; but, for all its freshness and clarity, it is not as yet particularly striking as the expression of a characteristic and uncommon musical idiom.   The middle section, however, coming between the other two slow, sustained ones, is notable if only because its leading theme is note for note the same as that which occurs at the opening of *La Bohème*, and bubbles up in so many scenes of that opera, with its exuberant, headstrong rhythm, and the often slightly exaggerated and giddy merriment with which it passes into three-eight time; while the lyrical episodes, too, in which are to be found phrases of great grace and poignant charm, already possess all the fragrance, the bracing, ozone-like freshness, the wealth of precious colour, the throbbing heart-beat and strange magic of the melodies in *La Bohème*; they are, as it were, buds from the same ornamental plant, and it is as though, in the springlike profusion of the opera, one saw a number of them in full bloom, whereas in the *Capriccio* they are still shyly opening their first tiny flowerets.   We feel how intensely, if unconsciously, Puccini had already lived through the inward experiences of the *Vie de Bohème*, long before Murger's

E

romance first came into his hands.   Its prototype existed within
his soul, even before he knew anything at all about Mimi,
Musetta, and Rodolfo, and we can now understand how it was
that, in his impatience with his librettists, who never worked
fast enough for him, he wrote down long passages of his work
entirely without any accompanying text, urged on by the compelling atmosphere of the dramatic situation, and then demanded
that his literary collaborators should subsequently fit beautiful
verses to what he had already written.   He often had to
break the tissue of his work, from another motive than that
of Penelope, afterwards fitting it to his characters again until
they emerged from the pattern constructed in his dreams and
became breathing human creatures, with all the sufferings and
joys of mankind.

It is a remarkable fact that the symphonic *Capriccio*, which
certainly had nothing overwhelming or of the nature of a
revelation about it, but was a thoroughly impulsive, audacious
work, full of happy inspirations and, at the same time, of bold
experiment, was never heard again in the concert hall, in spite
of the initial success of the first performance, and that there
is not even a printed score in existence of this youthful
production, fascinating though it is from more than the
merely biographical point of view.   The manuscript, which is
likewise preserved at Torre del Lago, is interesting both
from the psychological point of view and from that of the
artist's script.   We reproduce the first page of it among the
facsimiles in the present work, and the stiff, careful, neatly
written notes and the laborious clearness of the verbal indica-
tions enable us to draw the most interesting conclusions with
regard to Puccini's state of mind at various times of his life,
when we compare them with the careless notation of the later
manuscripts, crowded together, erased, inked in again, and
thrown on the paper all awry, with a supreme disregard for the
copyists' and engravers' eyesight.   But, what is more, this first
page, and many others after it, allow us one of those fleeting and
fascinating glances at the musician while at work, which reveal

so much about his nature as a creative artist. We can see that, in spite of the well-marked character of the music heard by his inner ear, the young *maestro* is not yet altogether sure of having achieved the brilliant colouring that he desired. He is still feeling his way, and quite at the foot of the page, below the double-bass part, he adds yet another one for the cornet in unison with the principal theme played by the rest of the brass. Had this been intended from the first, it could easily have been included on one of the vacant lines, whereas the almost shaky writing, far paler and less resolute than that on the lines above, would in itself suggest doubt and hesitation. But this addition is not the only sign that he could hardly do enough to make this opening passage brilliant: the hastily added direction that triangle and cymbals are to be used, too, suggests the same thing; and all this scrupulous detail tells of an artist who intends thoroughly to deserve the fortune brought him by this happy hour. Unfortunately this particular page does not reveal much of his characteristically individual harmony, which already seems to be symptomatic of his nature as early as this work. His predilection for frank consecutive fifths and the subtle introduction of dissonances to form a transition, the fondness for secondary chords, the addition of notes extraneous to the scale, and all the other 'special signs' that are among Puccini's most important identification marks, are already present in the germ. The outlines of his artistic personality are already established, and before very long its essential characteristics received their final stamp.

This *Capriccio* ought now to be rescued from oblivion, engraved and performed, if only in order to evoke the memory of a turning-point in the Master's life and work, and add it to the picture of him as a whole. It is Puccini's own fault, indeed, that this has never been done up to the present. He was deterred by the very thing that now forms such a fascinating incentive to us to do this: by the fact, that is, that the principal motive was incorporated in *La Bohème*, together with other anticipations of the later work. It is true that he had learnt by experience of what his beloved fellow-countrymen were capable when a phrase in one of his new operas recalled one in an earlier one; for on this occasion he was hissed and abused. However this may be, it was on account of this similarity between the themes that he refused to allow this fiery youthful work to be published, or even played, after the edition arranged for two pianos that was published shortly after the first performance had been exhausted. Nobody nowadays could possibly accuse him of having had such a scanty flow of invention as to be unable to avoid borrowing from himself. If would be a piece of false piety towards his memory if, for the sake of this judgment, due to his over-sensitive artistic conscience, all those who love Puccini and desire to possess him as a whole, with his weaknesses as well as his irresistible qualities, were to be deprived of a work that suggests an imitation of his own manner, dating from the period when he was growing to maturity, yet in which breathe so much resolution and courage to be himself, and such fine inexperience and freshness of feeling; and in which his light yet sure hand proved itself for the first time. By this time he had discarded all that was not adapted to his own purposes, and in this work not only did the spring sing in him, but he sang to the spring.

CHAPTER IV

AN EXCURSION INTO THE LAND OF ROMANCE ('LE VILL')

WE might almost be suspected of trying to be funny when we say that the first operatic work written by Puccini, that inveterate 'verist', regarded as worthy of the greater damnation by the high-souled banner-bearers of idealism, was an opera on a subject drawn from German legend. But, as a matter of fact, *Le Villi* (The Witch-Dancers) [1] takes us straight into the heart of the fairy-lore of the Black Forest, a region hitherto exploited by none save German composers such as Weber, Marschner, and their contemporaries. It seems as though Puccini had meant not only to revel in the Swabian Romanticism of the text upon which his work was based, but also to suit the style of his music to the German folk spirit, at least in the choruses and a few distinct numbers in *Lied* form, and by this means to capture something of the atmosphere of woodland fantasy, as well as of a simple people in whose imagination natural events have been embodied from remotest antiquity in supernatural beings, dwarfs and giants, will-o'-the-wisp-like spirits and ghostly huntsmen. We need hardly say that he was bound to fail, if only because he was still too young, and had not yet conceived the idea of doing as he did in later years, when he wanted to master the exotic elements in his subjects and all the distinctive idiosyncrasies of their folk colour: that is, steeping himself in German folk-song, so as to strike root both intellectually and spiritually in the region of his choice, or, at least, following the example of those works in which this fantastic folk element,

[1] TRANSLATOR'S NOTE.—Meyer's *Konversationslexikon* explains that *Wilis*, or *Willis* (rendered by Fontana as *Le Villi*), are a variety of vampire, formed by the spirits of betrothed girls who have died as a result of being deserted by faithless lovers.

53

racy of its native soil, had succeeded in producing something living and convincingly real. At that time, however, he knew as little of Weber and Marschner, Schumann and Mendelssohn as he did of Wilhelm Hauff or of the traditional songs collected by Arnim and Brentano in *Des Knaben Wunderhorn*. His German forest is an Italian *pineta*, his villagers are opera singers, his *Villi* are neither the unquiet spirits of betrothed girls who have been abandoned and died, nor flickering marsh-lights such as have their home by lonely mountain pools, but are at home only in the chorus-girls' dressing-room and the ballet school. To-day, as when he first completed it, this feeble composition contains only one character whose voice has any compelling force and spontaneous vitality—and that is the young composer of six-and-twenty. Nor was the tumultuous success scored by this, his first opera, in Italy due to any traditional lore by which the composer might have grasped the national characteristics of a foreign people, or to any genuine ballad note or imaginative rendering of the moods of nature. Least of all was it due to the libretto itself, with its disarming helplessness in dealing with primitive emotions. Nor, to my knowledge, did this success ever go beyond the frontiers of its own country. It was due solely and wholly to Puccini's amazing talent and the way in which it wells forth spontaneously in music—though not such music as is inevitably associated with the characters, or gives them, as it were, their due colour, for, as compared with his chief masterpieces, it here produces a poor and colourless effect. As yet, however, it is by no means dramatic in quality, being only, as it were, hung upon the events and people as upon a peg. But what causes it to move us so strongly is the impression it leaves upon us that it is the expression not merely of the composer's intentions, but of an inward compulsion. This is music that simply forced its way forth from a young man who could restrain it no longer. He would have set the very alphabet to music, had no other text been ready to his hand. As it was, in his unappeasable longing for a libretto he set to work on this one because he could get no other; though whether it was fortunate for him that its action chanced to be laid in the land of German legend and faery remains very questionable.

But was this mere chance? I think not. I have expressed the opinion above, in a different connexion, that the choice of a libretto is a fateful act for which the composer's own nature is responsible; and though, so far as *Le Villi* is concerned, the choice was not a free one, so that the element of responsibility is excluded, it was certainly fateful. The higher order that, in chosen natures, governs the relations between the man, his life and his work, can be traced here, too. The series of Puccini's operatic works starts with *Le Villi* and ends with *Turandot*: that is, a succession of thoroughly realistic works, characterized by a spirit of everyday reality that is often positively brutal, is set between a couple of quite a different nature, which carry us into the realm of the supernatural and legendary. This fact is significant of an organic process of development in the artist's nature, immune from the workings of caprice and chance, and marks the completion of a cycle. In the magic circle of this symmetrical career of achievement, beginning and end are linked together as in the symbolic figure of the sacred serpent.

It was Amilcare Ponchielli who, after many tentative efforts, introduced his favourite pupil to the writer Ferdinando Fontana, and, as we have already related, induced him to compose the libretto for *Le Villi*, as well as for Puccini's next opera, *Edgar*. Ghislanzoni, the librettist of *Aïda*, was no longer available. This remarkably gifted, but eccentric man, who had been employed by turns in writing novels and short stories and as librettist, critic, and singer, had now, by way of variety, become the owner and landlord of a modest inn, at which he entertained principally artists; for he loved them as a class, their society was a necessity to him, and he took a delicate pleasure in feeding all these clever and jolly but needy people. The only ill-feeling that arose was when the inevitable moment arrived for settling the accounts that had mounted up, and this affected both those who had to pay and the good-natured landlord, who felt pained and ashamed at accepting money from his 'colleagues'. It is hardly to be wondered at that such an excess of delicacy should have led in the end to a disastrous bankruptcy. In spite of everything, this odd creature could not be induced to compose a libretto for Puccini, evidently fearing lest he might again come off rather badly from collaborating with a musician who had no means and a highly precarious future. Had he had any idea how very much to his disadvantage his refusal would be, and what a resounding success Puccini's music was to obtain throughout the whole world, he would certainly have decided otherwise. But the only result probably was to make him consume a few more bottles of Chianti, accompanied by furious imprecations.

Perhaps, too, it was really fortunate for Giacomo Puccini that at the very outset he happened upon such a literary collaborator as Fontana, compared with whom Friedrich Kind, who composed the words for *Der Freischütz*, was a perfect Shakespeare; for it compelled him to put forth his whole strength and concentrate his musical powers to the utmost during that phase, in order to make up for the poverty and lifelessness of the text by infusing music into it. For what the worthy Fontana produced for *Le Villi*, and still more so for *Edgar*, constitute very nearly the worst specimens extant of the preposterous, machine-made type of libretto that is long since effete; while *Edgar*, in particular, beggars the most absurd productions of the *Trovatore* school. In addition to all this, the worthy gentleman was crassly vain and stubborn, and so sure of his own literary infallibility that he was deaf to any of the sensible objections and suggestions for modifying the libretto advanced by the young composer; besides which he made him so nervous by his unctuous explanations that Puccini, who was quite inexperienced and innocent of any sham culture, conceived a fatal respect for the merits of this composition—and Heaven knows it was pretentious enough—and set everything to music exactly as he received it from this self-satisfied author who had arrogated the authority to himself. The subject had been chosen by Puccini himself in the course of a consultation lasting four days, which also took place in Ghislanzoni's boarding-house. The young composer, who, though inconstant, was never unscrupulous, was the very man to be fascinated by the legend of the dead girls who had been abandoned by their lovers and died of grief, but whose unsatisfied longings will not allow them to rest quiet in the grave. They hover round, unable to find repose, in the form of whirling will-o'-the-wisps, and lead faithless men dancing to their death. Not till one of them has succeeded in bewitching her own treacherous lover, and enticed him into the fatal dance till he rushes giddily upon his end, is she able to find eternal peace in the depths of the earth. Such are the outlines of this legend, with its rich possibilities and weird beauty, well suited to an imaginative and warm-hearted poet, and certainly the right one for a young musician who had already known many passing adventures of the senses, and whose spirit may, perhaps, have been clouded by a fleeting shadow of remorse in moments of serious thought. Fontana was, however, nothing but a skilful verse-maker, devoid of either imagination or warmth of feeling; and this subject, which might have inspired a real poet with a strong, stirring drama, full of colour and meaning, compounded of human happiness and sorrow, passion and infatuation, and diversified by the intervention of natural forces embodied in uncanny forms, became in his hands no more than a set of pictures worthy of a child's story-book. It is, in fact, no more than a rhymed scenario, having as its setting a village in the Black Forest. Roberto and Anna love each other and are betrothed. The wedding-day is approaching, but Roberto has first to go to Mainz to receive some property that he has inherited, for there is a stipulation that it must be handed over to him in person. Anna, her father, and the chorus—which, we need hardly say, has already appeared *en masse* to offer its congratulations—utter a prayer calling down every blessing upon the head of the departing lover, and bid farewell to him as though he were starting for the North Pole. They go off to escort him on his way, and none but his betrothed, with whom he has once more plighted his troth, remains tearfully behind, waving him her last greetings. And they are her last indeed, for by the second act she is already dead.   Roberto has fallen into the toils of a beautiful siren at Mainz.   The betrayed girl's father curses him, and the ghostly voices of the *Villi*, the spectral, supernatural beings, are already heard in the distance.   Roberto appears on the edge of the forest, driven, exhausted and tortured by the pangs of conscience, while the avenging dance of the will-o'-the-wisps draws nearer and grows more terrible, for the form of Anna floats before them, reproaching him for his broken faith and blaming him for her premature death, whereupon he is drawn into the wild dance, collapses and dies—and that is all.   The effect is rather as though one were to set down a pair of quotation marks, and omit the phrase between them.   The main action, which is, in any case, rudimentary, is relegated to the intermezzo, and, what is worse, there is not a single moment of strong emotion, not an accent that goes to the heart, not a single word of genuine human feeling, not a single character with warm blood; nothing but paper figures, puppets with the mechanism of a musical clock instead of a beating heart.   The stilted phraseology of the average libretto triumphs over every situation.   Even Wagner or Verdi would scarcely have been able to breathe life into such words and figures, and Puccini was far from being a Wagner or a Verdi.   But his vigorous handling of the whole subject, and the amount of music that he succeeded in drawing from this paltry trash, none the less remains a notable proof of talent.

Far be it from me to proclaim *Le Villi* to be a fine, or even a noteworthy work of Puccini's; on the contrary, it is a weak production.   The music does not either grow out of the action or adapt itself to it; the separate numbers are like a charming tissue draped round mere dummies—indeed, the librettist has produced nothing but dummies for the composer to clothe. We have already indicated that the music confines itself to expressing mere outward events, and fails to grasp any of the atmosphere of the country-side or of those phases of inanimate nature that soon becomes so paralysingly alive; besides which, it entirely misses the German Romantic spirit, without which legend remains no more than a mere story, and never speaks to the soul with the force of real experience.   But this should not be imputed to the young *maestro* as a serious fault.   He would not have been himself if he had 'made up' (*gemacht*) German music, and thus belied the Italian within him.   In many places, indeed, it looks as though he had tried to attempt something of the kind by approximating to the Swabian folk tunes; but these are the dullest parts of the opera.   His richest and most spontaneously individual note is always to be heard in *Le Villi* when his prayer becomes an operatic *preghiera*, the dialogue between the lovers a regular duet, and the sounds of nature and the wild, whirling pursuit of the dancing, elemental beings a sort of ballet music.   And its attractiveness is greatest when his own characteristic traits throw off the conventional and indeterminate elements that hamper them and appear with their own well-defined outline—though it is true that these Puccinian themes are still, so to speak, in their early childhood. All this is undeniable; yet there is already an infinite fascination in observing how Puccini's prodigious talent and amazing instinct for the theatre keep forcing their way through what is merely traditional.   This is shown, above all, in the sure sense of proportion and of the dramatically essential which enables the composer to feel in what points the librettist is deficient: that is, in throwing the real conflict and its tragic consequences plainly into relief.   The librettist has taken every sort of liberty with the subject, relegating all the exciting scenes—the seduction, the treachery of the lover and the death of the abandoned girl—to the interlude between the acts, the audience being left to supply the necessary links in its own mind.   Puccini meets the situation by simply composing this interlude, providing for the ear that which has not been revealed to the eye, and thus restoring the defective equilibrium by a method that is, however, rather that of symphony than of drama.   In a symphonic intermezzo consisting of two sections he represents Anna's tender, pensive sorrow, her pining away for grief, her death and funeral; we hear her companions singing their chorus: 'O pura virgo, requiesce in pace',[1] to the same melody as afterwards predominates in the scene where Anna's ghost upbraids her faithless lover. In the second section of this intermezzo, the wild, grim dance of the *Villi* whirls in a persistent, monotonous, beating rhythm above heavy, skeleton triads hammered out in the bass parts, lashing, hunting, and driving him pitilessly to madness and death. Moreover, in order to make his intention quite clear, Puccini has resorted to the rather dubious expedient of prefixing to each of the two sections some verses in the spirit of a German folk ballad, which he intended to be recited at the performance for the purpose of relating what has happened in the meantime and anticipating what is to come, though even with the orchestral or pianoforte score before one's eyes one can hardly make out what is happening. We are even told the name of the beautiful harlot of Mainz, Karit, who has reduced Roberto to beggary, and we are informed that Anna has died of a broken heart, after which the legend of the *Villi* and Roberto's expiation are related. Any one wishing for a few minutes' hearty laughter would do well to read these verses, which are worthy of a Christmas card. Furthermore, Puccini has the curtain raised before the second section of the interlude, showing us the Black Forest in winter and the pallid dance of the ghostly *Villi*, floating like trails of mist among the trees covered with hoar-frost, the whole forming a mixture of programme music, melodrama, and pantomime. Though it remains questionable whether such effects as these are to be regarded as artistically justifiable and really dramatic devices, yet, as an expedient for saving the situation, it is a brilliant example of Puccini's extraordinary dramatic instinct, and the drastic way in which he could use it when necessary. The proportions of this intermezzo alone show what importance he attached to it. It comprises nearly a fifth of the entire opera, and is repeated almost in full in the last scene. Apart from this experiment of the

[1] 'O virgin spotless, sweet peace enfold thee.'

intermezzo, which, though picturesque, is none the less open to criticism, there are few passages worthy of note in the work. Among them are the short prelude, with its graceful, yet grave beginning, and the melody of the middle section, which already bear, to some extent, the sign manual of the composer, the neat little waltz of the peasants, and one or two phrases in the otherwise somewhat stereotyped song with which Anna makes her appearance, and, in the first duet, Roberto's ardent though flowery melody in C major, which is afterwards treated with greater intensity and more direct effect in the epilogue to the first act, and again in the second act, when it rises from the lips of the dead Anna like a shadowy, desolate lament. In the second part of the opera, apart from the motives of the intermezzo there is little of importance save the fervent longing and concentrated grief of Roberto's *canzone* in B flat minor, 'Per te quaggiù sofferse (Back to the vanish'd days)', which likewise bears the unmistakable stamp of Puccini's individual manner. All the rest is thin and derived from tradition, and might equally well be any one else's work. In spite of all, however, this first little work of his might almost be called a horoscope in music, foreshadowing a future that was soon to be fulfilled. It still contains too much that is naïve and timid, and the real problem of opera is barely approached, while the purely orchestral element still preponderates over the vocal and dramatic. We can understand why old Verdi, who had greeted Puccini cordially as the rising representative of true Italian melody, none the less sent him a warning not to disregard the principles governing symphonic and operatic composition respectively or to confuse them: for each of these two styles, he said, has its own laws, and a composer must choose between them. Nor, he added, did he think it a good thing to interpolate a symphonic passage into an opera, merely in order to give the orchestra a chance.[1] And this advice bore fruit.

[1] TRANSLATOR'S NOTE.—Verdi's actual words, as quoted by Fraccaroli, were: 'L'opera è l'opera, e la sinfonia è la sinfonia; e non credo che sia bello fare uno quarcio sinfonico pel solo piacere di far ballare l'orchestra'.

CHAPTER V

For the purpose of writing *Le Villi*, Giacomo Puccini had taken refuge from the senseless, noisy bustle of Milan in his home at Lucca, where, watched over solicitously by the mother whom he had longed for so much and missed so sadly, protected from all interruptions and lovingly crammed with all his favourite dishes, he found peace for his work, true understanding and stimulation, and often, too, that loving over-estimate of his work that no creative artist has ever found so excessive as to put him to shame or weigh upon him.   In this atmosphere of home comfort, surrounded by the admiration of his relatives and fellow-townsmen, about whom he troubled very little, except to make fun of their sudden reverence for the returned hero, and all the while consuming masses of his inevitable cigarettes, which he did not have to ration so severely here as under the draconian laws of his Milanese budget, he was able to produce his work without difficulty, and with the utmost concentration and care, so that the 'operetta', as 'Mamma Albina' called it, was completed in a disproportionately short time—disproportionate, that is, as compared with after years, for in the future, as his sense of responsibility increased, Puccini worked far more slowly and weighed his effects far more cautiously.   But when an artist is still young and full of unbounded confidence, he does not yet grasp the real difficulties involved, and knows nothing of checks and hesitations, but overleaps all the obstacles that obstinately confront the mature artist, with the unconscious audacity of the legendary 'Reiter über den Bodensee', the horseman who rode across the frozen Lake of Constance.   And Puccini, too, did not know till later all the dangers that the creative artist has to overcome, his doubts and fits of despair.

But as soon as he had written the last note of the score of *Le Villi*, and signed the date at the foot of it with a sigh of relief, there was no longer anything to keep him at home. Nor was this only because he now wanted to have his mute notes rendered into living sound, and was eager to enter for the prize competition for a one-act piece announced by Sonzogno, with a confidence of success in no way impaired by the fact that he had waited till nearly the last possible day for sending it in. But everything combined to drive him away. As soon as he was no longer absorbed in his work, he found the confinement and close quarters of his mother's house hard to bear, and equally hard was the lack of anything to inspire him in the middle-class society of his little native town. He longed to rejoin his companions in the great city, with their eventful and adventurous life, especially now that he was returning with a completed work. Milan, the starting-point of every Italian composer's fame, could, should, and must be that of his own, too; and so he went forth, in spite of his mother's tear-stained eyes, for she loved him too much and was far too wise to try to keep him at home. Had he had any idea that in the very next year he was to lose this devoted mother, who worked herself to death for him and his brothers and sisters, he would certainly have stayed with her longer.

On his return to Milan he resumed his former modest life. Now that he was no longer burdened by compulsory attendance at the Conservatorio, he had far more free time, and his days were spent in making music, studying operatic scores both ancient and modern, searching for a new subject for his own use, and all sorts of consultations, all of which only served to blunt the edge of the unbearable impatience with which he awaited the result of the prize competition. He was still permanently short of money; but at the Osteria dell' Aïda, whose very name exerted a magnetic attraction over all needy musicians, and where Giacomo, too, was in the habit of consuming his

frugal midday meal, consisting largely of soup, it was the
tradition never to ask for payment, but to 'chalk up' everything on the spot, even when these infinitesimal sums had
already swelled to quite a considerable total, and nobody was
ever dunned for payment.   It is said to have made quite a
sensation, arousing the indignation of the artists habitually
taking their meals there, and causing the proprietors an almost
wounded astonishment, when, after the first performance of *Le
Villi*, Puccini changed a thousand-lira note with the unconcern
of a *grand seigneur* in order to settle his debt.   From that time
onward an unmistakable coolness is said to have made itself
felt in the hitherto good-natured and motherly tone of the
proprietress towards this uncomfortable person who would insist
upon paying her.

But his evening hours were given up to the Galleria, that
great glass-covered arcade in the shape of a cross, from whose
spacious central hall, crowned by a glass cupola, brilliantly-
lighted tunnels of houses run towards the four points of the
compass, forming regular glass-roofed streets, with one fine
shop-window after another, restaurants patronized by the
nobility or the bourgeoisie, cafés, bookshops, motor show-
rooms, shops full of wireless apparatus or musical instruments,
travel bureaux and jewellers' shops.   Here every luxurious
want can be satisfied, while even those whose empty pocket-
books condemn them to be mere shop-gazers can enjoy all this
superfluity without any temptation to envy.   Here, in the later
hours of the day, at least, is the centre of Milanese life.   Somewhere or other outside the tumult of the streets surges through
this noisiest of all Italian cities; but here people stroll up and
down, or sit, protected from sun and rain, eating their meals or
sipping a cup of 'special coffee' (*espresso*), or transact business
and discharge various social duties, while the young men follow
with a pretence of unconcern the charming ladies and young
girls who have come to show off their new dresses and hats—
for it is also a 'love parade', and not that of venal love only.
Seductive adventures are here to be found, connexions are

LUIGI ILLICA   GIUSEPPE GIACOSA

COMPOSERS OF THE LIBRETTI FOR *La Bohème, Tosca,* AND *Butterfly*

lightly made and painlessly severed, for 'serious business is for the future, but for the present life is an easy-going affair'. Small wonder that all the young poets, painters, and musicians prefer this place above all others as a meeting-place, quite apart from the fact that a regular superstition has grown up, to the effect that the Galleria is the easiest place in which to make one's fortune, as has, indeed, happened to many. And so Puccini too was to be found every evening in this enchanting Vanity Fair, smoking his inevitable cigarettes one after the other, hoping to meet a princess, or else somebody who should have a first prize in the lottery of life in readiness to give him. Meanwhile he chattered with his companions, and if it so happened that one of the band did not possess even the forty *centesimi* for the glass of punch that would serve as a pretext for sitting a good long time at a table in a café, then either his friends clubbed together for him, or else he enjoyed their society in the peripatetic fashion; for serious business is for the future, but life is an easy-going affair.

Among Puccini's friends at that time he had a particular affection for Pietro Mascagni, who was five years his junior. (The reverse was true of Ruggiero Leoncavallo, whom he absolutely detested, in spite of the fact that for a time they lived on friendly and neighbourly terms, and in whom he could not admit the existence of a single redeeming quality.) The young musician from Leghorn, who at that time was also at work on his first opera, entitled *Ratcliff*, and based on Heinrich Heine's execrable dramatic imitation of Byron, was then as slender and handsome as a young god. His wild, spirited, boyish face and dense shock of black hair, his flashing eyes, fine, powerful nose and defiant mouth, might have been those of some shepherd from Hymettus or some Dionysus roving through the forests, and was spoilt by one detail only, the moustache, which Mascagni, like Puccini and the other musicians of this band, wore as a sign of mature manhood, and of which they were all inordinately proud, though this luxuriant ornament could easily have been removed with an india-rubber instead of a razor.

F

A day came, however, when, for some reason or other, an oblation had to be made to the gods, whether by way of thank-offering, expiation, or propitiation remains obscure, and all of them took a simultaneous oath to shave it off, so that on the same evening a 'clean-shaven club' appeared in the Galleria to the admiration of all, wearing a superior smile. Mascagni was the man of fashion among them, though, like the others, he possessed only one good suit, however much he might romance about the marvellous wardrobe that he had left behind him at Leghorn. A few years later he really did possess one, and dressed so fashionably that he was a perfect dandy. On this occasion, at at any rate, he discovered that his Apollo-like head looked remarkably well clean-shaven, so he remained faithful to this fashion. The others, however, including Puccini, soon broke their oath and once more wore this adornment on their upper lip with extreme dignity, responding to Pietro's adverse verdict with contemptuous abuse.

I do not relate these innocent, childish doings because I consider them particularly worth recording, but because I feel that this delight in nonsense—which is, by the way, common to all simple artist natures—this habit of seeking relaxation in merriment, and the jocular pretence of taking absurd trifles seriously, tell of the good comradeship prevailing among this band, that showed itself both in friendly practical jokes and in sincere interest in each other's affairs. But I also recall them because I seem to hear in them all something of the music of *La Bohème*. They would sit together, smoke, drink, criticize one another, abuse non-existent enemies, and intoxicate themselves with exuberant hopes rather than with the inferior punch; and if one of the circle suddenly disappeared, they all knew the reason why, and exchanged a meaning smile. The little chorus girls from the Scala, the dear little flower-girls and embroideresses, were so charmingly easy to please, so complaisant, so touchingly affectionate and grateful for a little fun, and even, in their way, so loyal. Their names were not yet Mimi or Musetta, but Concetta or Peppina, and if there was a tragedy in May, with tears and farewells, it was forgotten by June. It was all so youthful and light-hearted, and cried out to find expression in music.

But what were his disappointment and despair when he learnt that *Le Villi* had been rejected in the prize competition, and that he had not even obtained the meagre consolation of an honourable mention! Perhaps, indeed, the jury did not so much as look at the work, if only because that they simply could not, or would not, read Puccini's slovenly script, which in the course of his work degenerates into absolute chaos. Zuelli, who won the prize, but of whom nothing was ever heard afterwards, declared years later with praiseworthy honesty that Puccini's opera was incomparably finer than his own, and superior to it in merit, though he was far from wishing to disown his own work and the pleasure he felt at its success. But Puccini could not live on the recognition of his fellow-artists. In his em-bittered frame of mind he may even have suspected that it concealed a spiteful pleasure at his failure, so he found their consolation and encouragement rather unsatisfactory. He was desperate, and once more withdrew into himself in the blackest melancholy.

But at this point Fontana conceived a plan. Whether out of pity for the composer, who had felt his failure a severe blow, or because he, too, was not very anxious to see their joint work pushed aside so ignominiously, he managed, by the aid of some friends and lovers of art, among whom was Arrigo Boito, to raise the sum required for getting the orchestral parts, the score, and the various roles copied out; and, with the active support of Ponchielli and Boito, he and Puccini succeeded in making arrangements for a performance of *Le Villi* at the Teatro dal Verme, Milan. It took place on 31st May, 1894, with d'Andrade as the tenor, and was received with wild enthusiasm. The finale of the first part had to be repeated three times, the applause increased with every scene, and at the end Puccini, attired in his coffee-coloured suit, was tumultuously called before the curtain eighteen times. A few hours earlier he had indignantly rejected the suggestion that he did not know what was proper, and ought to appear in a black evening coat; but he omitted to mention that this coffee-coloured suit was his only sound one. That evening, however, he might have appeared in pyjamas without causing any particular sensation. This was one of those hours when the public, which is often so recalcitrant, and particularly unmerciful to those who are as yet unknown, is intoxicated with its own power, and delights to shower honours on a new-comer, thus enjoying the pleasures of a new discovery, and deciding once and for all, on a first hearing, the merit of a work whose reception has been uninfluenced by extraneous factors. By the end of the orchestral prelude the success of the piece was assured. The weaknesses of the text were excused; the rather thin passages, such as are generally received with rage and contempt, were indulgently forgiven, and the music as a whole, which now strikes us as so feeble, and, as it were, stunted in its growth, was received with unbounded enthusiasm, as the springlike bloom of a novel type of melody, and the sign of a great and promising talent. The very public which, more than twenty years later, howled down ruthlessly and with the most insulting contempt *Madame Butterfly*, by the same composer, by that time the spoilt favourite of fortune, on this first occasion showered laurels with exuberant enthusiasm on the composer of *Le Villi*, which was shortly afterwards to be an utter fiasco at Naples. But with what overwhelming force this new talent and unaccustomed musical idiom must have made themselves felt, for the mere hint of them, the diluted, infinitesimal dose of their new quality, to score such a brilliant success! It is hard to decide whose verdict carries the greater weight: that of the retrospective judge, looking back after the dust raised by the first sensation has cleared away, when the new type of musical expression, at first strange, or at least surprising and provocative, has become a familiar habit, and the intrinsic merit of the work itself has asserted its full value; or that of the men who had the fresh experience of what was at the time a hazardous venture, whether pleasing or startling, and witnessed

its victory over the style that had gone before, and the unexpected effect of a new phenomenon different from all that
had preceded it.

The critics, too, joined in the general chorus of enthusiasm:
they gloated over the discomfiture of the unfortunate judges in
the prize competition, who had passed over what had been
described by a leading critic as 'the best, yes, enormously the
best among the works of our young composers (*il migliore, ma
a distanza immensa il migliore dei lavori dei nostri giovani maestri*)',[1]
and had not considered the composer's name worthy even of an
honourable mention. They poured scorn upon those com-
mittees which always confer prizes on works in the old familiar,
threadbare styles, and hesitate to recognize genius; and they
extolled Puccini's imaginative and inspired music, with its noble
workmanship, rising to the level of Bizet and Massenet, and
hailed him as the master for whom Italy had long been waiting.
It is true that when they imagined they could detect the influence
of modern theories, of recent German opera, and, above all, of
Richard Wagner in the style of *Le Villi*, they were merely
proving that they knew nothing of these things except by hearsay. As a matter of fact, it was not till much later that Puccini
penetrated into the world of Wagner, to which he surrendered
himself with deep emotion and rapture, and especially to *Parsifal*,
which was in his eyes the most sublime and consummate of all
Wagner's works. But neither the problems of style, nor the
processes of construction, nor the musical idiom of these works,
whose metaphysical and symbolic element and intellectual
superstructure he was quite unequipped for comprehending,
produced any effect upon his own mode of composition, or, at
most, they did so only indirectly, perhaps through Verdi's *Otello*,
or through *Carmen*, which possibly bear traces of having been
influenced by Wagner and his principles in the mutual reaction
upon each other of music and words, in the way in which the
music is interwoven with the drama, and in their more expressive,

---

[1] TRANSLATOR'S NOTE.—Gramola, of the *Corriere della Sera*, quoted by
Fraccaroli.

richly coloured, and animated treatment of the orchestra as a running commentary on the text and an interpretation of it. But even in these works, and still more so in Puccini, another factor was at work; that is, the secret and mysterious relation that exists between the various phases going to make up the whole intellectual development of an age, as a result of which absolutely similar modes of expression may exist in different places, remote from one another, and in isolated artists existing quite independently—so much so, indeed, as often to produce absolutely similar types of style—inexplicable currents which sweep away what is out of date in manners and art, and inaugurate a new epoch, the symptoms of which are common to a whole quarter of the globe, and affect its every part. Least of all could an artist of Puccini's subtle flair escape such influences as these, even when he was quite unaware of their sources.

However this may be, the first step had been made. The young composer of twenty-six had made his public début with a short operatic work on a subject foreign to Italian taste, and in a musical style showing notable differences from that consecrated by routine and familiar to the public on every barrel-organ. As yet everything in this music was undeveloped and lacked freedom; but it had none the less commanded instant attention. Scarcely had the first chord been sounded of the tender, passionate witches' song which was soon to enchant both old and young, when everybody became aware that the ill-omened voices which had joined in a dirge over Italian operatic music like so many ravens had croaked too soon. A new hope had dawned and the public saluted the youthful master.

CHAPTER VI

DAYS OF DEPRESSION ('EDGAR')

PUCCINI's friends had gathered together from far and near for the first performance of *Le Villi*, and even those living in other parts of the country had come to Milan to share in this celebration in honour of their friend Giacomo and take part in the rejoicings over his success; besides which, it is legitimate to assume that they had come quite frankly as a voluntary *claque*. Young artists are not, as a rule, yet prone to envy, and do not grudge a comrade the best of everything if they cannot have it themselves; it is only the experiences and intrigues of an artist's life that make them self-centred and envious as they grow older —a truth which many notable examples go to prove. Pietro Mascagni, too, was present, and cordially rejoiced in his fellow-student's triumph—indeed, he is said to have burst into tears as he pressed his friend's hand; though even the Maestro himself would find it hard to say now whether his tears were due to the emotion caused by the work itself, to joy at the composer's success, which exceeded all expectations, or to depression at his own affairs, which were still in a very gloomy state. No doubt they were due to a mixture of all three causes. Not only had the whole confraternity of musicians appeared at the Teatro dal Verme, but all his acquaintances in both Lucca and Milan as well—cordial supporters of the modest and likable composer, who beamed with gratification, every one of them giving himself airs as though it were a piece of his own. That evening the Galleria must have been half empty.

Only one spectator was missing from Giacomo Puccini's first triumph: his mother. She had looked forward to this performance with greater hopes and fears than anybody else, having

71

sat at her son's side for whole nights on end, darning stockings and mending clothes while he was feverishly engaged in composition; for he always liked to know that there was someone near and dear to him in the room while he was working. But a few days before the first performance, which she would have loved to attend beyond anything in the world, she had fallen ill. Possibly it was the excitement of joyous anticipation and anxiety, as much as anything else, that caused, or at any rate hastened her collapse, for she had worn out her strength, and kept up chiefly by will power. She had never desired anything for herself, but had worked for her children's sake till her little slender hands were rough, lavishing all her affection upon them with silent love. The absence of his mother, whom he knew to be praying for him fervently in her quiet room during this critical hour, threw a shadow of grief over this brilliant evening, and, escaping from the theatre while the people were still applauding tumultuously, he rushed to a telegraph office, and spent the last lira he had left in his pocket upon sending her the longed-for telegram for which she had been waiting through the night: 'Successo clamoroso—superate speranze—diciotto chiamate—ripetuto tre volte finale primo (Tumultuous success, exceeding all hopes, eighteen calls, first finale repeated three times)'. We can imagine with what a sigh of happy relief and gently exultant thankfulness the sick woman must have clasped this joyful message to her weary heart. By the next day Giacomo was at her side. Once more he could kneel at her bedside, feel her hand stroking his hair in blessing, and thank her with heartfelt tears for all her love. But it is doubtful whether he managed to deceive her about her own condition by all his soothing and comforting assurances, in which he held out to her the prospect of a near future in which he would at last be able to take care of the convalescent and make her life brighter. All she could do was to gaze at him with her quiet, resigned smile, and give one last kiss to the son who had caused her great anxiety, but still greater joy; and both of them knew that it was for the last time. After which all that remained for him to do was to close her loving eyes, dimmed by many vigils, which had never been turned on him in anger or reproach, but always with tenderness and love. Not till now was his childhood really at an end.

He returned to Milan and threw himself headlong into his work. By a piece of unprecedented good fortune for a raw young composer, Giulio Ricordi had bought *Le Villi* and also commissioned him to write a new opera that should fill a whole evening, though unfortunately this time, again, it was to be to a libretto by Fernando Fontana. This implied the guarantee of a first performance at the Scala, as well as prestige and an existence free from anxiety. It was such a moment as brings a rising artist greater happiness than any other piece of good fortune in his whole life, and it was an injustice of fate that it should have happened to Puccini at the moment when he was deeply overshadowed by grief at his mother's death, and consequently almost indifferent. A month earlier he would have jumped for joy, and so one of the fairest moments of his life passed by, and gave him hardly any pleasure. The experienced publisher was, however, of the opinion that *Le Villi*, which had been written with a view to the competition for a one-act piece, and consequently compressed into a single act, would have more prospect of surviving on the operatic stage in a two-act version. Puccini at once threw himself into the work of rewriting it, and the unbounded success with which the work met at Brescia in its new form shortly afterwards confirmed Ricordi's judgment, though this seemed to be invalidated again not long afterwards by the catastrophic failure of the piece at Naples. Not that such events mean very much: it is in keeping with the irrational atmosphere pervading everything connected with the theatre, and still more the opera, that one town may make a point of refusing to see any merit in a piece, and even abuse it and give it a bad reception, for no better reason than that another place has acclaimed it as a masterpiece. In spite of his youth, however, Puccini was shrewd enough not to let himself be upset by such unfortunate incidents; and it is certain that he took part with great satisfaction and the best of appetites in the banquet which awaited him at Lucca after this disastrous performance.

Giulio Ricordi, the founder and head of the great world-famous house of G. Ricordi and Co., is an exceptional pheno-menon among publishers. He not only published his artists' works and acted as their impresario, but he was also a friend to them, of an almost brotherly or paternal kind, and, what is more, their best adviser. He was well qualified to be this, for he was himself a remarkable artist. The view that publishers, like critics, must be born with a vocation and themselves possess the creative faculty is still not widely enough held. A man who is not himself in some sense a creator will never succeed in entering into the productions of others, divining the inner law of a work, or arriving at a true understanding of the often rather elusive workings of the artist's mind, and the mysterious processes by which his work comes into being; and, what is more, he will be a bad prophet with regard to the potentialities of the artist's life, and a bad psychologist in dealing with the capricious and sensitive children that almost all musicians, poets, and painters are. He need not be a great master him-self, or produce anything of permanent value, nor need he trouble the public with his own artistic work, but if he desires to have a true critical insight into the real nature of a work and its creator, he ought to be capable of such work himself, for the publisher must also be in a definite sense a critic. Giulio was a publisher of this type. He was a composer with abilities far above the average, and, under the curiously German-sounding pseudonym of Burgmein, wrote a number of remarkably charm-ing little compositions, dainty and uncommon in character, exquisite in taste, perfectly polished in workmanship, choice in invention and piquant in their harmony, which has a subtle aroma and a delicate, never over-emphatic audacity almost anticipating the charm of Debussy. They are regular musical miniatures, including short pianoforte pieces, often no more than a page long, light pantomime music, marionette scenes and serenades, the motives of which always have something of the grace of the *commedia dell' arte*, the languishings of Pierrot and the coquetry of Columbine. He had literary ability, too, and, in particular, a feeling for the essentials of drama, so that his interest in the libretti of Verdi's operas and those of Puccini, too, often went far beyond mere advice on the composition of the drama. In *Manon Lescaut*, in which so many cooks had a hand that it is a wonder the broth was not entirely spoilt, Ricordi had the decisive voice in settling the general scheme. During the composition of *La Bohème*, at those stormy meetings of the authors where the poet Giacosa was amiable and serene, while Luigi Illica, ranting and improvising, would pour forth whole acts at a time from his copious imagination, and Puccini would sit in despairing silence, savagely biting his nails, it was 'Sor Giulio's' word that often decided the plan of many a scene, while many passages in both Verdi and Puccini's works were modified and assumed their final form on his advice. All who followed his counsels, however unwillingly at first, were grateful to him in the long run. The fact that, in addition to all this, he possessed rare practical shrewdness and foresight and business ability of a high order, may have prevented him from becoming an artist of note; but he did better and more lasting service to art by being what he was than if he had been merely one composer the more.

It is all the more to be regretted that no use was made of his dramatic insight in Puccini's second opera, *Edgar*; and it is surprising that he should not have dissuaded the composer, who was perhaps prompted by a sense of gratitude, from again collaborating with the librettist of *Le Villi*—an omission he must surely have regretted often enough afterwards; for this time Fontana accomplished a positively stupendous feat: he succeeded in producing an even more stupid text than the first, almost incredible though this may appear. In it, in fact, we find a complete collection of all those features of Italian *opera seria* which might have been supposed to be most thoroughly dead and buried; for it belongs to the type of opera whose real plot may best be expressed in the words: 'the tenor and the soprano, the contralto and the baritone'. In *Edgar* the contralto is only lacking in appearance, the heroine's rival, who is at the same time the chief female villain, being a mezzosoprano. I may perhaps be excused for not entering in detail into the contents of this piece of fussy emptiness, which, if performed in a cabaret as a parody, quite seriously and without the slightest relaxation of the performers' gravity, could not fail to provoke peals of the heartiest laughter. I will confine myself to indicating that it contains the startlingly novel situation of a man torn between two women, one tender and true, who could have no other name than Fidelia, and the other as fierce and dangerous as a wild cat, who, by a conventional symbolism worthy of Nestroy's dramas, is condemned to be ticketed with the name of Tigrana. We see the hero going off to the war, his pretended death, his return, disguised as a monk, to attend his own funeral, his revelation of his identity and his ardent avowal of his love for Fidelia, his only love, who has remained constant and proved her fidelity to him even in death; next comes the exposure of the demonic mezzo-soprano as a spy and a traitress to her country, who, in her natural chagrin, ends by ridding the stage of her pure and innocent, but inconvenient competitor by stabbing her with a dagger, as a result of which she herself is promptly led away *a morte* (to death), accompanied by exclamations of '*orror!*' of a lapidary simplicity from the chorus, while the inevitable final *tableau* is formed by Edgar, who has thrown himself sobbing on the corpse of Fidelia, and the peasants, who group themselves about him, struck dumb by emotion. The reader will hardly desire more details; the whole thing is almost touching in its feeblemindedness. We pity the unhappy composer who was condemned to deal with such trash, and, without discussing what is not worthy of being discussed, we may relegate the book to the shelf of the theatrical library marked 'Curiosities'. . . .

The unfortunate Puccini should never have been expected to do such a thing; but on this occasion he was indeed to be pitied, and not blamed, for the question was decided not by his own will, but by necessity. He made every effort he could to save himself from the libretto of *Edgar*, and implored Fontana to make far-reaching alterations, but naturally without success. Every sensible proposal or reasonable objection glanced off the author's impenetrable cuirass of stubbornness and conceit, as he condescendingly rejected them all; and on the whole this was immaterial, for it was beyond salvation by mere verbal alterations. It remained to be seen whether the music could work the miracle. Every nerve would have to be strained if it was to do so, but this was, after all, a forlorn hope. Such a problem might well have proved stimulating to a composer of such youthful and audacious energy as Puccini; in spite of this, however, he found the greatest difficulty in making up his mind to set to work. But he had no alternative. He had by now signed his contract with Ricordi, and knew only too well what insensate folly it would have been to break it, thereby jeopardizing his whole future, and, at best, having to start all over again. He accordingly accepted the situation; but he had little heart to deal with a libretto in which not a single word appealed to his feelings. For four long years he worried over the luckless *Edgar*, though it is true that this is no proof of his antipathy for the libretto; for he was always a deliberate and conscientious artist, and required to spend a very long time over every one of his works, the period increasing as he reached maturity. He often took from five to seven years composing, touching up and polishing his work; he never sat down to his writing-table unless he felt himself in an inspired mood, and stopped work at once if he felt his inspiration running dry. While he was working at *Edgar*, however, considerable periods would elapse during which ideas would not present themselves at all, or only with great difficulty. Nor was this due only to the uncongenial libretto. Once more he was weighed down by grievous depression, and he could not turn to what is the salvation of others so afflicted, by taking refuge in music, and finding release through it during such periods of lowered vitality.

Perhaps the real significance of *Edgar* is that, this time, he had to apply himself to his music by an effort.

He was alone in the world. Not only was his mother dead, but death had also torn from him his younger brother Michele, whom he had dearly loved, and whom the life of merry poverty that they had shared in their cramped student's lodgings in Milan had drawn very close to him. Now, however, Michele had died overseas in America far from his home, and his favourite sister Romelde was preparing to enter a convent. It was her sweet, melancholy image that Puccini delineated many years later in his *Suor Angelica*. He was so much older than his other brothers and sisters that they were almost strangers to him, and the friends of his youth were scattered through various small towns in the pursuit of their various professions. He was quite alone.

Even Mascagni had long since left Milan, for he could no longer find any means of subsistence there. The allowance made him by the Count de Larderel, for the purpose of enabling him to live while he pursued his studies, had been stopped, perhaps because he had ceased to attend the Conservatorio before he ought to have done. He therefore went on tour as conductor of a light opera company, during which he found his way to Cerignola in Apulia, where he managed to exist with difficulty by giving piano lessons and conducting the little municipal orchestra, and from whence he wrote his friend Giacomo piteous letters on the subject of the unworthy decline in his fortunes, alternating with others that seemed still to have flashes of his former lovable self-confidence. Both of these moods are quite comprehensible: he had taken refuge in composition from his wretched everyday drudgery, and was once more aflame with ardour, so that he felt the journeyman's toil in which he spent his days doubly shameful and degrading by contrast with the flame that burnt in him by night. He had once again resolved to enter for a prize competition for the best one-act opera, which this time, too, had been announced by the publishing house of Sonzogno, and had induced two writers who were friends of his to construct a concise and powerful libretto based upon a play written by the Sicilian Giovanni Verga and made famous by Duse; and he was working at his opera like one possessed. My friend Guido Menasci, who composed the libretto of *Cavalleria* in collaboration with Targioni-Tarzetti, and made a present of it to Mascagni, declining to enter into any contract with regard to it, has often described the curious circumstances in which the opera came into being. The librettists were simply unable to keep pace with the composer, who was at a white heat, but every evening the verses roughly drafted during the day were jotted down on postcards and sent off to him. As a rule there was only one card to send at a time, so that it was like a drop of water falling on a sunbaked rock. The music for a scene was often in existence before the words, and had to have the text fitted to it afterwards. It is evident, then, that in a certain sense the ever-recurring question—whether the music is prior to the words or vice versa—that is always being put to famous operatic composers, and rouses their derision as showing the ignorance of the uninitiated, is by no means so foolish as it seems at first sight. I may add that Menasci also told me, with a good-natured irony devoid of all animosity, that a valuable self-winding watch was the only piece of gold that ever fell to the lot of the unselfish librettists out of all the unforeseen showers of royalties that descended in an inexhaustible stream upon both composer and publisher. But no sooner had the opera been sent to Sonzogno than Mascagni was assailed by a torturing restlessness. His work suddenly seemed to him a failure, insignificant, devoid of ideas, and entirely lacking in individuality, and his life in that little Apulian hole now appeared simply unbearable. Once more a letter arrived for Puccini, but this time, instead of mere lamentations, it contained a definite request for his friendly assistance: even the smallest post in Milan, said Mascagni, would be his salvation, buried alive as he was in a little provincial town—even a place as double-bass player would do, at the Teatro dal Verme, where Puccini might perhaps have some influence. As to Sonzogno's prize, he had no hope of it. His letter is the wail of a desperate man.

Puccini's prompt reply to this despairing appeal was to summon Mascagni to Milan at once. He then made every effort he could on his behalf, but without success. There was no vacancy for a double-bass in any of the orchestras. When *Cavalleria* was played to Ricordi, it made no very strong impression upon him, and he rejected the work on behalf of his firm. Mascagni was utterly disheartened and at a loss, and his friend shared in his feelings. At that time there were as yet no cabarets or cinemas, and, apart from a little strumming on the piano and playing on the double-bass, the young musician had learnt nothing; besides which, he was quite in the dark with regard to his own talent. Great, indeed, was his distress.

But now the result of the competition broke upon the world like a lightning flash. *Cavalleria Rusticana* had won the prize, and the name of Pietro Mascagni, the hitherto unknown young composer of twenty-seven, was on everybody's lips. On 17th May 1890 the epoch of 'verism' was inaugurated in Italian opera, that epidemic of sanguinary one-act operas, concentrated dramas, stabbings and shootings, which mercifully did not form a whole evening's entertainment. But a lasting international success was also inaugurated. The performance at the Teatro Costanzi, Rome, was received with a tumult of delirious delight and frantic applause. Nor did the public notice that this peasant drama with its thrillingly realistic popular note, in which the tersely constructed scenes succeed one another with sensation after sensation, till they rush upon the final catastrophe, had been set to music like that of a good old-fashioned opera, with praying choruses, drinking-songs, and arias forming numbers complete in themselves and connected only by swift recitative. But this music was instinct with young and unimpaired strength, refreshingly popular, natural, and free from highflown pathos even in its most vehement moments. To the audience it all seemed new, and the originality of the prelude, with its novel idea of the serenade sung before the

THE VILLA AT VIAREGGIO

THE VILLA AT TORRE DEL LAGO

rise of the curtain, which strikes the note of the whole tragedy, determines the atmosphere of the whole performance, while the Intermezzo had to be repeated several times, and the tempests of applause at the end lasted almost as long as the whole opera. Puccini was frankly overjoyed at this turning-point in his friend's destiny, and the brilliant way in which the first performance had gone off. But he had more self-command than the gentle Mascagni had had at the first performance of *Le Villi*, for he was not seen to shed tears.

Yet he might have had some cause to weep on this occasion, for the *Cavalleria* mania threw all that approached it into the shade, and obscured the fame of all other operas for the next few years—even those of young Mascagni himself. He never again had the good fortune to find a libretto with so much dramatic effectiveness and power of conviction, or one that produced the same forceful impression by virtue of the popular customs it represented and the atmosphere of its home-land with which it was filled, and he had to pay dearly for the enormous success of his first work. This was quite unjust, for in Mascagni's later operas—for instance, in *Il piccolo Marat* and, above all, in *Iris*, whose strange, subtly vibrant harmony and exotic sequences of notes anticipate much of the delicate colour of *Madame Butterfly*—he produced music that was far more out of the ordinary and rich in invention than in his Sicilian peasant tragedy, which eclipsed all rivals on its first triumphal progress round the world. Though the truth of Nietzsche's *mot*, 'He who laughs best laughs to the last', is constantly being confirmed, even Puccini himself, for all his inward certainty of his vocation, could have had no idea that he would have the laugh on his side in the end, and that the final and permanent triumph was reserved for his own work. But a long time was to elapse first, and for the moment he was thrown into the shade.

Nor could *Edgar*, which he had meanwhile completed, do anything to change the situation. The show of applause which the work managed to command at its first performance on 21st April 1889 at the Scala, Milan, could cause no illusion

G

with regard to the artificiality and lack of vitality of this work, which contained nothing to suggest that Alfred de Musset, one of the most graceful and audacious of poets, had provided the suggestion for this confused production of a commonplace rhymester by his short drama *La coupe et les lèvres* ('Twixt Cup and Lip). The public received Puccini with every honour, vigorously applauded the music, and called the composer repeatedly before the curtain; but neither the loud applause nor the congratulations of the friends who crowded round him could deceive him and his own inward consciousness. Even in these early years he was not a self-deceiver. The rehearsals had already been a torture to him; he could not arrive at any satisfactory relation with his own composition, for even those scenes which had stirred him while he was working on them, and into which he had hoped to infuse some of the passion and sincerity of his own nature, now seemed to him alien to his true self, bloodless and lacking in sincerity. By this time he felt what was almost an antipathy for the work over which he had spent nearly four years of his life, and with which he had wrestled so hard. When the singers and the members of the orchestra spoke enthusiastically of the beauties of his music to the obviously dejected composer, he merely responded with a shrug of the shoulders, expressive of discontent, dejection and resignation.

But for all that, these good people were not necessarily dissembling. If we consider the music of *Edgar* by itself, apart from the insipid text, we are amazed at its wealth of ideas, the vigour of the soaring melodies, the variety of rhythm, the piquancy of the pungent harmonies, the personal idiosyncrasies of colour shown in the blend of instrumental timbre—which at times only is a little too crude, and tends to be drowned by the massive tone of the brass—and, last but not least, at the almost astounding degree to which the composer has asserted his artistic independence, in such a way that all that was previously latent in him has sprung into growth and blossomed, as though in the heat of early summer. Between *Le Villi* and *Edgar* he had advanced by leaps and bounds. It is true that this music still seems, like Gretchen in Faust's vision at the end of the *Walpurgisnacht*, to advance *mit geschlossenen Füssen* (with dragging gait, as though fettered), like some hypnotized person forced by suggestion to carry out a task entirely opposed to his own nature, and even repugnant to it. The music has to obey the capricious vagaries of the text, yet it rebels and tries to find its way according to its own laws, shaking off the leaden trance that paralyses its limbs, so that it may advance with light and dancing step, free and with wakening consciousness, at the dictates of its own native grace. We can trace this effort on almost every page of the score, and it is frequently successful. The introductory bars at once, with their terse, characteristic phrase by way of overture, are such as might occur in any of Puccini's later operas. This constant repetition of a figure formed of the notes of the common chord, first unaccompanied, then referred to their key by the addition of the tonic and the fifth, above which runs an insistent accompaniment of scale passages on the strings which forms part of the theme, bears the unmistakable stamp of the composer of *La Bohème*, with its persistent, nerve-exasperating monotony and the unusual use of the augmented fourth. Fidelia's innocent *pastorale*; Tigrana's entrance, accompanied by feverishly agitated *tremoli* on the strings and the wild, rushing energy of the cello motive; the voluptuous seductiveness of the words in which the courtesan addresses Edgar to an accompaniment of soft strains on the organ—which may be regarded as the original germ of the similar contrast in the church scene at the end of the first act of *Tosca*—followed by her stinging, contemptuous accents in the dialogue with Frank, her toy whom she has cast off, and whose imploring, plaintively humble song is effectively set off by Tigrana's cold irony—all these passages are simply effervescing with talent, and already show a decided individuality. In the neat workmanship of the songs sung by the pious congregation Puccini shows what he had learnt at the organ in Lucca about the composition of church music, while Edgar's canzone, 'O soave visione (O entrancing vision)', his duet with

Tigrana in the second act, pulsing with ardent vitality and sparkling with fire, the heartfelt, vibrant accents of Fidelia's song over the bier of the lover whom she believes to be dead, and even the great, impetuous choral ensemble in unison in the first act, already show the characteristically Puccinian rising line, constantly working up higher and higher, and the vehement, insistent accentuation, sometimes rising almost into a shriek, but also the warm, singable quality and suppleness of his melodic curve.   It is notable that there is an almost entire absence of recitatives, which are here absorbed into the melodic element, and given the dramatic accompaniment of a symphonic orchestral tissue.   Another thing worthy of note is the tendency to florid passages in Fidelia's part, which occur here for the first and last time in Puccini's work.   The old formal divisions of the Italian aria, such as the *stretta* and *cabaletta*, are dispensed with, while that mere virtuosity on the part of the singers, whose vanity and attempts at brilliance, in the form of ornate cadenzas, interpolated roulades and trills, still indulged in perfect orgies even in Verdi, finds no place in this music, which requires to be sung with the soul, and not with the throat only, and at once loses its sincerity, and, indeed, its most essential character, if the insolent, almost ineradicable caprice and insincere craving for effect of the operatic star change so much as a single note of it, or venture to indulge in interpolations claiming to be more 'effective'.   'Son' io che fò la musica, Lei ha da cantare ciò che ho scritto (It is I who write the music, it is for you to sing what I have written)', as the fierce old Verdi once shouted out at a rehearsal to Battistini, though the latter was already famous, because he had ventured to interpolate a dashing flourish into an aria in *Un Ballo in Maschera*; and impertinences of this sort on the part of singers never failed to rouse Puccini, too, to unbridled fury.   It is, moreover, striking to see how this very opera, *Edgar*, in which Puccini follows the manner of Verdi more closely than he ever did either before or since, clearly demonstrates the fundamental difference between their two natures, and Puccini's entire independence of the older master, though the latter was incomparably the greater and richer genius, inexhaustible in his power and inspiration. Not that the difference is always to the disadvantage of the younger composer. For all its torpedo-like impact, Verdi's melody, with its sombre glow, its fiery, soaring rush and its lavish profusion, seldom touches the heart as does that of Puccini, which is more tender, nervous, and genuinely human, more keenly sensitive, and certainly marked by a greater economy than that of Verdi. Verdi's melody loves, as it were, to parade in 'period' costumes, while Puccini's goes thinly clad, and often seems to shiver with cold, wearing that suffering expression, that 'faccia povera' which Puccini's children so often noticed, with such tender grief, in their own father.

Edgar never found a permanent home on the stage either in Italy or abroad. The Maestro gave this hybrid type of opera one more trial when he produced it at Buenos Aires in a revised version; but it failed to make at all a lasting impression, and after this he threw it aside as dead.

Puccini did not disown his *Le Villi*, any more than Wagner did his *Rienzi*. Thirty years after composing it he wrote some jesting verses to Zuelli, his victorious rival on that occasion, in which he recalls his first work without any regrets or qualms of conscience. A long time before this he had referred to his second opera as 'warmed-up pottage (*minestra riscaldata*)', and he was almost glad at its lack of success. 'What is wanted,' he said, 'is a subject that palpitates with life and is convincing —and not inflated nonsense.' [1] In accordance with which sentiments, he did disown *Edgar*.

---

[1] TRANSLATOR'S NOTE.—Puccini's actual words, according to Fraccaroli, were 'Ci vuole un soggetto che palpiti e ci si crede, non le panzane'.

CHAPTER VII

IDYLLIC SCENES ('MANON LESCAUT')

By an odd discrepancy in Giacomo Puccini's nature both as man and artist, this composer, whose music seems to be the product of an over-cultivated, luxurious dweller in great cities, sentimental, inclined to worry, and anything but simple, had, as a matter of fact, a horror of life in large towns. It is quite comprehensible that he should have been unable to work amid the noise and ugliness of their bustling commercialism, and have felt their stuffy houses and the crowded promiscuity of life in the stony wastes of streets and squares to be soul-destroying and a death to all atmosphere; but, more than this, in the long run he simply could not live in town. He was always slipping away and seeking refuge in little villages in the country, amid the open-air life of nature, where he could find himself once more, whether in composition, shooting or pure relaxation. It was as though he felt a secret dread of losing his real nature amid the vortex of town life, remote from nature, and sacrificing those qualities that were peculiarly his own. But here we come upon yet another discrepancy, for his music reflected none of this delight in open air and sunshine. Puccini's world of music has no affinity with the country-side; we hear in it the music of humanity, but never that of nature. And when, on occasion, he becomes a tone-painter, and tries to catch the atmosphere of a particular region, desolate wintry wastes, the break of day, or the dreamy, starlit nights of the Far East, and reproduce their image in music, what we hear consists chiefly in the sounds of nature and their reaction on the human mind, rather than nature's mystery. This music knows nothing of cosmic phenomena, the procession of the clouds, the patter of the rain, the

86

quiver of rustling trees in the moonlight; it leaves all these things to the scene-painter, contenting itself with what can be grasped by the ear. It does not, like the music of Wagner or Richard Strauss, teach us to see by means of our ears. When, for instance, at the beginning of the third act of *La Bohème*, Puccini shows us the *Barrière d'enfer*, what he depicts is not so much the melancholy monotony of the falling snow, the freezing mist that envelops all living things, the motionless branches covered with rime, all the death-like quality of the winter landscape, used as a symbol of love growing cold; what he prefers to represent—and he does so in masterly fashion—is the winter of the heart, as heard in the cries of the toll-house keepers, the peasants, the lamplighter and those drinking in the tavern. We can hear all this shivering in the light, sharp, dripping effect of the bare fifths on the flutes and harps above the frozen, rigid pedal point of the shuddering *tremoli* on the cellos. It is as though the exuberant, resonant motive at the opening of the previous act were dead and covered with ice. This is a picture of the human soul, and not of nature. Similarly, in the introduction to the last act of *Tosca*, the awakening of day in Rome is simply indicated by the blended sounds of the morning bells, tinkling cow-bells, and the melancholy song of the shepherd, and is in no sense a song of dawn. Again, the love-duet at the end of the first act of *Butterfly* does not aspire to be any more than a symphony of the throbbing Japanese night, with its exotic fascination, its heavy perfumes, its hovering fire-flies and strange, voluptuous voices; the same thing might equally well be heard at Capri or Taormina. This is not an adverse criticism, but merely a statement of fact. It is possible that Puccini defined the bounds of music with greater purity, in his own fashion, and preserved its dignity by very reason of all that he renounced; for he proves himself equally capable of the other method at the beginning of *Il Tabarro*, where a single theme serves to express, with an incomparably convincing and harmonious atmosphere, at once the night descending upon Paris, the hush that falls over the working day, and the stolid, resigned weariness that reigns on board the tug on the Seine. But if we think of the two sunrise scenes in *Die Götterdämmerung*, the forest murmurs in *Siegfried*, the whisper and flow of the night music in *Tristan*, throbbing with ardent longings, or even the nocturne, woven, as it were, out of moonbeams, at the close of the first act in Berlioz's comic opera *Benedict and Beatrice*, with its surging warmth and thrilling elation—a passage that would alone justify the revival of the work—we cannot but ask ourselves once more whether Puccini the musician and Puccini the man did not live entirely separate lives, and how it is possible that nothing should have found its way into his music of all the wonders of his beloved lake, the distant thunder of the sea, and the wonderland of the woods, whether glowing with sunshine by day or full of the whispers of night—the whole of his everyday surroundings, in fact, which he missed so much when he was far away that he was positively homesick and really unhappy without them.

He had at last attained a modest independence in material respects, so that he was able to satisfy his desire for freedom of movement by leaving the town and leading a life suited to his modest wants amid the quiet and simplicity of country life. He was no longer alone. The presence of the woman whom he loved, and of two children, a girl and a boy, had brought brightness and happiness into his house, and now lent his existence an object and a meaning. He was not born to be either an ascetic or a hermit; such a poet of love, singing of the simple, unheroic emotions of the much-tried human heart, as Giacomo Puccini showed himself to be in his music, longed for the cherishing warmth of a woman's presence in his everyday life as well, for tender affection, the company of a beautiful woman and her patient understanding, upon which, thanks to his careless and masterful sense of his own rights, he often made heavy demands. He needed a companion always at hand, and an ever-present affection and indulgent companionship such as can never be possible in those youthful adventures which end as rapidly as they begin. Till now home had been to him no more than a temporary abode; but now what had started as a passing phase had developed into a home. He had found that for which he had been seeking: an intimate bond, an *existence à deux*, a refuge and peace. Wherever he might choose to pitch his tent during the following years, his happiness in his family and work made it an island of the blest to which none of the temptations or enmities of life could penetrate, and to which, after all his experiences in the outside world, the world of appearances, to whose summons he had time after time to respond, he always returned unchanged, as though to his real existence.

Just as Cosima Wagner had had the courage to brave evil repute, social ostracism, and the legal consequences of her action when she left her first husband and restored to the most powerful genius of that new epoch the peace for creative work that he had lost, by bringing a loving security into his harassed existence and comforting his loneliness by her wonderful self-abnegating love, so now, with the same high courage, Elvira Bonturi attached herself to the young composer, whose personality and artistic qualities she was unable to resist. And Puccini reciprocated the tender, passionate affection of this beautiful young woman, a year younger than himself, with her delicate, grave profile, her soft, fair hair, her great, sad eyes, shadowed by long lashes, and the set mouth, which suggested the many things it had had to leave unsaid, and wore a quiet smile that had something touching about it. But she was united to a husband whom she did not love, in a marriage arranged for reasons of worldly suitability, which had so far been childless, and in which man and wife lived a joyless existence side by side, with no really deep bonds of union, though without any mutual dislike, since habit had blunted all desires, but also all antagonisms. This colourless existence was suddenly illuminated, as by a lightning-flash, with an irresistible love, which swept away the whole stable basis of everyday existence and decided the fate of two people. The flames closed over them, they belonged to each other, and knew that they were bound together till death.   But Elvira Bonturi was not one of those women who are capable of existing amid lies and treachery.   She confessed the situation to her husband, concealing nothing from him, frankly confronted him with the fact of this irrevocable, compelling bond, and begged him to obtain the dissolution of their marriage.   Her husband refused, whether through fear that his social position might suffer in consequence, or because he really did not care to live without her, or have his life upset, for, though it was only an outward form, this merely external bond had none the less become a necessary part of his life.   She had therefore to make up her mind to remain with him.   A year later little Fosca was born; and it is not altogether surprising that Elvira's renewed request for her freedom was rejected even more decidedly than the first.   This wearing state of affairs lasted for four years, but by that time she was at the end of her endurance.   In the long run she found the continuance of these equivocal relations and the necessity of keeping up an unworthy pretence unbearable.   She wanted to be not only the lover, but the companion of the man of her choice, and to live with him and for him; and she accordingly resolved to take the irrevocable step.   Since her requests for the dissolution of her marriage had been repeatedly rejected, she left her husband's house with her children and fled, panting like a fugitive, to Giacomo Puccini's home, with the intention of sharing his existence for the future.   To the credit of Bonturi it must be said that he had the good taste not to cause an open scandal or lay claim to the child, and did nothing to disturb the life of the pair who were at last united; but nothing would induce him to consent to a divorce.   Not till after his death, which took place after eighteen interminable years, was it possible to legitimatize this union, of which a boy, Tonio, had also been born shortly afterwards, by both official and religious sanctions.   This was a mere matter of form, and, what is more, almost superfluous. From the very first Elvira Puccini had been esteemed by everybody as the Master's rightful and worthy mate and equal, and she had every claim to be so treated.   She was both wife and mother, friend and counsellor to him, the court of final appeal in every problem of his life, and in very deed and truth the 'honour of his house' (*Hausehre*, the ancient German expression for a man's rightful wife), his first and last thought till the day of his death.

Intimate friends of Puccini's are familiar with a snapshot of him on his knees before his wife, with his head upon the ground and her foot on his neck, and, written beneath it, the jocular lament: 'And this is my family life!' It goes without saying that this was a mere jest; he was far too proud to show anything personally disparaging to him to strangers, even in joke, had such a thing been true. But the little germ of truth contained even in this little jest against himself none the less enters into the mosaic that goes to make up our image of him. To an artist with Puccini's imagination, easily agitated nature and inflammable temperament, whose almost defenceless nerves reacted immoderately to every impression, a normal bourgeois marriage would have been an impossibility, and the crises and conflicts of such a union were the price that had to be paid for all it did to enrich his existence and raise it above the every-day level, lending fullness and graciousness to his life. Even if mutual forbearance and indulgence sometimes failed and there was a slight storm, yet with natures such as his, which, though easily roused, are quite as easily appeased, these things need not be taken too tragically. Yet for all that, in such situations the woman has the harder part to play, and one that demands great tact and diplomacy in matters of the affections, especially in dealing with such a wayward and childlike character as that of Giacomo Puccini, who could never be persuaded to abandon the naïve 'butterfly morality (*Schmetterlingsmoral*)' of one who 'sips each flower and changes every hour'. 'Il giorno in cui non sarò più innamorato,' he would often say, 'fatemi il funerale (On the day when I am no longer in love, you may hold my funeral)'. And he would add: 'If it were mine to command, upon my word of honour, I would make a law allowing all composers to take a new wife every five years; and even that seems to me moderate'. Yet for all that, he would himself have chosen the same woman every five years, and she would always have been his dearly loved Elvira.

In all things pertaining to love he was as ingenuous as a child of nature, and in all his escapades he never had the least sense of doing anything wrong or forbidden, but felt that he himself was being wronged if he had to endure reproaches and tears. I repeat that, not only in his shyness and embarrassment, which was always ready to change abruptly to a refractory mood, but also in his view of what was permissible or not in his amorous vagaries, he remained a great boy, and similarly, when he was found out and forced to confess he showed the defiant confusion and injured obstinacy of a boy who is being scolded. Donna Fosca Leonardi-Puccini, of whom the Master made his chosen confidant while she was still quite a young girl, has often told me how *il babbo* (papa) would come to her in an irritable, excited state and complain of the tyranny he had to endure, of his wife's lack of perception, and the incessant scenes of jealousy to which he had to submit helplessly, and which were driving him to despair; and, though taken aback for a moment, he would burst out laughing when the young girl replied: 'If I were in mother's place, I should not scold you. I should pay you back in the same coin'. It never entered his head that his wife might be allowed to behave as he did, and he was quite incapable of seeing that there was anything to find fault with in his own conduct, and that he might cause serious pain to his life's companion, but regarded her reproaches and tears as merely idle and vexatious.

The book *Giacomo Puccini intimo* (The Intimate Life of Puccini) by his friends Marotti and Pagni, which appeared two years after his death, has a few essentially absurd and insignificant episodes of this sort to relate, but shows a perfect understanding of the Maestro, who was often placed quite helplessly and innocently at the mercy of amorous suggestion. Thus some talk was caused by the very long trips that he suddenly began to take in his motor-boat, ostensibly only in order to try whether he could reach the open sea through the canal that led to it from the lake; for he would return from them later and later every day, always with some fresh excuse, till he was seen at Viareggio being upset from his boat in full view of everybody and saved from capsizing by a charming young lady. Or there was an agitating episode at Vienna, the city of all others of which Puccini spoke with the most enthusiastic delight. 'If I were ever to move from Torre del Lago or Viareggio,' he used to say, 'my home would have to be in Vienna'. While he was there he stayed at one of the best hotels, where he was besieged by admirers, ladies, and reporters, though he displayed a cunning worthy of a Red Indian in eluding these exhausting encounters, and was only too happy when, comfortably clad in pyjamas, he could abandon himself to the undisturbed enjoyment of his beloved cigarettes in the quiet ease of his handsome room. On this occasion there was a ring at the telephone, and he was informed that a lady urgently desired to speak to him. 'What is she like?' he replied. The porter assured him that she was young and charming, and received the order, 'Show her up!' A shy knock was heard, and a brother and sister appeared at the door, a really beautiful girl and her little brother—but, horrible to relate, the boy had a roll of music in his hand. The girl allayed the Master's consternation by saying that the boy had to go to his music-lesson, but that, if the Master would allow her, she would stay with him in the meantime and let her brother call for her on his way back. Puccini good-humouredly raised no objection, being far from averse from a pleasant conversation with this attractive creature. He merely requested that, while the brother was taking his departure, he might change from his sleeping-suit into some more formal costume, during which time he asked the young girl to wait for him in the hall. She promptly consented; but when, a few minutes later, he came out of his dressing-room in an elegant visiting costume, he was transfixed with amazement, for he found the young lady standing before him stark naked. 'Una povera pazza!' (a poor madwoman) was the idea that flashed through his mind, and for a moment he hesitated whether to ring the bell or not, and commit the poor creature to the servants' care. But next he reflected that, after all, it was not without danger to oppose the will of a lunatic—and he decided that it would be better not to do so. It was no wonder, then, that this well-built man, with his frank, handsome, tanned Italian face, who was inordinately fêted all over the world, was absolutely idolized by the women, who thronged round him till he had no need to seek adventures, for they positively rushed into his arms of their own accord. One day he was overcome by a longing to hear *Parsifal*, for which he had a passionate enthusiasm, and felt that he simply must go off to Bayreuth— alone, naturally, for Donna Elvira took but little interest in German art. But the visitors' books in the little festival town do not contain the name of Giacomo Puccini. The one at the hotel where he stayed merely has an entry: 'Archimede Rossi, merchant, of Milan, with his cousin'. But it is no easy thing to preserve one's incognito in Bayreuth; it so happened that an acquaintance, sitting with Frau Cosima in her box, caught sight of the Maestro and pointed him out to her. She eagerly expressed a desire to make his acquaintance, for the sight of a famous Italian operatic composer at *Parsifal* was a notable one, which pleased her. She therefore sent her companion to Puccini between the acts, with the request that he would visit her in her box; whereupon the following dialogue took place: 'What do I see? You, Puccini, in Bayreuth!' 'Hold your tongue! I am not Puccini.' 'Ah, you must have your joke!' The composer began to be annoyed: 'Listen! I must preserve my incognito here, for reasons that it would be tiresome to explain!' 'I quite understand,' replied his friend, 'but just excuse yourself to your reasons for a few minutes, and come with me to the Wagners' box. Frau Cosima wishes to make your acquaintance.' 'You are mad!' was the reply. 'If I go to her box, my name will be in all the papers to-morrow, and then the fat will be in the fire. Say that you have made a mistake, and that I am somebody else.' 'But I have already said that you are Pucci——'

'You infernal ass!' hissed the Maestro into his ear, 'I am Archimede Rossi, merchant and Wagnerian!' 'I see. A double?' 'Yes, a double.' Whether Frau Cosima's messenger pretended that he had been dreaming or had seen a ghost, or whether he confessed the truth, remains unknown; but the last alternative is the most probable, and Frau Cosima's woman's heart surely understood and forgave with a smile. But after this the straiter sect of the Wagnerians, who had no sense of humour, had yet another pretext for contemptuously dismissing the frivolous Puccini and doubly underlining his name, which had long been on their proscription-list.

It can well be understood that Donna Elvira was not precisely pleased when she heard of such little comedies as this, though essentially they were of no importance and were soon forgotten. Perhaps it would have been better, and it would certainly have been wiser, if she had taken things more lightly and in silence, or at least passed them over with indulgent forgiveness. She must, after all, have known her great child, and known that nothing could make her lose him, while a sensitive amorist, such as he was, is simply defenceless against the attacks of charming femininity. But she had suffered too much in her life to be able to retain her confidence in the power of conquering serenity. A poet with much experience of love has said that 'The true and only fidelity consists in always returning to the same woman'—and in this, and in every spiritual sense, Giacomo Puccini remained true to the woman whom he always continued to love. All these insignificant episodes, which only bourgeois prudery and hypocrisy could judge severely, would have been unworthy of mention, and any reference to them would be no more nor less than prying indiscretion, were it not that, after all, they throw light upon the Master's music. Had it not been for his encounters with all these women, whether hot-blooded or coy, gay or melancholy, provocative or reserved, generous or possessive, he would never have been capable of creating either Manon, Mimi, or Musetta, Cho-Cho-San or Turandot, and giving such true and convincing musical expression to their meretricious charms, their constant love, or their haughty cruelty; nor could he ever have come to be the most popular poet of feminine charm and tenderness, the great artist of small things.

After *Edgar* Puccini was silent for a while; for he could never write down mere notes, but had to hear music sounding within him, or else remain mute. But he found these pauses in his work hard to bear, and envied the composers of symphonies their independence of the accursed librettists, without whom an exclusively dramatic composer, such as he was, was like a fish out of water. During such times as these he attempted several times to jot down smaller pieces when the inner voice was prepared to make itself heard. But no operatic subject was forthcoming to make him fruitful, though he needed one as the dry earth needs the warm summer rains. The song-like *Malinconia* (Melancholy), with the languid grace of its melody, but no very characteristically Puccinian traits, dates from June 1881. His *Inno a Roma* (Hymn to Rome), which we have already mentioned, a work in the style of a fiery festival march with vocal parts, was written later, after the completion of *La Bohème*, besides two other marches, one dating from September 1896, and written, curiously enough, in D minor, which has an animated movement, though it does not exactly carry one away, and has more energy in its title, *Avanti!* (Onwards!), than in its rhythm; and the other a gay, brilliant, spruce *marcetta brillante* entitled *Scozza elettrice*, in which the electric shocks promised in the title lead to a lively dislocation and breaking up of thematic material that is not very distinctive in itself. We have also four small pieces, entitled *I Crisantemi* (Chrysanthemums), delicate, plaintive memorials to a dead friend.[1] It is hardly surprising that he could find no satisfaction in things of this sort, feeling them to be, at best, scrappy productions of merely incidental interest, and not even fragments left over from his

---

[1] TRANSLATOR'S NOTE.—In one of his letters, printed in the *Epistolario* (ed. G. Adami), Puccini says that they were written on the occasion of the death of Amedeo of Savoy.

PUCCINI IN HIS MOTOR-BOAT

PUCCINI AT HIS STUDY WINDOW

operatic music. 'My kingdom for an operatic libretto!' was his cry. It often happened, too, that he thought he had discovered one, and was fired with enthusiasm for it, only to discover all of a sudden that the flame of his enthusiasm had consumed it to ashes, because it failed to appeal to his heart.

His ill-luck in connexion with *Edgar* had not discouraged him, for he knew that he had made progress. It now remained to find a subject that should lend him wings and set free all that was best in him, not another one which he would have to force himself to treat, so that it would be a violent strain on his powers. This time he was fortunate. Once again he fell in love, not with a living woman, but with Manon, the incarnation of seductive womanhood, light, yet capable of love, playful, yet capable of passion. He was really in search of an *opéra comique* when fate willed it that the Abbé Prévost's novel should fall into his hands. Now, for the first time, he found himself in that sphere of noble sentimentality, free morals, and graceful gallantry, ready to flutter from heedless happiness to beribboned griefs—the whole rococo world, with its tender dalliance, equally ready for the rites of love and for dagger-thrusts, which he was once more to call to life in his strains, like some Fragonard or Lancret of music.

At last Puccini had, for the first time, chosen his own subject, and played a large and determining part in framing the libretto. Hence for the first time he was able to direct his efforts towards a coherent unity and create a work imbued with his most essential qualities, with the result that it possessed the strength necessary for survival. I am never weary of proclaiming that no subject for an opera that has not first taken root in the very soul of the composer, is really capable of lasting—quite apart from the other requirements that are indispensable: the power of making its meaning clear through pantomime without preliminary explanation, and the human sympathy and fellow-feeling inspired by its content, which are the true fostering-ground of music. Puccini was well aware of all this at an early age; his dramatic insight was extraordinarily acute, to the

H

sorrow of his harassed librettists, who could hardly ever fall in with the exacting composer's stubborn objections. And apropos of this, it remains simply incomprehensible why Puccini did not become his own librettist; he often wrote really poetical verses, whether in jest or in earnest, and a comparison of his librettists' original drafts with the final version which he himself imposed upon them proves how strong was his talent for effective stage grouping, vigorous terseness and the inexorable extirpation of all that was superfluous, not to speak of his skill in eliminating all that was merely stagy and tasteless. Possibly he lacked confidence to give his subject poetic form himself, as Hans Pfitzner did after going through many unfortunate experiences of the attempts made by other writers to produce libretti, only to discover, in his *Palestrina*, that he himself was his own best poet, and one of distinction and genuine lyrical ability too. Or perhaps the idea simply did not occur to Puccini, though he might at least have learnt from the prolific example of Arrigo Boito, a member of his immediate circle.

The story of the vicissitudes through which the libretto for *Manon Lescaut* passed is a curious one. Somewhat like the author of the original work, the unfortunate Abbé Prévost, who experienced the hideous fate of being dissected while he was still alive, the libretto was cut to pieces, dismembered, and fitted together in various ways over and over again; and if, after all, it has been kept alive chiefly by the magic philtre of Puccini's music, its life has been rather an artificial one; and the operation, in which a dangerously large number of surgeons took part, did not precisely result in strengthening the whole organism and preserving the beauty which it was naturally destined to possess. But there were other reasons for this, as well. Puccini was not in the least worried by the fact that the same subject had been used for an opera with extraordinary success by Jules Massenet, the very man as whose follower he is regarded by many people, though most unjustifiably. Massenet was merely his prede-cessor, just as Dittersdorf was the precursor of Beethoven, though there is, of course, no comparison between Puccini and Beethoven. Before writing a single note of his work the Maestro knew that he need hardly fear comparison with Massenet; and rightly so, for Puccini's opera stands in somewhat the same relation to that of the Frenchman as bright red blood does to insipid perfume, and they are as little comparable as a picture by Watteau is with a volume of sickly gift-book poetry. In spite of the attraction that Massenet's work still continues to exert in a few places, in the long run Puccini had no cause to fear for his own opera; but he had the weightiest reasons for avoiding all resemblance to the text upon which the other one, written seven years before his own, was based. We can quite understand why this principle was consistently carried out, but it is none the less regrettable; for it was greatly to the detriment of the opera, and especially of its title role, which was left with hardly any of the hovering grace, the almost innocent corruption, the fascinating frivolity and lovable candour of the Manon in the French opera, not to speak of the original figure in the novel. Nor was it to be expected that it should, for the many writers who collaborated in the libretto, supplementing one another in rotation, and among whom were the dramatists Marco Praga and Giuseppe Giacosa, followed by Domenico Oliva, Giulio Ricordi, and Puccini himself, together with a few more or less unknown assistants, have succeeded in avoiding too marked a similarity between the two operatic libretti by the simple device of enacting upon the stage the events taking place between the acts of Massenet's work, and relegating to the intermezzo the really essential events represented in the body of Massenet's opera. The result is that, with the exception of the first act, which follows very much the same lines in both works, and in which the flight of the young couple, Des Grieux and Manon, to Paris forms a sort of prologue to the whole action, nothing is left of all the scenes in which Manon appears as the lover, the little enchantress, who has a good heart and is unfaithful only reluctantly—the Manon who renounces splendour and money for the sake of her love, and, though as fickle as a butterfly, is none the less permanently attached to her Des

Grieux in the depths of her heart. In Puccini's work, on the other hand, she is at first no more than a little provincial simpleton, but afterwards turns into a bored coquette with a passion for dress and money, who seems, as it were, deliberately to work herself into an almost feverishly exaggerated passion for her lover, and to attach more importance to collecting all her jewels in a hurry than to escaping with him in time, with the result that her ultimate deportation and wretched death in the American desert fail to stir us very deeply. During the composition of this libretto, the too numerous collaborators seem to have taken it in turns gradually to strip this Manon of one attractive quality after another, leaving her a mere shadow, and not even a very pleasing one. Unlike Prévost's Manon, who had only one father, but a number of energetic lovers, Puccini's heroine has a number of fathers, but such a passive lover that we are almost surprised when she chooses to follow him, instead of preferring to remain with old Geronte, who is, after all, chivalrous and generous.

All this will always prejudice the work in the eyes of the public; and this is a pity, for *Manon Lescaut* is perhaps the richest in inspiration of all Puccini's works, though possibly this is to the detriment of the dramatic element in it. If it is a fault to overload the subject with music—that is to offend against the artistic unity between words and music, which is undoubtedly a fault—it must be admitted that the composer has offended against this unity. *Manon Lescaut* overflows with genuine music, with a soft brilliance and a youthful impulsiveness, on which there lies, as it were, a soft bloom like that on a butterfly's wing, and through which gleams a brightness as of spring. It has a few themes which seem, as it were, to wear powdered hair and patches, and three or four numbers with a dainty, measured gait and the graceful, courtly bows and curtsies of the age of gallantry; and these amply suffice to shed the silvery light of the rococo epoch over all the rest. And 'the rest' is made up of the music of love and longing, which is for ever young and belongs to no age, the music of

overweening hope and disconsolate grief, still with a frequent
sprinkling of the suddenly interpolated flourishes and perfervid
ejaculations characteristic of the often artificial and laboured
modern Italian operatic phrase, but for the most part filled with
a natural ardour, throbbing with life and the joyous magic of
the senses.   One inspiration follows hard upon another, crowd-
ing upon it and almost smothering it, and the piece is almost
too compressed and overfull, so that the composer resembles
that king who used to have his guests smothered in flowers.
Not till later did Puccini learn to be less profuse, and to observe
a due economy and balance in the distribution of his musical
patrimony.   In this opera he spends himself lavishly; ten years
later he would have made two or three operas out of the musical
material in *Manon Lescaut*.   Let those who choose find fault
with a defect that consists in over-abundant wealth and a plenitude that has no need to be parsimonious; it is an irresistible
delight to allow this cataract of melody to pour over one.   It is
like a garden with an unending profusion of bloom.

It starts in the very first bar of the short introduction that
ushers in the opening scene; this is like a supple minuet, that
has wearied of the mannered repose of its graceful, dignified
gait, and now flings itself into the light, brilliant movement of
the *allegro brillante* with head on high and flashing eyes.   This
theme is full of the purest *joie de vivre*, the accustomed symmetry
of the eight-bar phrase being prolonged by a rhythmic exten-
sion into a curious eleven-bar phrase, and further heightened
to a perfect abandonment of gaiety by the wayward elegance
and variety with which the motives are developed, the joyous
syncopated accompaniment that adds precision to its rhythm,
and the ornaments and varied accentuation with which it is
liberally sprinkled, heightened to unrestrained gaiety, till we
almost see the capricious image of a dark-haired young lady of
the rococo period, tossing her white perruque laughingly into
the air; and we are reminded that Puccini had at first intended
to write an *opéra comique* on the subject of Manon, in which he
would have aimed at expressing in music only the lively and

diverting side of this light-hearted world. It was only afterwards that, instead of treating a series of light episodes from Manon's life, he found himself forced to choose the method of contrasting these with the gloomy close of her frivolous existence, which is dreary, rather than tragic. The whole of the first scene is full of this sunny, morning atmosphere. Young people are singing and loitering about, while the motive of the orchestral prelude gradually dominates the scene and swells into a chorus of *joie de vivre*, over which floats a supple tenor voice, celebrating the fleeting hours of happiness spent in light loves, while four girls' soprano voices, like the twitter of swallows, accompany the love-motive played by the orchestra. All of these motives are quite slight and sweet, and filled with the breath of May. They insinuate themselves, as it were, ingratiatingly into the whole, and merge once more into the sparkling, animated fireworks of the introductory music, which pervades the whole of the first act, and only once falls silent in this first scene, when Renato des Grieux strikes up his madrigal, which then develops into the finale of the act in a broad, swaying chorus, which is one of Puccini's most charming inspirations, a melody with which we cannot but fall in love, as it flutters like a rosy garland in some picture, upon which the kindly young deities of spring have lightly scattered little flowers and leaves. The graceful pastorale in B flat that accompanies Manon's entry is not only a short, pleasing ensemble number, but at the same time sketches the portrait of the simple, inexperienced, charming girl from the small provincial town. Her next motive, 'Manon Lescaut mi chiamo (Manon Lescaut they call me)', which is afterwards interwoven with Des Grieux's aria, is combined with an allusion to the love-motive, hitherto heard only in passing, in a thematic development that is full of significance. Puccini's tenderly exalted, ardently pulsing *cantilena* swells forth for the first time with all the passionate *rubato* of its vehement accents in Des Grieux's song, the heart-felt theme of which becomes the most important symbol of love in the whole work. The following scenes flit past in a fluent, melodious *parlando* style, but are always firmly based upon the orchestral accompaniment, with its clear, sharp contours and rhythmical variety, which forms a background, slight in colour and full of agility and *brio*, for the conversational recitative which only occasionally combines with the instrumental melody.   In the dialogue between the lovers can be heard whispers and murmurs of mortal dread and awakening desire, and though the suave, pastoral, oboe-like *amoroso* melody into which it overflows is like an echo from the peaceful realms of childhood, yet out of this melody, like a rustic lullaby, there springs, like a flame, a fatal passion, at first merely glowing and smouldering beneath the surface of shy hopes and timid, dawning attraction, like a warning hint of future menace, till it breaks forth abruptly and bursts into a blaze as the two young people flee together.   Next, after the rapid passage of buffoonery between Manon's drunken brother and the furious, baffled old Geronte, who had meant to carry off the fair Manon himself, the act closes with a song of youth, the bright, spring-like melody of the madrigal sung by the chorus, at first in unison, being, as it were, a sort of manifesto of light love.   Puccini never wrote an act with a more perfect and well-rounded unity than this one, for in his later works his method was more mosaic-like, consisting in the marshalling of a whole series of short phrases and disjointed scraps of melody one after the other, with a constant, restless change of time and key—a method which, with its incessant, and sometimes purposeless repetitions of themes and fluctuations of tempo, is more impressionistic and rhapsodic than that of this opera, the treatment of which, in the first two scenes, at least, is more architectural. Never again, till, perhaps, in *Turandot*, did he raise such a solidly constructed and well-articulated structure as in this act of *Manon*.

The beginning of the second act has points that anticipate the delightful *lever* scene in *Der Rosenkavalier*, and is full of Boucher-like colour.   It is a delicious period study in a golden frame, from which Manon steps forth with an almost impersonal air, like some allegorical figure in a rococo painting.   It would, however, be unfair to deny that Massenet's historical

sense is more convincing, and that he finds a more genuine
note to suggest the fragrance of that epoch; while, similarly,
the two principal motives in his *Manon* are more adequately
suggestive of his hero and heroine, possessing, above all, the
sensuous sweetness and abandonment, and the insouciant in-
fidelity of his lovely courtesan, and a more genuine perfume of
society in the age of the *Roi Soleil,* that outwardly charming,
though inwardly decadent world of abbés and gamblers, frivolous
marquises and courtly men of learning, adventurers of genius
and servile comedians, who delighted in playing at shepherds
and shepherdesses, and knew no god save that of self-indulgence
and pleasure.   His subtle hand possessed the exact degree of
lightness required to depict a captivating fascination.   Moreover, the essential point is that, in the French musician, this is
the heritage of birth and culture.   But Puccini is the more
richly endowed and vigorous of the two, and so succeeds in
doing something different, which marks an advance on Massenet.
Not only does he set old dance-rhythms to produce their spontaneous music, but he is conscious of those spiritual overtones
and simple human emotions which have remained unchanged
from of old.   His music has blood in its veins, not lemonade,
like that of Massenet, though the latter is superior to him in
intelligence—or rather, in sprightliness of wit.   Yet there is
no dearth of historical colour in Puccini's work either.   The
way in which, in the delicious scene of Manon's toilette at the
beginning of the act, he from the first accompanies the swift,
prattling dialogue by a charming symphonic *scherzo,* in which
he seems to take his motives, arrange a curl here and place a
patch or pin on a flower there, or underline a phrase as it were
with a make-up pencil, is masterly in its swift, rippling movement
and the light colour which he seems to dust on rapidly, as with a
powder-puff; and so is the art with which, in the dialogue
between the Lescaut brother and sister, which begins almost
in an indifferent tone, but works up to a fever of interest, the
somewhat insipid *arioso,* which seems almost to droop with
melancholy, conjures up the figure of Des Grieux, who has

meanwhile been abandoned by Manon and become a gambler; for the melody, first given out by Lescaut and then passionately taken up by Manon in tones of remorseful recollection, is a variant of the arcadian motive from the lovers' duet in the first act, and in its clear incisiveness is like a portrait in miniature. Again, the boredom with which Manon listens to the five-part madrigal that now begins is strange in one so fond of her image in the looking-glass; for the madrigal reflects her nature quite as well as does the minuet that she dances, being fascinatingly soulless, yet sentimental music from the realms of Watteau, suggesting the tunes played by a musical clock, or a decorative drapery of melody and formal grace, though through its tinkling notes, like silver bells, there none the less breathes here and there a gentle touch of feeling. In the trio of the minuet, in the minor key, which afterwards appears in the music accompanying Manon's death, like a touching reminiscence of brighter days, there is something of the weary beat of a little lost bird's wings, and the expiring breath of these vanities has a childlike pathos. All the more violent is the contrast with the breathless rush of the duet between the passionately imploring Manon and the bitterly contemptuous Des Grieux, who none the less succumbs once more to her spell. Never did Puccini reveal such indebtedness to *Tristan* as in this fevered duet, with its rising sequences, its yearning chromatic figures and imploring sevenths, the mounting swell of whose melodic line is as unmistakably characteristic of the composer as are the narcotic or pungent effects of his sophisticated harmonies, the high lights obtained by introducing notes extraneous to the scale, the blend of disparate and fragmentary chords and the effects of refracted light that these produce. But never, too, was he so full of fire as in this scene, hurled forth, as it were, with volcanic power, though its melodic treatment is still not quite free from hackneyed turns of phrase, and is still a little short of breath. Only gradually did Puccini's characteristic traits reveal themselves. On the other hand, its construction is far more compact and strongly articulated than is to be noted in

the works that followed, and the *fugato* passage, which is, however, not developed at any very great length, is a splendid
touch, for, in accordance with the literal meaning of the word
'fugue' (*fuga*, signifying flight), its perplexed hurryings and
trippings in the upper parts, and the long striding movement
in the bass parts, picture the renewed preparations for flight on
the part of the two fugitives, who are caught this time. It
provides a heightening of the dramatic tension to the pitch of
panting haste, a characteristic background, and, last but not
least, a powerful and effective contrast with the weighty
emphasis of the melody in Des Grieux's bitter and despairing
outburst against Manon, who finds it so hard to leave her
money and finery and her easy, pampered existence. 'Sempre la
stessa, Manon (Always the same, Manon)', he cries, a reproach
which might also be brought against Puccini's music, in view
of the sameness of his devices for expressing love and grief.

The intermezzo serves, as it were, to separate two worlds.
It is melancholy in its beauty, opening in a mood of Tristan-
like sadness; the disconsolate, tearful desolation of its melody
foreshadows that of the death-scene, after which it broadens
into a passage of sequences of ever-increasing intensity, finally
ending on the love-motive, charged with quivering passion.
As the quotation prefixed to it indicates, it is intended to express
Manon's imprisonment and transference to Havre; but it might
equally well—or badly—represent some other event, without
attaching a credible and unambiguous interpretation to music
that is capable of a number of interpretations. It may be
regarded far more convincingly as an instrumental transcription
of the words of piteous longing placed by Puccini at the head
of this intermezzo, in which, in Prévost's novel, Des Grieux
cries out for his Manon. The last two acts, to which it forms
a transition, have an atmosphere quite different from that of the
preceding ones. The rococo spirit is gone, the strains of dissolute frivolity and amorous dalliance have fallen silent, and all
that is left is human misery, the lamentations of the victims
of violence, the cries of distress of creature's in agony, and in

these we find Puccini's own most essential nature. This is his own true domain, both as man and as artist, and here, in the wails of the defenceless, in the silent tears of helplessness and abandonment, in all that makes the hearer thrill with sympathy and fierce indignation against the brutal caprices and abuse of power, he has achieved a feat that is unforgettable. The great ensemble in the third scene, in which women, both guilty and innocent, are denounced by their seducers, who have grown either jealous or simply indifferent, and are driven from their country and shipped off on a voyage to inhospitable regions, stings us to the most violent emotion. Puccini has written few things more penetratingly moving than this scene, with the cold, callous, business-like tone in which the sergeant reels off the names of the women to be deported, the voices of the spectators, whether indifferent, mocking, pitying, or even flirtatious, the quiet, argumentative tones of Manon's brother as he tries to rouse the crowd in her favour, and, floating above all this, the fruitless, bewildered lament of the hapless pair, who cannot bear to part. At the same time, we may here note a characteristic idiosyncrasy of the composer's, which is like-wise to be found both in the choral scenes of the earlier acts and in many of his later works: though Puccini cannot tolerate anything that tends to check the action, yet in these massed numbers it seems to come to a standstill, because he always interweaves the voices of the principal characters, whose words carry on the action, or at any rate provide its motive, into the general tissue of the whole, so that these words are hopelessly lost in the ensemble. After all, we see that his autocratic musical instinct was stronger than the artistic insight of the dramatist. Moreover, the situation here is so clear that it stands in no need of elucidation, and the progress of the weary, hopeless duet, now hardly concentrated into melody, but in which the voices merely float in a toneless whisper above the thematic tissue of the orchestra, in itself suffices to express the sombre atmosphere, heavy with destiny, that hangs like a black cloud over the path of the two lovers. The closing act, too, is made up of a single duet; and here, too, as the approach of death is heard in the music, combined with a suggestion of the grim, unending distances of the American plains, the exhaustion and tortures of thirst endured amid the burning wastes of the waterless prairie, Manon's collapse and fever, and her companion's vain hopes of rescue, we find the same atmosphere of gloom and pitiless anguish, which communicates itself to the exhausted listener as well. This act would be better omitted. The prospect of it, as indicated in the previous one, is enough —indeed, this would possibly make a more powerful ending. Nothing can exceed the desolation of the deportation scene, yet even this does not really move us. And if we ask the cause of this failure, the answer is that it is impossible to feel any real sympathy for the foolish, slavish weakling, with his unmanly apathy, who here stands for Des Grieux, or for the silly, vain, lustful, vacillating harlot, dazzled by gold and jewels, who represents Manon, and only succeeds in arousing a little sympathy because of her constant affection for her first lover. These are mere operatic puppets instead of human beings; and, though they are the principal characters, they remain purely episodic. Puccini fell in love with Prévost's Manon, and his spell has drawn all the music possible from this lovely, almost flowerlike figure, who abandons herself to every passing love as the flower does to the butterfly. But in doing so he failed to observe that the Manon of his opera has retained scarcely a single lovable trait of her original, but only the repulsive ones. And even music such as this is hardly enough by itself alone.

Yet in spite of all this, it will continue to live. But it has to be admitted that Puccini's music, unlike that of the great masters, knows nothing of God or of spirituality, nothing of the mystery of existence or the significance of life; and, unlike theirs, it gives no answer to questions concerning the relations between this world and the next. It does not rise to any high plane, or hear the call of any mysterious powers. It knows nothing of dreams or presentiments, nothing of the Idea, but only of its semblance in the material world of waking life. But it does know mankind. And though it may fail to bring release to the spirit and lend it wings, or to widen our inner vision, and though it lacks the power to transform the soul, it knows how to touch and move the heart. The voice of God is silent in it, but the fraternal voice of humanity, the *vox humana*, is clear and resonant.

Yet, by a contradiction hard to parallel, this fraternal voice issues from the mouths of puppets, and when they rend their hearts in pieces, we see that they are made of tow. All that Puccini attempts is to make men in his own image, He is indifferent to conventional style and exalted pathos, and cares only for the simple, touching emotions of creatures like unto himself, suffering and rejoicing as he does. Rhetorical heroes wearing the tragic buskin mean nothing to him. Thus, full of heart-felt expectation, he plumbs the depths of human existence as a whole, yet he fails to see that the features of it that he grasps are the purely theatrical ones. He has no desire to build a temple, but only habitations for human beings, yet their walls prove to be merely stage scenery. But his incredible fascination and, at the same time, his paradoxical quality lie in the fact that, in spite of his phenomenal instinct for stage requirements and stage effects in his music, he was absolutely unaware of all this, for, though his inward eye was always fixed upon the stage of life, and not upon the theatrical stage, with its painted scenery and the deceptive illumination of the footlights, and though he wrote for the theatre and was versed in all the subtlest tricks of his profession, he succeeded in remaining sincere, unconstrained and true-hearted, and in pouring forth streams of sincere, unconstrained, and true-hearted music.

There are melodies which, though genuine in feeling, do not wear well, and there are others that live for ever, and retain their youth. Puccini wrote some of both kinds, as well as some that from the first originated in deliberate intention rather than in spontaneous inspiration, yet that, none the less, possess

remarkable vitality.   It is hard to decide what laws determine
whether melodies will take permanent root or die out; this may
possibly have something to do with the words associated with
them, and it may be that many of them might awaken to real
and lasting life for the first time, if they could be separated
from their present words and linked with others better suited
to them, which might prove their predestined complement,
whether they treat of a similar subject or of quite a different
one.   An almost incalculable service might be rendered to
Edgar if a new and really poetic librettist were to arise for it to
be regenerated or even reborn; the same is true of many parts
of *Manon Lescaut* in which the words are a failure—though,
be it observed in passing, for the benefit of those German
judges who are always ready to reject Puccini as the very negation of an artist (*Unkünstler*), that, with regard to this question
of his operatic libretti, it is doing him the gravest injustice to
judge them by the translations, and not by the original text,
which, at any rate from *La Bohème* onward, reaches a level
quite capable of satisfying any artistic standards, not as regards
the subject-matter, which is often most crude and repulsive,
but as regards the quality of the language and the supple,
animated dignity of the verse, which is often genuinely poetical,
and almost always melodious, easily set to music and worthy of
a musical setting.   While, on the other hand, the translations
really are of an execrable, not to say grotesque and barbarous
clumsiness, that is an outrage upon sense and taste, and makes
them quite unsuited for declamation, besides which they are
absurdly feeble, distorting the original with unintentionally
comic effects; so that even when they try to do justice to the
meaning, and do not distort every sentence, they at any rate
destroy the distinctive quality and charm of the Italian original,
or at least rob it of its individual savour.   Even the best of them
lose a little of the living quality of the Italian text—as though
we were to speak, not of Giacomo Puccini, but of Jakob or
James Puccini.

While looking through the original drafts of the Master's

operas or operatic fragments I constantly came across a certain word: when he had written down a passage and rejected it afterwards, making it almost illegible by striking it out and scribbling over it, only to discover, after all, that he could not improve it, and might as well restore it again, he would write beside it in his firm, bold handwriting, '*Vive!*'—as though some creator were to exclaim, 'Let there be life!' Every time I came upon it, this word affected me strangely. And when I had the manuscript score of *Manon Lescaut* before me, I felt that, at the end of the opera, after the date of its completion, he ought to have written this same '*Vive!*' For it was the first of his works that he might with justifiable pride have sent out into the world accompanied by this superscription.

Puccini wrote every act of this opera, which was finally to confirm his reputation, at a different place, whether at Lucca, Milan, or Torre del Lago. Curiously enough, the third was written last, in a little Swiss retreat at Vacallo, a mountain village situated high above the frontier station of Chiasso. He liked to live a primitive life at times, and besides, it was as well for him to economize. We can see how much truth there was in the reports of his supposed wealth from a passage in one of his letters dated 1893, in which he describes with absolute delight how he had bought a bicycle, which he could only manage by paying for it in modest monthly instalments. It was not till much later, after the success of *La Bohème* and *Tosca*, that he acquired any property worth mentioning, but then it descended upon him in a perfect avalanche. At that time, however, during the *Manon* period, he was glad to make a living that would prevent him from being harassed by anxiety, and lived quite a simple life with his family. The little house at Vacallo looked as though it might have been bought at a toy-shop, for it consisted of three tiny rooms and no more, piled one above the other like boxes. On the ground-floor was a kitchen, above that the parents' bedroom, and on top of all the attic in which the children slept. As for the parents' bedroom, the Maestro said contentedly that it was a nice, accommodating apartment, that did not mind how it was used[1]; for during the daytime it served indiscriminately as dining-room, study or reception-room, but chiefly as a music-room, for Puccini sat from morning till late at night over his work, which he wanted at all costs to finish while he was still there, to the supreme disgust of Tonio and Fosca, who were bored to death in these mountain solitudes, remote from the world and with no play-mates, and, having long since exhausted all the resources of childish mischief, could hardly wait for the return to their beloved Torre del Lago. But they had to be patient, for the work had not yet advanced far enough, and they kept listening eagerly to the fragmentary chords that reached their ears from the rather dubious little piano in their father's room, and followed them with feverish anxiety. Their interest, however, was not in the music, but was merely due to *il babbo's* promise that they should start for home at once so soon as they heard a certain theme with certain closing chords full of wild despera-tion. He had played them the love-motive, which seems to break off, dripping with blood, at the end of the third act, closing, as it were, with a sudden shriek, and they had heard it so often that it was quite familiar to them. No wonder, then, that they were on the look-out for it day and night. Little Fosca was particularly annoyed, for she had only one frock, which did not remain clean long when she was at play, so that whenever it was washed she had to stay in bed till it was dry. Yet still those wretched chords which they longed so eagerly to hear failed to ring out again.

At times, too, the children would loiter about the neighbouring house as well, for music floated forth from it too; besides which, on their arrival it had been most amusingly decorated. Over the door had hung a clown and from the window opposite Puccini's room had fluttered a flag upon which was painted a gigantic hand. For Leoncavallo was staying here, and had greeted his fellow-artist with this play on the name of the works

[1] TRANSLATOR'S NOTE.—Puccini's words, as quoted by Fraccaroli, were 'una buona camera indulgente, che lasciava fare'.

LOST IN THOUGHT

THE COMPOSER AT TORRE DEL LAGO

upon which the two of them were then engaged; his own
Pagliacci (Puppets) and Puccini's *Manon* (signifying in Italian a
big hand).   At that time the two composers were on amicable,
if not very cordial terms.   It was not till later that strained
relations arose and alienated them from each other for good;
nor were these due exclusively to Puccini's at first unconscious
dislike of this composer who wrote the famous opera on the
life of a clown ('Bajazzo'), a dislike which he afterwards displayed more and more aggressively, and which was, moreover,
cordially reciprocated by Leoncavallo.   But during that summer
of 1892 harmony still prevailed, and they lived peaceably as
neighbours, vying with each other in the progress of their
composition.

   Then at last, late one night, the love-motive rang out, together
with the abrupt chords symbolic of fate, and made their way
even into little Fosca's slumbers.   She woke up, jumped out
of her little bed, hurried downstairs with bare feet, dressed in
nothing but her nightgown, and rushed into the room where
the Master was working, with cries of: 'Now, *babbo*, now!'
Puccini was still dreamy and absorbed, being in that state of
subsiding agitation that accompanies the close of all creative
work.   He stared at the child as she stood stammering with
excitement.   Surely, he thought, at her age she could not
possibly understand the happiness experienced in the hour that
sees the completion of a piece of work.   'What do you mean
by "Now"?' he asked.   The thin little arms were clasped
about his neck as she cried: 'Why, now—now we are going
away—away, away, aren't we?   You promised!'   Puccini
looked at the little childish face, all aglow with expectation,
smiled, and simply nodded his head; but both of them knew
that, though this moment meant such different things to the
two of them, it would be an ineffaceable memory.   And on the
next day they did really return to Torre del Lago.

   Here a paradise awaited the Maestro and his family, the lake
of Massaciuccoli, the Pineta—the pine-forest, which stretches
for some fifteen miles, from Pisa to Viareggio—and the little

I

village which, when he first settled there, numbered some eighty inhabitants, simple people who attach little value to autographs or signed photographs, and still less to conversations about music, the theatre and publishers. It was a godsend to him, the fulfilment of a desire that he had cherished all his life, a refuge for the artist to whom social life was a torture, who felt at his ease in a shooting-coat and uncomfortable in evening dress, for his shyness was so insuperable that he would turn tail at the door of a café where he had meant to go and look at the latest newspapers, simply because he could not pluck up courage to sit down among all those people. As we may remember, he was even incapable of stammering out a few words in response to a toast at a banquet, though in a *tête-à-tête* conversation he was both animated and talkative himself and stimulating to those with whom he was conversing. Here, at Torre del Lago, he felt quite at home. When he had to stay in Paris or New York for the purpose of supervising the production of one of his operas, and was surrounded by people who gushed over him and pestered him for souvenirs, reporters who bothered him for interviews, or fascinating ladies whose ready complaisance he found it hard to resist, his letters were always full of an almost morbid homesickness for Torre del Lago, and no place on earth was dearer to him. Here he was entirely himself, living a peaceful life in his family circle, free from all constraint, and could shoot, fish, or lie dreaming in his boat. It was here that he composed almost all his works, with the exception of *Turandot*, and it was to this spot that his heart always returned. Even in after years, when he was driven from this refuge, partly because his fame attracted too many curious strangers, and partly because a factory had been built close to his villa, and its steam sirens were a torture to his ear, while its abominable smells tainted the whole neighbourhood, he could not bear altogether to abandon the place which had become his home, looking like the bungalow of some great captain of industry. He built himself a roomy house not far away, among the pine-woods of Viareggio, but as often as he could, he would walk or ride through the Pineta as far as Torre del Lago—and not only when he was shooting, either. A magic power seemed to draw him to the simple white house on the banks of the lake, where his days of melancholy had gradually become rarer, where he had been happy and lived for his work, and where his mortal remains found their last resting-place.

At first he had rented a little house, which he occupied with his young family. Later he had a house built for him, a long, one-storied building stretching along the shore close to the water, and surrounded by a handsome garden with a wealth of shrubs and trees; and for more than twenty years this house formed the centre of his world. The rooms have been left unchanged, and the study still shows signs of his presence, as though he had only just left it. On the large table next the little piano is lying some music-paper, upon which is the eye-glass used by the composer, who had become short-sighted. Over the piano are photographs of Mahler, Nikisch, Caruso, Franz Schalk, Madame Jeritza, Miss Geraldine Farrar, and other artists who had been associated with the composer. In a corner is Troubetzkoy's splendid bronze statuette, instinct with life, of Caruso as Ramerrez, and opposite, against the wall adorned with frescoes by artist friends of the composer's, and below the life-sized portrait of Puccini, stands the table round which his friends smoked, drank, or played cards, while he sat at the piano humming and striking chords, occasionally calling out some racy remark to them, or, if the members of the round table fell silent, asking them whether they were asleep. He encouraged them to call him by the brotherly *tu* because it 'gave him back his youth'.[1] It is almost as though he were still there, sitting as was his habit, with his hat on his head, as he sought for his precious harmonies, or walking over to the window, deep in thought, when inspiration languished—for he never tried to force it—or else striding through the garden to

[1] TRANSLATOR'S NOTE.—Puccini's words, as quoted by Fraccaroli, were: 'Dammi dal tu, ché mi ringiovanisci'.

the terrace overlooking the lake, so as to loose a boat from its moorings.

Unlike most creative musicians, Puccini did not work in the morning; the evening and the night-time were his more productive hours of composition, and he would often sit at the keyboard by the open window till daybreak, playing and singing a melody with a dozen different variants, accompanying it now by one harmonic progression, now by another, till it could at last be written down. Thus it often happened that these strains penetrated to the bedrooms of the girls and young men living in the neighbouring houses, so that they would sing many of the melodies before Puccini's veranda long before the opera was finished. He was always delighted when this happened, for then he knew that his inspiration had been a happy and a living one, and that his music was capable of striking root in simple souls. But he had to be very much absorbed in his work to decline a summons to go shooting, and even the soundest sleep would not prevent him from waking up immediately and jumping out of bed when Giovanni Manfredi, the worthy peasant and poacher—nicknamed Lappore, in the local dialect, on account of his white eyelashes—would throw up a handful of pebbles at 'Sor Giaomo's' window some night when there was no moon, thereby informing him that he had sighted some water-fowl, that the wind was propitious and that he was waiting for him. On these occasions Puccini would hastily slip on his bed-jacket over his undervest, and above that a woollen jersey, adding coarse canvas trousers and thick boots, for preference each belonging to a different pair; then, having knotted a handkerchief round his neck and crushed a hat down over his cap, he would creep quietly downstairs in this picturesque shooting-costume, swearing as the steps creaked, lest he might wake Donna Elvira—which he would not have done for anything—and, having got his guns out of their case, he was off! The result was not always worth all the trouble, and it may be doubted whether Puccini was a good shot. There is a story of a shooting expedition in Brazil and of the Master's disgracefully bad shots at partridges, which flew gaily away, that would tend to prove the contrary, and legends vary as to whether he was a wild huntsman or rather a tame one. It may well be supposed that the creator of Scarpia was not entirely devoid of cruelty, and that the composer of *Gianni Schicchi* pitied the poor slaughtered beasts from the depths of his heart, while devouring them with an excellent appetite. He took a special delight in trespassing beyond the area reserved for his own shooting and in playing tricks on the watchful *carabinieri*. It is said, however, that on one of these occasions his life was in danger, for these good fellows, who would not have touched a hair of their beloved 'Sor Giaomo' even if they had met him face to face in a forbidden path, discharged a few shots at his boat as it glided away into the darkness, and hit the water immediately in front of him. On another occasion he was actually arrested as a poacher and brought before the courts. It was a most amusing business, for the judge trembled at the prospect of having to convict the world-famous Maestro, the consequence of which would no doubt have been his own transference to some such place as Sicily. The counsel for the defence, who was a friend of Puccini's, delivered a pleading full of flagrant sophistries, claiming that he ought to be discharged on the ground that not a single bird had been found dead anywhere near the spot, and that without some such *corpus delicti* none but the most imbecile administrator of the law could possibly talk of poaching and infringements of the game-laws; the double musket-shot which had been heard, and had provided a pretext for this abominable prosecution of the Master, was, he said, merely a trial shot with Puccini's new gun, and he could hardly have been expected to try such a dangerous experiment with powder and shot indoors. Moreover, being in his own boat, he was standing on his own ground and inside his own property. Though everybody in court knew perfectly well that Puccini really had infringed the game-laws, this judicial comedy ended, not in a conviction, but in a solemn luncheon—an incident symbolic of the undisturbed serenity and perfect immunity from interference in which the universally beloved Maestro lived at Torre del Lago.

Possibly his love of sport had something symbolic about it, too. It was most certainly a case of repression in the Freudian sense. Nobody can say what reactions may have been set up in the course of these roamings through the forest and excursions on the lake, in a musician who was capable of composing *Tosca*, and not only wrote the music, but himself planned the dramatic action in the last act of *The Girl of the Golden West*, which had been on quite different lines in Belasco's play, the hideous man-hunt and the threats of torture being added on Puccini's own initiative. Had it not been for his love of sport, these reactions might have produced an unpleasing effect, not only on his art, but perhaps on his everyday life too. But it was a distraction to him, for the pastime, and the delight he took in forbidden things, were a relaxation to his nerves; yet at the same time it was no doubt a symbolic substitute for intellectual sport. When he was in pursuit of an idea which refused to be caught, when a motive flitted out of his reach before he could catch it on the wing, when an intellectual close-time circumscribed his musical inspiration, or when he had spent months on end, exasperated and discontented, in his search for some operatic prey, and no new libretto was in sight, it was the silly fishes that he would catch in his hands, or the clumsy tame hunting-owl, whose neck he wrung on the spot, or the wretched water-fowl that bore the brunt of his temper.

As we stand on the terrace constructed in front of the house, overlooking the lake, where Puccini festivals are now held every summer, we can understand the Master's love for this peaceful spot. The broad, shimmering surface of the lake, whose waters find their way to the sea near Viareggio, the majestic chain of mountains fading away in the green and blue distance, with snowfields on many of their peaks, the dazzling gleam of the distant quarries of Carrara, from which Michelangelo obtained the blocks for his gigantic statues, the little villages scattered along the shore, with the red roofs of their huts in the sunshine—all formed a landscape in which he felt himself to be a man, and was able to live like one. When he went down to the miniature harbour that he had himself planned, and, having chosen the smartest among the little flotilla of skiffs and motor-boats that rose and fell on the water, sped like an arrow across the waters, accompanied only by Tonio, or by one of the peasants who understood machinery, or when he rode on his bicycle through the pine-forest, or pursued his meditations in the garden, with his eternal cigarette in his mouth and his head, wearing the inevitable hat, sunk on his breast, with his coat unbuttoned, one hand stuck in the front of his waistcoat, and the other in his pocket, as he was usually to be seen, he felt like a little king, at home in his own kingdom. But his 'subjects', too, the inhabitants of Torre del Lago, were well aware of all that he meant to them, and were absolutely devoted to him. They might know nothing of his real nature, and it was only incidentally that they heard of his operas and their glorious progress round the world; perhaps, indeed, they valued him only as the natives of Carlsbad do their springs— that is, as an attraction to strangers, and a sort of natural wonder. But even their simplicity recognized his superiority, and requited his sojourn among them with respect and trusting affection. When his dead body was brought home from distant Belgium, the crowd thronged to the spot and stood there for hours in the streaming rain, weeping loudly, while the bier, upon which the coffin was laid, was lifted from the railway carriage and borne over all their heads into the black-draped villa, which was now to become the Master's resting-place. They were all loath to leave him; every one had brought a flower from his humble garden to lay upon the catafalque, and all of them felt that they had suddenly grown old. They knew that not only had the glowing spring ceased to flow to which they owed their humble well-being, and of whose gushing waters they had felt as proud as though they had been due to some merit of their own; but they also felt dimly that Torre del Lago, from which such streams of tenderness and love had flowed forth in music to the world, was no longer the blooming place that it had been, but only the mausoleum of the man whom they had seen in his days of happiness, whether laughing or swearing, whether good-natured and jocular or harsh and angry, whether cordial and expansive or laconic to the point of morosity; but always smoking like a chimney.

CHAPTER VIII

MELODIA AMOROSA ('LA BOHÈME')

Zart Gedicht und Regenbogen
Wird auf dunklen Grund gezogen.—GOETHE.[1]

ON 1st February 1893, *Manon Lescaut* was performed for the first time at the Teatro Regio, Turin. Its success was sensational, sweeping, and triumphant. At first the audience was reserved, not to say cold and mistrustful; but as soon as it came to the irresistible, sensuously graceful madrigal, a storm of applause swept through the house, and the tenor Cremonini had to pause and bow his acknowledgment repeatedly, hand in hand with Puccini, who, according to Italian usage, had to appear upon the stage too, and respond in person to the audience's expressions of applause. At the close of every act, moreover, the public, now in a perfect uproar, called him before the footlights more than thirty times, together with the singers, who were weeping with delight.

We may here comment, by way of parenthesis, that, though this is a matter of minor importance, it cannot but astonish non-Italians that Puccini, who had such a sense of the theatre, and regarded a strong plot, full of progressively heightened dramatic tension, as the most important condition requisite for producing his music, should interrupt the action in this fashion and destroy all illusion by so far complying with tradition as to appear upon the stage in modern costume, surrounded by the singers in their stage attire, to acknowledge the spontaneous bursts of clapping. This very fact is significant of a racial difference, and marks an essential distinction between the Italian operatic public, and, say, the German. In Germany

[1] A tender poem, like the rainbow, is traced against a gloomy background.

it would be regarded as a serious breach of propriety if, on receiving applause, the singer were to lapse from his role and become a private individual in order to bow his thanks; and if any composer were to take it into his head to suspend and upset the action by appearing from the wings to make his bow, thus trying to attract the applause to himself as well and share it with the actor on the spot, instead of waiting till the fall of the curtain, he would provoke such serious annoyance as to deprive him of any desire to repeat the experiment. In Italy, however, the contrary is the case; and if any composer were to fail to respond to applause immediately, this would be interpreted as conceit, and would give offence. The Italian public is far more naïve, and dramatic continuity in opera is of less importance in its eyes; or else its imagination is so lively that, especially in moments of ardent enthusiasm, it simply does not notice the material interruption, and can switch its attention on again immediately. Moreover, in its eyes the composer is simply a part of the whole, like the conductor and the orchestra; and the fact that the latter are visible might equally well be regarded as detracting from the spell of the stage. The contrast between the Festival Theatre at Bayreuth, on the one hand, with its hidden orchestra and prohibition of applause during the progress of the piece, or even of curtain calls, and the Italian opera house on the other, where on occasion it is possible to encore even a death-scene, a conductor who refuses to do so being liable to be pelted with fruit, is significant not only of two different national temperaments, but also of two different ways of approaching life in general.

The criticisms that appeared on the morrow of the first performance of *Manon* were unreservedly unanimous in their extravagant hymns of praise. 'Great though our expectations had been,' wrote Giovanni Pozza, the distinguished critic of the *Corriere della Sera*, who had been sent to Turin expressly for the occasion, 'the opera astonishes us by its great artistic merit, the power of its musical conception, and its dramatic effectiveness (*teatralità*). . . . The human and at the same time romantic quality of the Chevalier des Grieux's love for Manon, with her sweetness and ingenuous depravity, has unsealed well springs of the freshest and most artistic inspiration in Puccini's genius'—though it is curious, at least, to note that the writer of this dithyrambic report is actually capable of asserting that this opera, half conventional and half directly drawn from life, and delineated, as it were, partly in silver-point and partly in sanguine, fulfils more than any other opera of the present day the cry of 'Back to the antique!' and may be called classical in character. Criticism really seems to suffer from the hereditary curse that, when confronted with a new work of art, its paths are as obscure as are its leading representatives, and that even the well-meaning ones among them are thrown into such confusion as to make it possible to describe a work of a high class (*ein Werk von Klasse*) as a classical work—that is, one displaying grandeur, austerity of style, and an antipathy for naturalism—everything, in fact, that, in spite of all its attractive qualities of a different order, is entirely lacking in Puccini's *Manon Lescaut*, and indeed in all his other operas. But we cannot but be glad when a work of merit meets with cordial approbation, instead of the usual carping criticism of conceited superiority; and leading musical opinion in Italy granted it this approval, sometimes even to the point of exaggeration. It was a long time before it reverted to a superior tone in criticizing Puccini. The critic Berta admitted, in the *Gazzetta del Popolo*, that he had seldom found himself so much at a loss to collect and sort all the confusing impressions of the evening and the ideas suggested to him in the course of the work, but characterized the effect that it produced upon him as great, unforgettable and of high merit (*eccellente*), and referred to Puccini as one of the most able (*forte*), if not the most able of all young Italian operatic composers. And Giuseppe Depanis of the *Gazzetta Piemontese*, not content with enthusiastically trumpeting forth the fame of the work in his criticisms and celebrating its honourable triumph, which had not been won by intrigue or advertisement, also took the greatest pains to obtain the *cavaliere's* cross for the composer, and was overjoyed when his efforts succeeded, and he was able to announce to the Maestro that he was about to receive this distinction. Instead of embracing him, however, the ungrateful Puccini merely assumed a rather self-satisfied expression and remarked with crushing irony, 'Think of that, now! (*Oh, guarda!*).' For the unfortunate composer thought less of orders, medals, and diplomas than he did of a promising libretto or a living and inspired melody.

Since the production of *Manon Lescaut* Puccini was recognized as possessing the most outstanding ability among the modern operatic composers of his country and as the legitimate heir to the genuine and unfailing Italian gift of melody. But, as always happens, he was not only recognized, but immediately given a label. It was taken for granted that in future he was to write nothing but operas of the rococo, or, at the outside, of the Renaissance period. He was, indeed, in a difficult position, for if he so much as appeared to repeat himself, or if one of his vocal phrases even seemed to be reminiscent of an earlier one, the public was furious, and behaved most insultingly; while the critics, on the other hand, were furious because, instead of high tragic plots and grand, exalted passions, he turned more and more lovingly to the 'little things' of the human heart.

Not that he troubled about either of them. He now felt strong enough and rich enough in internal resources to go his own way without troubling about the precepts of others, listening only to the voice of his own soul.

There is one amusing detail that we must not omit to mention, for it casts a sidelight upon the psychology of rival operatic composers. Massenet, whose *Manon* has maintained its precedence over Puccini's work outside Italy—in my opinion, I must repeat, only on account of its superior libretto—evidently felt it so impossible to endure the brilliant success of the 'other' *Manon*, that he made a supreme effort, and came forward, a year after the first performance of Puccini's opera, with a new one-act *Portrait de Manon*—a portrait of which the paint was hardly

given time to dry, for it was at once relegated to the lumber-
room for ever—a failure in which there is a certain retributive
justice; for hatred may make an artist productive, but envy never.

We have already intimated in passing that, while still engaged
upon *Manon*, Puccini was possessed by the idea of composing
a *Buddha* as his next work.   This shows a curious lack of self-
knowledge in an artist who was usually so honest and clear-
sighted with regard to himself and his own limitations.   In
this case, however, he seemed unaware that, apart from all the
other faculties that he would have required if he was to succeed
in depicting in music the human sublimity and love of such a
figure as Buddha—a love lavished upon all the world, and
rising superior to all selfish impulses—as well as the Indian
exoticism of the background, he lacked one essential quality:
that of spiritual exaltation, the raising of material experience
to the metaphysical plane, and the power to infuse into his
music that mystery without which Prince Gautama and his
renunciation of the world could never have been made convincing.   It is hardly possible that Puccini could have heard
of Richard Wagner's project of sketching the plan for a drama
dealing with Buddha after his *Parsifal*.   The knowledge of this
intention alone would presumably have been sufficient to deter
him from following in the footsteps of that mightiest of all
composers of music-drama; but it is probable that the aspect
of Buddha he would have chosen would not have been that of
the universal sage and teacher of humanity, but of the young
prince who abandons splendour and pleasure and passes through
life with his eyes fixed upon poverty and misery, so that Puccini
would have stopped at the point where we have reason to sup-
pose Wagner would have begun.   Puccini revered the Master
of Bayreuth with an admiration verging on humility.   Even
in his mature years he felt his own comparative insignificance
so deeply that once, when he had been reading the score of
Tristan for hours, he pushed it aside with bitter resignation,
exclaiming in his chagrin: 'We are nothing but mandolin-
players and dilettantes: so much the worse for us if we allow

our feelings to be stirred. This terrific music reduces us to nothingness and admits of no imitation!' In his eyes *Parsifal* was the one work of all others, so much so that he allowed himself to be drawn to Bayreuth (as we have seen, in pleasurable circumstances). He was fond of playing the Prelude, the Grail music and the Good Friday music from memory for hours on end, and when he was in Vienna, instead of hearing one act on each of the three successive evenings on which *Parsifal* was performed, as he had intended, in order to enjoy it without fatigue, he remained spellbound every time from beginning to end. He was always studying *Die Meister-singer*, and had analysed it in the minutest detail. Hence he would have felt it presumptuous to venture to carry out an idea of the great Master's, though, in spite of all his unbounded reverence for him, he none the less managed to remain inde-pendent of his influence to an extent which may almost be considered admirable. However this may be, Puccini's lucky star preserved him from venturing upon a Buddha opera, which would have led him into an intellectual and artistic sphere where he would have been doomed to failure.

Nor is this the only subject whose treatment we are sur-prised to find the Maestro contemplating; and this warns us to be cautious in our view of Puccini's nature as an artist, and perhaps even to revise it. I have already intimated that he applied to poets of note, and not merely to the ordinary run of librettists, in the hope of obtaining collaborators suited to his true nature. He requested Maeterlinck to suggest subjects to him, but did not receive any proposals that bore fruit. He entered into correspondence with Gabriele d'Annunzio, whose sketches, proved, however, unfit for his purposes. He asked Alphonse Daudet's permission to turn *Tartarin de Tarascon* into an *opéra bouffe*, nor did he abandon this desire till it was seen that the figure of Tartarin himself and the possibilities of framing a plot with him as its centre were both too slight. But the idea that engaged his attention longest was that of an opera based upon Émile Zola's *La Faute de l'Abbé Mouret*. He thoroughly steeped himself in the wondrous atmosphere of the book, in the luxuriant Eden-like bloom of its landscape, and the innocent love and ultimate lapse into sin of its characters; and he had already conceived the idea for a scenario, and even become so deeply absorbed in the subject as to start sketching the music, when he learnt from Zola that the subject had already been entrusted to the author's friend Alfred Bruneau, who did, indeed, compose the music for a few works of Zola's, some of which the composer had written specially for him. Puccini afterwards embodied in his *Suor Angelica* a large proportion of the sketches for this music of which he had dreamed in vain. As we see, it was not always his fault if he had to make shift with such texts as were accessible; and, we are bound to admit, it was thanks to him that these assumed a suitably terse and dramatically logical form that offered due scope for his music.

He took incessant pains to find the right subjects, and carried several scenarios about with him for a long time, testing them by describing them to others, only to discover that, though he had at first been full of unbounded enthusiasm for them, they had lost their hold on him and no longer touched his heart; and so far as he was concerned that settled the fate of any proposed opera for good, however tempting it may have been. It is quite in keeping with his temperament that the fate of the hapless Queen Marie Antoinette should have occupied his mind for years, and that the contrasting vicissitudes of her life, sufferings, and death should have moved him deeply both as man and artist; but in the long run this subject, too, lost interest for him, and so did Pierre Louÿs's sentimental and passionate tragi-comedy of modern life, *La Femme et le Pantin* (The Woman and the Puppet), which for a time produced a violent, though not a lasting impression upon both the French and the German stage. Puccini was strongly moved by it, and approached Maurice Vaucaire with a view to the drafting of a libretto based on the play, which was forthwith translated into Italian. The work was even announced in the papers as Puccini's next opera under the title of *Conchita*, but Minnie, the 'Girl of the Golden

West', ousted the girl of the Paris pavements and ended by suppressing her entirely. The Maestro's mind was exercised even longer by another subject for an opera, in which what chiefly attracted him were the unbridled passions of Sicilian life and the power of the 'jettatura', or evil eye. Immediately after the completion of *Manon Lescaut* he was irresistibly attracted by *La Lupa* (The She-wolf), a crude drama, full of brutal vigour and bloodthirsty bigotry, by Giovanni Verga, who wrote the libretto for *Cavalleria*. He even went to Sicily, came to terms with Verga, studied the people and their songs, and wrote a quantity of music for it. Yet all the while he felt a secret doubt. There was something within him that protested against certain scenes, especially the last, in which blood is shed while a procession is passing by, singing its holy litanies. On his way home he met the Countess Blandine Gravina, Cosima Wagner's daughter, on board the boat; and when she asked him about his projected compositions he described to her the subject of *La Lupa*. She was horrified: 'Beware, Maestro,' she exclaimed. 'It will bring you bad luck to associate your music with deeds of blood and sensuality, and with a religious procession as a background! How horrible!' [1] That settled the question. In terms of sincere regret he notified Verga that he had irrevocably abandoned the idea. But this music, too, was not lost. That which he had laid aside as dead in Sicily woke to life in the Parisian garret of *La Bohème*, and Rodolfo's very first *arioso*, 'Nei cieli bigi (Lazily rising)', revives a melody which was born beneath the blaze of the blue southern skies, darkened at times by the smoke of Etna, only to become an address to the grey, overcast sky of Montmartre; though, strictly speaking, it is as little expressive of the one as of the other, but rather of merriment and care-free youth.

But dissimilar though the two scenes are, 'extremes meet'.

[1] TRANSLATOR'S NOTE.—The Countess Gravina's actual words, as quoted by Fraccaroli, were: 'Ah, Maestro, non voglia mischiare questo dramma di sensualità e di delitto a un episodio religioso! Le porterà sfortuna!'

A PAGE OF *La Bohème*, ACT III (reduced facsimile)

Instead of the fierce peasant tragedy of a frenzied woman, *Manon Lescaut* was followed by the 'old, yet ever new' story of young lovers, starving yet full of hope, who do not take hunger and cold too seriously or love too lightly, who have fits of jealousy, but are quickly reconciled, and whose hearts 'break in two', as in Heine's poem, when life or death robs them of that which they hold most dear.   Henri Murger's *La Vie de Bohème* had fallen into the Master's hands, and kindled him to enthusiasm.   This time it was not the man, but the musician who found himself between two women: he became the hopeless slave of Mimi and Musetta, and with fiery impatience urged Illica and Giacosa (the latter of whom he also meant to interest in his *Buddha*) to compose an operatic libretto in which the rich abundance of scenes in Murger's book would have to be condensed into four.   The choice was a difficult one; the abundant wealth of the story was so rich in matter, and the unrestrained imagination which Illica brought to supplement it was so exuberant, that *La Vie de Bohème* yielded from fifteen to twenty acts.   They had regretfully to omit much that was charming and much that was very funny, and many outbursts of rage on the part of the choleric Illica had to be appeased; while even that which had already been decided upon had to be constantly modified, rearranged, and often presented in quite a different fashion.   Ten times the weary librettists threw up their work in a rage before the four acts were finally completed, in a supple form with well-balanced contrasts, as well-constructed and ready to be set to music as Puccini could desire.   During this period Giulio Ricordi hardly knew whether he was a publisher or a consulting librettist, so incessantly was he called upon to settle quarrels and deliver judgment, like a very Solomon. As a matter of fact, his word was almost always final, and thanks to him the often discouraged composer was enabled to have his way, and the book to attain a final form in which it had satisfactorily shaken off all tendency to hypertrophy.

By a curious parallelism of events, Puccini came into collision with other composers over all three of his operas that first became

K

famous: in the case of *Manon* with Massenet, in the case of *Tosca* with Franchetti, and in the case of *La Bohème* with Leoncavallo. But whereas the conflict over the first two took place only behind the scenes, and, so to speak, without bloodshed, there was a serious clash with the author and composer of *Pagliacci*, and it is not altogether easy to discern what motives were involved, and which of the two composers should be absolved of guilt. Things probably happened much as they do in the history of the world in general, in which conflicts are not always decided on ethical grounds, but the stronger carries off the victory. Leoncavallo was most likely in the right, but in the end Puccini vindicated his own claim.

While Puccini had still been at work on *Manon*, Ruggiero Leoncavallo had offered his fellow-composer an operatic libretto bearing the title of *Vie de Bohème*, which he did not want to set to music himself, at least for the time being. Whether Puccini's judgment was influenced by the fact that he did not much like the author of the text, or whether he rather distrusted the altruism of a colleague who, as a rule, always wrote his own libretti, and was now probably trying to dispose of a book that nobody wanted, and that was most likely too feeble for him to use himself, the fact remains that Puccini, who was at that time unacquainted with Murger's novel, scarcely looked at the libretto, but declined it, and in a week or two's time probably forgot the whole incident. About a year later the two composers met, exchanged amicable greetings, and fell into the usual conversation of composers, on such topics as operatic rivalries, singers, managers, publishers, and their own work; and Puccini—to follow, more or less closely, the account given in *Giacomo Puccini intimo*, by his two friends Guido Marotti and the painter Ferruccio Pagni—remarked with a deep sigh of satisfaction, simply for the purpose of annoying the other man: 'I have been looking for a good operatic libretto for ages, and now I have found one with which I am absolutely delighted'. Leoncavallo pricked up his ears. 'What subject is that?' he inquired. '*La Bohème*, by Illica and Giacosa, after Murger's

novel. . . . But what is the matter with you?' The stout
Leoncavallo had sprung to his feet, turning first as red in the
face as though he were on the point of an apoplectic stroke, and
then as pale as death, and spluttered: 'What? You are writing
a *Bohème* too? Why, I offered you my libretto last year, and
now you have the face to tell me that you are composing an
opera on the same subject, to a libretto by Giacosa and Illica?
But supposing I tell you that I have myself set my *Vita di
Bohème* to music?' 'Capital!' answered Puccini quickly. 'So
that means that there will be two *Bohèmes*.' 'Abominable!'
shouted the other. 'The idea came from me in the first place.'
'Very good! And the music will come from me!' 'Very well,
then,' replied Leoncavallo, foaming with rage, 'I shall go to
the *Secolo*, and insert a notice establishing my prior claim!'
'And I,' snorted Puccini, 'shall go to the *Corriere della Sera*!'
Without taking leave of each other, they both hurried off in
different directions, and in the morning the astonished public
heard of a *Bohème* that had been completed by Maestro Leoncavallo, while at midday it read of a *Bohème* to which Maestro
Puccini was just putting the finishing touches. For the time
the race was to Leoncavallo. While Puccini was still absorbed
in work on his opera, the rival one was performed in Paris, and
a little later in Vienna, with but little success, to the fury of
Gustav Mahler, who, with much gnashing of teeth, had had to
abide by the contract signed by his predecessor, and, what is
more, to look on while the neighbouring Theater an der Wien
was simultaneously performing Puccini's work, of which he
was particularly fond. A little while later he took it over and
staged an enchanting production, as a result of which Leoncavallo's poor opera was finally consigned to oblivion. So Puccini's
supposition that there would be two *Bohèmes* was not confirmed.
After all, there is only one.

While Puccini was working at his opera at Torre del Lago
with greater fervour than ever, the band of friends who were
bidden every evening to the Maestro's villa formed itself into
a club bearing the name of the new opera—an expression of

genuine esteem which, pleasing to relate, did not take the form of inflated language and solemn offerings of incense, but assumed the mask of nonsense and jollity. I quote the statutes of this 'La Bohème Club', because they seem to me typical of the atmosphere by which Puccini was surrounded, as well as of the artist's love of exuberant fooling in his hours of relaxation. He was naturally assigned the hilarious office of honorary president of this light-hearted society, which included some distinguished members.

Article 1. The Members of the La Bohème Club, true knights of the spirit, for whose benefit the club has been founded, take an oath to cultivate well-being, and still better eating.

Article 2. Those indifferent to the Muses, pedants, those with weak stomachs or of little wit, grumblers, and other deplorable persons of the kind, will not be admitted, but will be indignantly expelled by the members.

Article 3. The President acts as arbiter in disputes, but pledges himself to prevent the treasurer from collecting the members' subscriptions.

Article 4. The treasurer is empowered to abscond with the funds.

Article 5. The lighting of the club-room shall be by means of an oil-lamp. Should there be a shortage of oil, it shall be replaced by the brilliant wit of the members. (The play of words on *moccoli*, which means both candle-ends and swear words, is untranslatable.)

Article 6. It is strictly forbidden to play fair.

Article 7. Silence is prohibited.

Article 8. Cleverness is not permitted even in exceptional cases.

And so forth.

A quantity of drawings, caricatures, sketches, and pictures from the hand of the painters who formed the majority of the circle, among them one of Puccini as the 'king of money', 'the least destitute of us all', bear witness that wit and intelligence were not excluded from their midst, in spite of all the prohibitions contained in the statutes. And the whole of this lively accompaniment to his work, which his friends' doings not only did not disturb, but actually encouraged, proved once again how great is the artist's need to find some compensation for the emotions and crises of creative work, and showed that it

is not change of occupation, but the mere pleasure of becoming
a child again, and indulging in nonsense to the point of absurdity,
that provide the true compensation for his hours of devotion
to his work.

There was one evening at the La Bohème Club that started
like all the previous ones, but ended very differently. The
book on *Giacomo Puccini intimo* gives an account of it, which
I reproduce here in a somewhat abridged form.

The date was November 1895, and the time late at night.
The friends were playing at cards, while the Maestro sat at his
Förster upright piano striking one chord after another. None
of the club members were troubling about him, nor he about
them. From time to time there would be a subdued cry of,
'Diamonds!' 'I trump it!' Next a murmur from the piano
of 'F-e-f-g-, no, that will not do; B flat minor—that will be
all right'. Then, from the table, 'Be careful, Cecco!' 'Pagno,
you might take the game seriously!' 'Of course not'—from
the piano—'Of course it must be C sharp minor.' From the
table: 'I trump it!' 'Che ha detto il medico?—Verrà (What
said the doctor?—He'll come)', hummed the Maestro, absorbed
in Mimi's death-scene. Suddenly he turned to his friends.
'Be quiet, you fellows! It is finished!' All of them threw
down their cards and crowded round him; and he sang them the
last scene of the opera, that of Mimi's peaceful death, with its
gently expiring music full of stifled tears and the grief of young
hearts. All of them wept, and Puccini, too, shed tears. They
embraced him in silence; and one of them said: 'These pages
will make you immortal'.

The next thirty years confirmed his verdict; and it is probable
that future years will continue to do so.

What is the secret of the spell cast by *La Bohème*, that *ingénue*
among operas, which appeals with equal force and the same
touching accents to both old and young? It is certainly not
to be found in its 'content', for its dramatic substance is of the
slightest. Two pairs of lovers come together, pass days of
merry frivolity, and also of bitterness, in company, and then

lose sight of one another. They meet again, only to watch one of the young grisettes, who has been drawn back by her desire to breathe her last in the garret that had witnessed her happiness, gradually dying, and to recognize the womanly goodness of the other, the human kindliness of whose heart has not been destroyed either by a life spent in alternations of poverty, transient luxury and renewed want, or even by her frivolous love of comfort and idle ease.

Perhaps, however, its attraction lies in the very fact that there is no violent action, calling for breathless sensation, and that the plot does not turn upon a homogeneous situation of gradually increasing intensity, but merely shows us detached moments in these people's lives in a series of episodic scenes. But its supreme attraction is to be found in the fact that it carries conviction, for normal life proceeds in exactly the same way. One thing about it, however, has a particular appeal to our sympathies: the figures in it are those of thoroughly young, good-hearted, natural human creatures, who endure hunger and deprivation courageously, spend their whole lives building castles in the air, and are always ready to help one another, feeling like kings the moment a little money happens to come into their hands. This produces a sense of warmth and close affinity with ourselves, and the word *simpaticone* (thoroughly sympathetic), which was always being applied to the composer, is equally true of his characters. The artist life of the Latin Quarter that provides their background adds a further touch. These painters, poets, and musicians live, love, shiver with cold and run up debts, yet manage to carry on a precarious existence, just as Puccini and his friends had done in the Galleria at Milan. When they feed the stove with their manuscript dramas, or while away hours of depression with all sorts of exuberant, childish nonsense, such as duels with the stove-rake or dancing quadrilles, so as to laugh their worries away, they are behaving exactly like the members of the famous club at Torre del Lago. All this is the fruit of real experience, and the whole thing teems with music—the music of youth, Puccini's youth and that

of everybody else. And, what is more, it makes the listener
young again.

Any one who has spent almost thirty years on end in the
drudgery of a critic's life, as I have done, goes through a
depressing experience in connexion with most works, for, by
the time he has heard them more than ten times, they begin
to wear thin. It is only what is absolutely genuine and truly
inspired that lasts, and even in the works of real masters all that
is not elemental, but due only to the artist's practised hand,
loses its directness of its appeal by the time we know every
phrase, every harmonic subtlety and every shade of instrumental
colour in advance, and are no longer surprised even by the most
striking touches of inspiration. I have heard La Bohème perhaps a hundred times, and know every bar of it—yet not a single
one has lost its freshness for me. If there is an impression
that has become blunted, it is that produced by certain
harmonies which caused an outcry at first owing to their
unprecedented and unpardonable audacity: the frank consecutive fifths, the double suspensions, the hybrid sixths, and
the many peculiar harmonies arising out of the use of the
secondary chords, though these have been so completely outdone by the atonal constructions, resembling reinforced concrete, of the extreme moderns, that nowadays—though perhaps
only temporarily—Puccini's combinations of tone seem to us
tame, and at times positively worn-out and faded. But what
cannot be outdone, because it cannot change, is his heaven-sent
melody, his genuine inspiration, the melody of the heart, as
distinguished from the element of mere technique and conscious
construction. It is feeling that discerns with unerring sureness whether a melodic or tonal idea is a gift of the gods, or
merely the outcome of the composer's personal idiosyncrasy,
which is, indeed, often capable of aping genuine inspiration to
the point of mimicry, even in the composer's own work, for he
may frequently alternate between the two. But in the long run
the only inspiration that holds its own is that which has come
'from above'. No fashion can supersede this, any more than

the blossoms of a fruit tree are superseded by the fruit every autumn, for it blooms again in the spring with the same fragrance and glory. Puccini's melody in *La Bohème* is of this order. It is thoroughly wayward, tending to dissimulate the four-bar periods by rhythmical modifications, preferring half-closes on the sixth or the mediant rather than on the dominant, upon which it tends to avoid coming to rest, in clever, though probably half-unconscious contrast with the composer's predilection for harmonic schemes based on the intervals of the fifth and fourth. The incessant *rubato*, the short and long pauses (*Haltungen*), and the sudden break into hurried successions of notes after sustained ones, all go to produce a sense of unrest that palpitates with life, though often, too, with nerves. In this sphere of warm and sensuous melody, this wooing, yearning, cooing, insistent atmosphere, even the merely accessory elements have a glow of vitality. When this unexpectedly occurs in passages of the libretto with no particular significance, it may lend them undue emphasis, to the detriment of the dramatic light and shade; but this apparent defect is compensated for by a terse neatness of treatment, and it always indicates an attempt to correct the tendency of a *parlando* passage to become too long, and provides a timely break in the dialogue, which may otherwise easily become monotonous in its constant alternation of short vocal phrases, answering one another like responses. Even in moments of supreme emotion the whole spirit of the piece is one of unfailing measure and equilibrium; while the piquantly provocative harmonies that spring to life with this wealth of melody, and seem, as it were, inherent in it, have a pungent tang and a perhaps over-piquant aroma (*Hautgout*) that deprive them of any sickly insipidity and lend them their characteristically refreshing quality.

This can be felt from the very first bar onwards, in the merry, leaping theme of the strings and wood-wind, which, once launched on its way with joyous impetus by the rebellious opening syncopation, dances waywardly onward, representing, as it were, the distinguishing sign of the *vie de Bohème*—a motive which, as we may remember, had already asserted its dominating character in the principal section of the amazing *Capriccio sinfonico*. How delightful, too, is the way in which Rodolfo's little arietta, 'Nei cieli bigi', originally included among the sketches for *La Lupa*, becomes a sort of heraldic badge of the young poet. The elegantly conversational tone and light gaiety of its *cantilena* simply refuse to adapt themselves to the prosaic words at first, but are better suited to the character of the charming poet. We realize this to the full when, in the final scene of the act, in the dialogue with Mimì, the little embroideress, this melody changes from the lively six-eight bar to the peaceful, swaying four-four movement, and develops into a dithyrambic, fervent hymn of praise celebrating the happy dreams that fill the poet's hours. Then, and not till then, it breaks into its full bloom in the fervent outbursts with which it continues: 'Talor dal mio forziere (Bright eyes as yours, believe me)', a model of its kind in the variety of its vocal line and broadly spaced climaxes, its unsymmetrical rhythmic plan, and its irregular alternation of sustained and accented quavers with hurrying triplets, besides which we may note how its soothing middle bars come at just the right time, and how enchantingly full and warm is the tone of the strings and wood-wind that form its accompaniment. Puccini's predilection for the bright, sparkling combination of harps, flutes, and clarinets, with whose swelling notes he loved to mingle the romantic glamour of the horns, produces the happiest results in this passage. And when this same soaring melody, sung in unison by the male and female voice, rises to an exultant expression of the mutual attraction that has sprung up so rapidly between the two, every heart is stirred by these strains, in which so much that is spring-like blooms in the midst of winter.

But before we reach this scene, with its tender ardours of youth and love, there is nothing but high spirits and sparkling exuberance: the entrance of Schaunard the musician, with his unexpected money, accompanied by the second *Bohème* motive, with its jingling vehemence and whimsical suggestion of effort, advancing with such confidence and jollity in six-eight time, the burlesque scene with the landlord, the departure of the joyous companions for the Café Momus, the musical symbol of which, the 'notorious' sequence of fifths repeated three times, is here suggested in a shadowy way, all go to make up one great scherzo, with the spontaneity of an improvisation, a sort of reckless humoresque, drowning want and the whispers of privation in its brilliance, and in which the recurring lyrical ritornelli take, as it were, the place of a trio. Perhaps this is why the spontaneity of Puccini's gaiety is not quite convincing in these scenes, any more than in those of the sacristan in *Tosca*, but always seems to be rather artificially worked up. It is not, indeed, till *Gianni Schicchi* that it seems to draw breath quite freely, and develop its full brilliance. For in the earlier operas we divine in it a hidden melancholy, and even in its most exuberant manifestations the impression of spontaneous joyousness is clouded by a curious feeling, as though of some boding evil, or as though it had its roots in an underlying sadness—a quality especially convincing in *La Bohème*, where it is peculiarly appropriate. But it cannot be denied that the purely lyrical scenes, full of tender, amorous emotion, are formed of quite a different substance from that which we have noticed in the characteristically bohemian motives, of a gaiety that is not altogether spontaneous, that typify the young band of artists. The insuperable melancholy which, even in periods of brightness, always forms the predominant colour of Puccini's nature, finds its truest and purest expression in passages of fervent emotion, shy longing and helpless lamentation, in the blissful love that pours forth from a full heart, or in the dejection of weary, suffering creatures. These melodies are propagated, as it were, by a plant-like process of growth. One germ springs out of another, blossom upon blossom pushes its way forth, and that which seemed at first to offer but a poor incentive for thematic development grows and develops into a luxuriantly clustering motive; though only as it unfolds can we recognize the scheme according to which the motives develop, which was at first merely hinted at. We may watch this process, for instance, in the closing scene of the first act, that delightful scene in which the two young people meet, and the candle carried by Mimi, with her longings for the modest pleasures of life, is extinguished not only before our eyes, but also in the music, while the little lamp of love begins to glimmer in the darkness. Next her bedroom key is lost, but that of two hearts is found; we see them both searching for it, groping their way closer and closer together till his hand grasps hers, and he exclaims 'Che gelida manina (Your tiny hand is frozen)'— words which have been repeated during the last forty years by hundreds of thousands of people all over the world; yet hardly anybody would call this music 'stale'—this music of simple hearts, this song of two grown-up children in love with each other, with its fresh fragrance as of green meadows. Or again, the tenderly passionate passage that follows it, in which Rodolfo tells of his poetic dreams and Mimi recounts her poor little life-story and her beautiful dreams over her embroidery, accompanied by such a graceful, flowery pattern in the orchestra. And next the unforgettable melody that blazes up, as it were, into a flame, the unfolding of the *appassionato*, the atmosphere of which is so cleverly broken by the shouts from the street, only to start again and gather power once more. If it had risen at once in an unbroken vocal curve, it could hardly have failed to degenerate into the banal pathos of the ordinary great operatic duet; yet, for all its glowing ardour, it remains firmly planted upon earth and true in sentiment, till it ends with a gentle, heart-felt emotion on the words, 'Che m'ami, di' (You love me? Say . . .)', accompanied by the motive of the *gelida manina*, which has in the meantime gained a little warmth, and concludes with the 'Io t'amo'—a little passage of imperishable beauty. But even if the melodic inspiration might conceivably seem to be exhausted, the preceding passages, up to the point at which the fluctuating and still formless *parlando*, in which the melody is, as it were, suspended, and hovers in tiny particles in the musical atmosphere, condenses into a firm vocal line, seem to me admirable, not on artistic grounds only. Indeed, the whole passage strikes me as a most happy inspiration, which may well be regarded as significant of future tendencies. Puccini discovered the music of everyday things. He detected the hidden potentialities of music in all that had hitherto been regarded as thoroughly anti-musical, and listened to the most homely phrases of everyday language, the sober prose of ordinary things, till he discovered that they vibrated in sympathy with the mysterious music of the universe, and demonstrated that music is to be found not only in that which is remote from us in time and space, in figures clad in the strange costumes of long past ages, and in those universal human elements that have receded into a legendary distance, but in the whole of life, too, even in its most primitive present-day forms, and in all the phenomena of the world as God created it, however much this music may be drowned at times by the din of everyday life and the cries of those buying and selling in the market-place. Puccini really succeeded in awakening the soul that exists in 'little things', in interpreting in music the gestures of daily life, and breathing music into simple, ordinary speech; and I must confess that nothing stirs or touches me more than the short, fragmentary phrases of this dialogue, in which, to my mind, he has found the tones that most move the heart. I may instance such phrases as 'Che ha detto il medico?—Verrà (What said the doctor?—He'll come)', or Rodolfo and Mimi's questions and answers in their first scene: 'Si sente meglio? Si, grazie (Do you feel better? Yes, thank you)', accompanied by the orchestra, first searching and groping in faltering, slightly indicated motives, only to fall silent again, then followed by little trifling remarks, which are none the less vibrant with suppressed emotion, and are accompanied by a slight, but clearly outlined melody, till the overflowing emotion assumes its form and contour in the vocal parts as well. The whole passage is a masterly inspiration. In former days, if passages of this kind were not swamped in operatic bombast as a matter of course, they were accompanied by a few meaningless chords, and relegated to the tedious, empty sing-song of *recitativo secco*. It seems to me true to say that Puccini has redeemed these passages by his sincerity of expression and living music, and that this is the really new feature of his art. For the future, even in merely subordinate and trivial dialogue, there are no longer any thin passages linking one number with the next, or anything that is not turned to eloquent melody, expressive of a deep inward experience.

The second act is rather disjointed and episodic. The fact that Rodolfo and Mimi join their friends and that Marcello and Musetta meet again is not of any particular dramatic importance, and provides too slight a subject for a whole act. Yet in spite of this the whole thing bubbles over with life. The Christmas bustle in the streets, the cries of the hawkers, the chorus of chattering urchins, the children's trumpets blown by the passers-by, and the merry or angry voices of the bohemians unite to form a symphony of incredibly diverting brilliance and remarkable finish, in which the principal characters are, however, condemned at times to a merely supernumerary role. Musetta's waltz, gracefully alluring and supplely coquettish and provocative, is the gem of the act, with its insinuating, enticing atmosphere and charm of line, leading up to the triumphant *canto fermo* of the great sextet that follows, in which Puccini follows his usual custom of giving no prominence to the words that illuminate the psychology of the characters or carry on the action, but allows them to be swallowed up in the mass of voices joining in the ensemble in a way that hardly tends to elucidate what is going on, for the listener's capacity for catching different sets of words is even smaller than his power of following the various parts, of which it is a matter of common experience that no more than three can be distinguished at the same time. But for all that, the sextet is a brilliant number, and, we may add, the only Parisian touch in the whole work. The words express the private sentiments of the various characters, whether these be love, jealousy, anger, or disappointment; but the music is all rustling silks and glittering lights, and this is justified by the fact that it was in existence first. Puccini wrote it with no words before him, or rather to whatever meaningless words he chose, and the text was fitted to it afterwards, not always very happily. It always strikes us afresh as incomprehensible that, though he was capable of writing charming and well-turned verses, he never wrote anything of the sort for himself. From the solo passage for the trumpets, with the ringing sequence of fifths sounded three times that opens the act, through the Christmas cries, the sprightly march of the children, and the gracefully lingering minuet-like number sung by the lovers, down to the waltz sextet, which outshines all the rest, and the lively tones of the old-world military march, with its squeaky fifes and cornets, advancing in time to the drum-beat, which brings the whole of the Latin Quarter to its feet, shouting and cheering, and, blending with the Christmas motives, brings the act to a close in a mood of most un-bourgeois gaiety, the whole thing is one great song of self-forgetting, care-free *joie de vivre*.

But the moment the opening bars of the next act are heard, all this is forgotten. I have already mentioned this passage in a different connexion, and remarked that the only landscape it depicts is that of winter in the soul, not the snowy scene of the *Barrière d'enfer*, in which a reminiscence of the once turbulent, unruly fifths on the trumpets at the beginning of Act II is here echoed in the glassy tones of the flutes and harps, that seem to drop downwards, wearily and emptily above the frozen rigidity of a pedal-point formed by shivering *tremoli* on the cellos. An infinite sense of desolation is felt when a sustained high note on the piccolo sounds above this monotonous, rushing bass, like the whistle of an icy wind, while the rough voices of the tipplers and the ring of glasses are heard from the inn, and the strains of Musetta's dainty, winning waltz suddenly seem to have acquired a meretricious suggestion, and descended to the level of a tune on the barrel-organ. We have a similar impression when, as we listen to the thin notes of the bells from the hospital near by, the monotonous cries of the toll-house keepers, peasants, octroi officials, and lamplighters, and the quivering, empty fifths on the muted strings, which sound like the singing of telegraph-wires, we seem to hear, like an echo of the past, the jolly, rebellious *Bohème* motive. The frost-flowers of the music seem to melt in the sad, imploring passage in which Mimi begs her friend Marcello to help her win back Rodolfo's heart, which has grown cold—a passage in which, we may note, can be found the only Mascagni-like echoes in the whole of Puccini's work. Then comes the duet between the two friends, with the heart-rending grief of its passionately despairing melody 'Mimi è tanto malata! (Mimi's so sickly, so ailing!)', amid which, like a beloved picture from happier days, Mimi's musical self-portrait from her song in the first love-scene gleams like a ray of light and the symbol of a heart-rending memory, after which its feverishly convulsive triplets break out, as it were, into stifled sobbing, penetrating the very soul with their sorrow—though it must be admitted that the association of this music, like hot tears, with the arid words, 'Una terribile tosse (By fierce, incessant coughing)', for which the unfortunate translator cannot this time be blamed, does not seem very appropriate. This is followed by the quartet, which is really a combination of two ill-assorted duets, the jangling, hopeless insolence of the squabble between Marcello and Musetta, and the tender hopelessness of the last reunion between Rodolfo and Mimi, forming an almost unbearably poignant song of farewell which, with the wild intensity of its vocal parts, clinging to one another, as it were, in despair, leaves an aching wound in the heart.

But the fourth act is even more heart-rending. It returns to the atmosphere of the first scene in the garret, which is also reflected in the music. But now everything is clouded with mourning and quiet resignation, with secret longings and anguish at the rapid flight of youth, and this *vie de Bohème*, outwardly unchanged but really overcast with gloom, is expressed in almost exactly the same motives. Puccini has learnt much from Wagner, and turns it to use in his own fashion. Above all, he has grasped the secret of reminiscence, and the power of memory to conjure up what is gone.   In the final scene of *Manon Lescaut* emotions that cannot be expressed in words had been suggested with the utmost insistence by quotations from earlier parts of the opera: by the love-motive, now broken, as it were, and wearily sinking, and by the sadly smiling grace of the minuet theme from the second act, whose dying strains illuminate Manon's closing hours like a happy memory of earlier and brighter days.   And similarly, in this last act of *La Bohème*, no newly invented theme, however great the genius that inspired it, could touch us so deeply as these hovering reminiscences of the past, reflected in the music.   How unmistakable and convincing is the way in which the harsher, and now rather brutal instrumentation of the opening motive, which is otherwise unchanged, expresses a mood of extreme tension, and a violent effort to work up an atmosphere of laboured good-humour; while similarly, the second *Bohème* theme, associated with the musician Schaunard, expresses the precarious situation of the young artists during their frugal meal of a herring by first hesitating, and then suddenly gliding into another key.   How simple is the process by which reminiscences of the squabbling duet call up the image of Musetta in Marcello's mind, while Mimi's motive, in an augmented form, suggests the appearance of the little grisette, who has been seen expensively dressed and driving past in a carriage, but arrives immediately afterwards to die in the arms of her Rodolfo.   With the exception of the stormy duet between the two friends, ardently evoking dreams of vanished realities, and the kindly pathos of Colline's song about his coat, there is scarcely a note to be heard in the whole of this act that has not been sounded before; and it is this that makes it such a revelation of the soul and so full of true human feeling as to bring hot tears to every eye.   It is indeed the crowning scene of the whole work.   Puccini was perfectly conscious of his reason for not introducing any new themes into the melodies of this act.   In a letter to Giulio Ricordi he expressly states that 'the whole act is constructed out

TOSCANINI

PUCCINI

of logical reminiscences. . . .'[1] But they are more than logical. They are so full of intimate feeling, and present such a convincing picture of mental processes, of the fluctuating thoughts and emotions of the characters, their sorrows and memories, that they produce the effect of an X-ray photograph: this is very soul, penetrated by mysterious waves that turn it to music. It is no wonder that, while Puccini was writing this farewell to life and youth, tears streamed from his eyes. How violent is the contrast when, after the exaggerated turbulence of the supper-scene, and the dance in which the friends take part with a gaiety too exaggerated to ring quite true, Mimi, now sick unto death, is brought to the garret by Musetta, and the poetic theme associated with Rodolfo marks her return to her poet-lover, while her love-melody accompanies the poignantly sweet embrace of the lovers, now reunited for a brief hour, and the once joyous *Bohème* motives become quite pensive and still. When Mimi, left alone with Rodolfo, draws him to her and tries once more to tell him all her love in a little melody of ineffably tranquil fervour; and when the sick girl, haunted by fleeting recollections of her former life with her lover, breathes out her tender little life in half-whispered reminiscences of her words in the earlier scene, after which the melody bursts forth into a poignant cry and sobs distractedly in an epilogue full of wild lamentation, it is as though a human heart were laid bare before us, and lay quivering before our eyes. The whole scene moves us as few other things have power to do.

We may here establish as a fact, once and for all, that, in the whole of opera, the genuinely moving, heart-stirring passages, that move us to tears, as distinguished from those which carry us away and uplift us, can be reckoned on the fingers of our two hands: among them are Lohengrin's farewell, Sieglinde's dawning consciousness of motherhood, Eva's outburst in the shoemaker's shop, and the 'Wach auf!' in the third act of *Die*

---

[1] TRANSLATOR'S NOTE.—Puccini's actual words, as quoted in the *Epistolario* (No. 48 to Ricordi), were: 'L'atto è composto quasi tutto di ritorni logici, salvo il duettino "sono andati" e la zimarra di Colline, e poco altro'.

L

Meistersinger, Kurwenal's exultant song when Tristan regains his consciousness, followed by the latter's death, the Minister's address in *Fidelio:* 'Euch, edle Frau, allein', the trio in *Der Rosen-kavalier* and the hush that falls before it, and possibly, too, Don José's terrible despair at his shame, degradation, and helpless love—with perhaps a few more. I may, for the moment, have overlooked some passages of this kind; but at any rate, it is no small thing that two or three of these ten supreme examples of pathos come from Puccini's hand. Others may aspire higher, possess greater power, and bring a greater sense of release, or may lead us to the summits of human experience. Puccini's name cannot be mentioned side by side with those of Bach, Beethoven, and Wagner. But he is unique among them all in the truth with which he renders the touching voice of the poor, suffering creature, and, for this reason, who can tell on what roll of honour a grateful posterity may not inscribe his name?

We may add a word about his instrumentation, which from *La Bohème* onward steadily increases in sensitiveness and lucidity, and becomes more personal in its tone-colour and subtle nuances, though even when it revels most luxuriantly in beauty of tone, it hardly ever blurs the significance of the words. Puccini is fond of those shimmering lights, delicate washes of colour, sparse effects (*Aussparungen*) and richly enamelled details to which the term 'Japanesque' might be applied in painting, and which do in fact rise to the most consummate finish in *Madame Butterfly*, with its subtly delineated miniatures. But as compared with the full brilliance and unsubtle lusciousness of tone that characterize the orchestration of *Manon Lescaut*, the blend of timbre has already become more discriminating, the distribution of colour more studied, though the use of colour as a means of dramatic characterization is still infrequent. The brutal crash of the massed brass is now kept mainly for moments of catastrophe, the *incalzando* effect of insistently accentuated strings in unison is now reserved chiefly for climaxes of passionate agitation, and the vocal parts are supported by accompanying instruments; but intimate gradations of tone predominate, with the shimmer of mother-of-pearl and the transparency of water-colour. I open the score at random—say at Mimi and Rodolfo's duet in G flat major in the third act, that song of farewell to young love and happy life in common, with its note of childlike sadness, and yet, as it were, of cloying over-ripe sweetness, and I note the perfectly masterly way in which the accompaniment, like dropping tears, with the alternating pizzicato and bowed passages on the strings, the soft murmur of the harp and the light, scarcely audible tones of the flute, grows into a theme, in which the various instruments often take up snatches of it in turn; while the scarcely perceptible syncopations of the clarinets seem, as it were, to mark the pulse-beat of the melody, and little quivering trills indicate how false is their pretended composure; after which the flute timidly accompanies the vocal part for one bar only, till the melody pours forth with the full resonance of the wood-wind and strings. Or the opening of Musetta's waltz-song, where the singer is supported by the muted violins, while the lower strings barely indicate the waltz rhythm in subdued tones, the flutes and clarinets wreathe a piquant little sextolet about the third crotchet, and the high notes on the harps add their soft sparkle. The same master hand shows itself at any part of the opera that we like to choose; the way in which Puccini uses the percussion instruments, and, above all, the much misused and hackneyed harp, would alone justify a separate study.

The apparently effortless naturalness of this music and its unconstrained flow no longer show any traces of the labour or the infinitely scrupulous and self-tormenting care with which Puccini used to work. A single word that checked the flow of his ideas or was contrary to his feeling might cause him a whole night of meditation and letters full of exhaustive detail to his faithful adviser Giulio Ricordi, who was constantly having to use diplomacy in order to wring from the now recalcitrant librettists concessions which the composer himself, whom they had come to regard as a cantankerous nuisance, had failed to

obtain.   His over-conscientiousness caused him to worry far
longer over the question whether, of the three trumpets in the
finale of the second act, one should be muted and the others
not, or two muted and the third not, than some of the facile
and nimble-fingered composers of to-day would do over orchestrating a whole symphony; and this is only as it should be.
Moreover, his practical stagecraft often influenced the plan of
the scenes.   For instance, he was anxious to give an opportunity
for a short solo to the singer taking the part of Schaunard, who
had been treated in rather a stepmotherly fashion, having been
given little more than a part in the vocal ensemble.   He saw
an opening for a solo in the drinking-scene of the first act, and
wanted to allow him an arietta in the form of a toast, or 'sentiment'.   But he had cause to vow that 'this toast will be the
death of me (questo brindisi sarà la mia morte)', for here the
harassed librettists failed him.   They would send him ten or a
dozen proposed stanzas, none of which were any use; or again,
he could not find the right point at which to insert this stupid
drinking-song so that it should be an organic part of the whole
structure; so that, after all the fuss, it had in the end to be left
out.   His next idea was to compensate the wretched Schaunard
for this by allowing him a political speech in the fourth act;
but it was obvious that this not very witty parody of an electoral
assembly was too much of a drag on the action, and impeded its
progress at a moment when it was urgent to press on towards
the conclusion; so that it too was left out, and once again the
composer said that it would be the death of him.   He repeated
this cry whenever Giacosa worked too slowly, or Illica im-
provised far too many scenes of every sort, or when he himself
found great difficulty in managing the instruments of percussion
in the passage of the third act where the bells ring.   If he had
been as good as his word, he would have had to die at least
twenty times while he was writing the score of *La Bohème*
alone.   But we can see how quiveringly sensitive his nerves
were at that time; indeed, they were often stretched to breaking-
point.   How illuminating it is to compare the various versions

and embellishments of the libretto, and then consider the final result arrived at by Puccini through cutting out all excrescences with his own hand, rearranging the text, pulling it together, and inserting new matter, and realize what torments he suffered in the course of his work, all of which is ignored by spectators, whether critical or uncritical, who listen, either complaisantly or with a smile of condescension, to .this 'musiquette', this 'light music' by the 'superficial' Puccini, and feel very smart as they eat *marrons glacés* to its accompaniment.

Like *Manon*, *La Bohème* was produced for the first time at the Teatro Regio, Turin, on 1st February 1896, exactly three years later. It took two years to reduce the libretto to its final form, and the music was completed eight months later. At the earlier rehearsals Puccini was very confident, but as the days went by he became more and more dubious and uncertain. He felt that none of those about the theatre believed in the success of the piece; for they all shrugged their shoulders, and, in response to the Master's questions, slipped away with an evasive 'Vedremo (We shall see)'. To quote Puccini's own words, he went to the performance like a criminal going to execution.

However, no execution took place. The public was friendly, though it was far from indulging in such enthusiasm as it had done at *Manon*, though the conductor was Toscanini, the Napoleon among conductors, as he is always being called, and Puccini's most consummate interpreter, of whom the Maestro once said: 'When the fellow gets a score into his hands, he digs into it like a miner in order to explore its every corner and discover its lodes. And when he finds them, or even when he does not find them, he exploits them in the most incomparable fashion, down to the last scrap. What a great artist!' This great artist had already been in charge of *Manon Lescaut*, and his vigorous, yet delicate hand, to which were afterwards entrusted the original productions of *The Girl of the Golden West* and *Turandot*, was exactly the right one to bring out with loving care all the delicate touches in the score, a quality in which he has had no equal save that remarkable operatic conductor Ernst von Schuch, whom Puccini may really be said to have revealed to Germany. Any one who has listened to the few bars of the orchestral epilogue, as rendered under his direction, knows what it is to hear the music of a heart bleeding to death, and will never forget it. Toscanini was supported by competent, if not outstanding singers: Madame Ferrani, who had played Puccini's Manon three years before, as Mimi, Madame Pasini as Musetta, the tenor Gorga as Rodolfo, and Moro as Marcello. In spite of the remarkable conducting, the performance was felt to be no more than a good average one, even by Puccini himself, though it is true that he was hardly ever completely satisfied with a singer. He must have had his own reasons for this; but we can see how exacting were his demands from a delightful little episode that took place at the beginning of the present century, when he met a friend and invited him to a rehearsal of *La Bohème* at which a new tenor was singing, but added: 'You will have to listen to a bad Rodolfo'. That tenor's name was Enrico Caruso.

Puccini had felt an intense conviction of the merits of his work, and was extremely depressed at the· indifference with which it was received. He could not disguise from himself that the applause of the public was more in the nature of a courtesy to the composer of *Manon* than of spontaneous approbation, and that all their plaudits had merely served to veil a *succès d'estime*. But he was so securely confident of the opera's vitality and power of survival that he could not be misled or depressed either by the verdict of the public on the first performance or, in the long run, by the critics, grotesque though the criticisms were. The very gentlemen who had been so prompt to hail *Manon* as a masterpiece, now vied with one another in disparaging *La Bohème*. Carlo Bersezio took the Maestro to task in *La Stampa* for having 'written his music in great haste, and without sufficient labour in selecting and polishing (*con poco lavorio di selezione e di limatura*)', and, not content with censuring it in the present, ventured to extend his condemnation to the future, hazarding the bold prophecy that, 'Just as *La Bohème* fails to leave any very strong impression upon the listener, so it will fail to leave any strong trace in the history of our opera, and it will be well for the author to regard it as a momentary error, to pursue the right way boldly in future, and to make up his mind that this has been a brief deviation from the path of art'. Another critic, Luigi Alberto Villani, considered that the music of *La Bohème* was not fit to be anything but the recreation of a moment; and a third, Signor Berta of the *Gazzetta del Popolo*, seized the opportunity for a nice little piece of revenge, for he had himself approached the Master and offered to write the verse libretto, but Puccini had had the bad taste to prefer such men of letters as Illica and Giacosa to this journalist of dubious capacity. He now revenged himself in the following words: 'We ask ourselves what it was that turned Puccini into the deplorable downward path of *La Bohème* (*spinse . . . sul pendìo deplorevole di questa Bohème*). The question is a painful one, and we do not ask it without a certain sorrow'; and he hypocritically implored the composer to return in future to the 'great and difficult contests of art'. Giovanni Pozza alone raised his voice in favour of the work and its composer, and predicted a great fortune for the opera upon the stage, on the ground that it had so much to offer both to the connoisseur and to the profane: 'The latter will say that the music is beautiful, the former that it is well written'.

How history repeats itself! What airs of importance these hack writers on the arts give themselves, and with what assurance they distribute their censures! Yet how ridiculous their verdicts and vaticinations have become after the lapse of only a few years! Their words have been forgotten or laughed to scorn; but the work still lives.

CHAPTER IX

THE CHAMBER OF HORRORS ('TOSCA')

Puccini did not allow the doubtful success of *La Bohème* to cloud his spirits very long. On the contrary, after moping for a few days he set to work to see how justice might be done to it. The fact that the sympathy of the public in Turin became more lively with every performance, soon increasing to a warm affection for the characters and music of the opera, merely increased his confident sense of having produced something good and of permanent value, though this consciousness of worth had to suffer yet another shock, when, a few weeks later, *La Bohème* was produced in Rome, with Mascheroni as conductor, and again met with a lukewarm reception, which was particularly surprising, for in no other city had *Manon* and its composer been greeted with such jubilant applause. Two months later, however, in April 1896, it triumphed at last, when Leopoldo Mugnone conducted the work at Palermo, for the unprecedented success of that evening carried the opera on to every stage in Italy and abroad. At first, indeed, it had seemed as though an unlucky star were presiding over this performance, at which we may note the curious fact that the part of Musetta was taken by Ada Giachetti, Caruso's first wife, and, in general, rather a mediocre artist. Mugnone, who, like many conductors, was superstitious, was afraid lest the date, 13th April—which was, moreover, a Friday—might prove doubly unlucky, and hesitated to take his place at the desk. There was yet another reason for this, for, as he had expected, a contretemps did occur, and the oboist, who is particularly important in this work, failed to appear. Puccini had almost to use force to make him give the signal to start. The oboist did arrive, after all, and the performance lasted a whole hour longer than usual,

152

as a result of innumerable calls and encores. When the curtain fell at the end, the public could not be induced to leave their places, and the clapping, shouting, and stamping went on till a thing happened that was most unusual even according to Italian usages: the singers had to be fetched back from their dressing-rooms, and Mugnone leapt from the stage into the now half-empty orchestra, collected the handful of musicians who were still there, and responded to the continuous shouts of '*bis!*' from the public, which had become absolutely uncontrollable. The pathetic scene of Mimi's expiring moments was therefore performed for the second time, with the *prima donna* in her everyday clothes and Rodolfo without a wig, so that that inconceivable phenomenon, the repetition of a death-scene, really took place on this occasion.

The Maestro always spent the winter in Milan. He was, indeed, one of those who are 'the sport of every change of atmospheric pressure'. Rain and cold made him feel positively ill. The state of the weather constantly recurs in his letters like a *Leitmotiv*. His physical condition, and, above all, his work absolutely depended upon the sunshine, and when the skies were overcast his soul was even more clouded by melancholy than usual. During the cold season he accordingly retired to the city, much as he loathed it, and there enjoyed some relaxation from his labours. He went to the theatres to hear plays and operas both old and new, and spent much time with his friends, of whom Carlo Clausetti, now director of the publishing house of Ricordi, was one of the most intimate. After finishing *Edgar* he had gone as usual to Milan, where Sarah Bernhardt happened to be playing at the Teatro dei Filodrammatici, and had seen her act the part of Floria Tosca in Victorien Sardou's drama *La Tosca*. He did not understand a word of French, but the play gripped him, and that decided the matter. A plot that can be clearly grasped through the medium of miming alone was exactly what he wanted. His criterion for a perfectly effective operatic libretto was precisely this: that it should be comprehensible without a single word being spoken. He applied the same test to *Madame Butterfly* and *The Girl of the Golden West*; for he and some friends who, like him, did not understand English, saw both these plays by David Belasco performed in that language, and the impression they carried away as the result of the merely scenic effect of the situations and the actors' gestures, which, in *Butterfly* especially, had a direct emotional appeal, sufficed to decide him to associate these scenes with his music.

He hesitated a long time, however, over *Tosca*, and when Henri Murger's romance awoke to music everything within him that sang of spring and love, the other piece was almost forgotten. The subject attracted, yet at the same time repelled him. He considered it strong, but, in point of fact, excessively so. The actress, Sarah Bernhardt, with her exaggerated slenderness, the impassioned clarinet-like timbre of her voice, and her cloud of fair hair, had, indeed, carried him away irresistibly at certain moments, but the piece as a whole had lacerated his nerves rather than appealed to his soul, whereas what he always wanted was 'la musica dell' anima', the music of the soul. On the other hand his interest was naturally stimulated by the fact that the aged Verdi, that great master, in declining the offer made him by the French dramatist of his *Patrie* as a subject for an opera, had added that, if he were not too old, there was one piece of Sardou's that he would have liked to set to music, and that was *La Tosca*. This made such an impression on Puccini that he talked the whole question over with Illica, discussing the adaptations that would be desirable in turning it into an opera, and the fundamental changes that would undoubtedly be necessary in the last act, which in Sardou's play takes place in the prison. After this, however, he became entirely absorbed in *La Bohème* and thought nothing more of the matter till he was alarmed by the report that Alberto Franchetti, a pupil of Michele Puccini, and the successful composer of *Asrael*, intended to set *La Tosca* to music, and had persuaded Illica to compose the book for him. It was even said that the completed libretto had been read to

Victorien Sardou in Paris, in Verdi's presence, and that the
Latin hymn sung by Cavaradossi before his execution had fired
the venerable old master to such a point that he had snatched
the pages out of the astonished Illica's hand and continued the
reading himself in a voice quivering with emotion.   Naturally
there was no turning back now.   Now that another was to have
it, the subject that Puccini had renounced for so long, and,
apparently, with so light a heart, seemed to him the most
desirable of all ideas for an opera.   A regular banquet of con-
spirators took place: Illica and Ricordi, who was Franchetti's
publisher too, but naturally preferred Puccini as a composer
for *La Tosca*, undertook to disparage the book by degrees to
the unsuspecting Franchetti, and, by raising doubts and objections with no apparent purpose, to deprive him of all eagerness
to work at it.   They succeeded with surprising rapidity, which
is not hard to understand, for in the form in which it was then,
the text was open to many weighty objections on artistic grounds.
Franchetti finally abandoned his plan, though he may often
have regretted this afterwards.   On the following day Puccini
signed the contract with Illica, Giacosa, and Ricordi, and set
to work.

This time, again, the first object of their labours was the book
and the proper shaping of it, and the process was again a stormy
and tedious one, which the two authors found no laughing
matter.   Puccini was really a perfect Scarpia towards his
collaborators, but it must be admitted that he was always in
the right, and that the points upon which he insisted were all
for the good of the work as a whole.   While comparing the
different drafts of this operatic libretto, I have once more been
forced to admire Puccini's rare insight into the essentials of a
musical drama, his sure instinct for the theatre, and the subtle
discrimination with which, over and over again, he stood out
against the authors of the book, with good reason, if at times
rather aggressively; for sometimes they followed the old beaten
track of operatic procedure, and sometimes they were incon-
ceivably lacking in taste.   I have not been able to resist

including among the facsimiles in the present work an excerpt from the first version of *Tosca*, which bears witness to both their bad taste and their adherence to antiquated operatic conventions.   It is hardly credible, but in this first version Cavaradossi sings a regular aria while he is being tortured, which is swelled to a quartet by the voices of Tosca, the judge, and Spoletta, the police agent.   This is but one example out of many, for these dramatic authors, experienced and talented though they were, indulged in a whole series of such incomprehensible vagaries, so that Puccini was forced to issue one ultimatum after another.   Every time he recast, abridged or interpolated a passage, or made verbal alterations, the change he made was a necessary one, and every one of his proposals was not only absolutely to the point, but profoundly significant of the requirements and character of this strongly individual musician.   He was a born stage manager and producer.

In spite of this—or should we say, because of this?—he failed to see that in this piece, more than in any other, he was not consecrating his music to the expression of genuine human feeling and soul-stirring emotion, but to the falsest and most commonplace melodrama, and to characters like wax puppets. The people in this play are at best conventional figures, not real human beings.   They are mere masks, Tosca of jealousy and love, Scarpia of cruelty and lust, and even Cavaradossi, who has personal traits that make him more like a human creature than the rest—even the fine young Mario is a mere marionette. I must confess that, as a work of art, *Tosca* is repugnant to me, that the torture scenes nauseate me afresh every time, and that, in spite of its popular success, it seems to me beyond redemption from the aesthetic point of view.   Hence the decision to set it to music seems to me to have been a mistake.   But I must also admit that, in the very first scene, I find myself becoming absolutely indifferent to aesthetic considerations, and that, after the duet between Mario and Tosca, I acclaim Puccini's error, for it wrung from him his most inspired music.

It is true that, before this result could be achieved, con-

ference after conference had to be held, and these were anything but amicable in character. Some were held in Paris, too,
in the presence of Sardou, at which that old Mephistopheles, a
past-master of all the most subtle tricks of the theatrical craft,
talked them all down. He started by trying to persuade
Ricordi that 50,000 francs was quite a modest advance on
account of his royalties, he bewildered Puccini and Illica by his
plausible proposals, sketched plans for the scenery and stage
effects, insisted that the harassed Tosca should end her life by
leaping from the Castle of Sant' Angelo into the Tiber, which is
nearly fifty feet away, and devised a whole series of new horrors.
'It looks as though Sardou means to kill Spoletta as well,'
wrote Puccini to Ricordi with a groan. But in spite of all this,
they finally reached an agreement. Indeed, incredible though
it may seem, Sardou declared that the operatic libretto was
perhaps even better than his own play; though this did not
prevent the seventy-five-year-old dramatist, sparkling with wit
and vitality, from terrorizing them all anew while the production
of *Tosca* at the Paris Opera-house was being rehearsed a few years
later. Puccini wrote a most amusing account of how the old
gentleman behaved as if he were not only the author, but the
stage-manager too, and almost as if he had written the music
as well. The only wonder was, said Puccini, that he did not
push the conductor out of his place and conduct the opera
himself.

'How can you achieve anything, if you do not put your whole
heart into it?' wrote Puccini on one occasion to his dearly
beloved Signor Giulio. How, then, did he himself manage to
complete his *Tosca*? It is out of the question that he should
have put his whole heart into it. The very fact of his reluctance
and hesitation in deciding upon the subject is conclusive proof
of this. It is out of the question that he should not have
realized the shocking, coarse theatricality of the subject, and how
little scope it offered for music with that truth of feeling and
sincere humanity that were always what he most required.
Puccini found two methods of doing justice to his music—

which, we must repeat, perhaps displays greater genius in this piece than anywhere. To quote his own expression, he has 'coloured (*colorito*)' [1] the drama rather than illuminated it from within. What he expressed in music was not people, but emotions: love, jealousy, fear, terror, nobility of mind, longing for freedom, brutality or gloating cruelty here find direct expression in song, the abstract essence of these emotions being, as it were, interpreted in a music that is, however, anything but abstract, whether it insinuates itself into our sensibilities by its sensuous charm, or subjugates them by its brutality. Seldom has the Maestro written music suffused with a more tranquil warmth and a gentler glow than in the first duet between Tosca and Cavaradossi, in which we hear none of the flaming passion and unrestrained exultation that usually characterize Puccini's *cantilena* in his love-songs, but only the voice of a steadfast, fervent union. Seldom has he risen to a grander intensity than in the finale of the first act, with its imposing *Te Deum*, which swells forth, glorious and magnificent, accompanied by the brazen clang of the bells and the thunder of the cannon—a passage in which, to ensure that it should be ceremonially correct, the composer asked the advice of his friend Don Pietro Panichelli, a priest in Rome. The sinister ardour of Scarpia's triumphant cry, 'Va, Tosca! (Go, Tosca!)', inflamed by a mocking frenzy of sensuality, drops like a hawk into the midst of this solemn, sonorous music, only to join with bigoted exaltation in the fanatically pious chant of the congregation and choir immediately afterwards. Seldom has he written anything so mortally sad, so bleeding with inward anguish as Cavaradossi's farewell to life, or so grimly terrible, like a chill hand clutching at the heart, as the sombre, incisive music to which the picket of soldiers march off to shoot Cavaradossi; we can hear death itself in these bars. The words of the famous aria in B minor were originally those of the Latin hymn to art, the *inno latino*, which had filled Verdi with such violent enthusiasm. Puccini,

[1] TRANSLATOR'S NOTE.—See Puccini's letter of 12 October 1899 to Ricordi, printed in Adami's *Epistolario*.

however, felt simply unable to write any music for them, for he felt reflections upon art to be simply inconceivable at a moment of such intense emotion, the only thought possible in these circumstances being an aching memory of the one thing that Cavaradossi felt any pain at leaving behind him—his Floria and her love.   He could never find inspiration in anything coldly intellectual, but only in spontaneously emotional impulses.   For this reason Mario's flaming 'Vittoria (Victory! Victory!)' was the most rousing and revolutionary thing that ever broke forth from the soul of a composer who was, as a rule, so far from revolutionary; and similarly, the burning ardour and wild lamentation of Tosca's *cantilena* passages during the hideous torture-scene are perhaps the most harrowing he ever turned to music —a passionate, wildly sobbing melody, which her excess of grief turns to a shriek, a distracted lament, now moaning, now raging, though even in its shrieks and wailing outcries it always expresses itself in phrases of truly Latin beauty and breadth, in whose very tumult we can trace a cultivated taste.   In all these impetuous outbursts of the agonized woman, of which 'Vissi d'arte (Love and music, these have I lived for)', known, perhaps not quite appropriately, as the 'Prayer', is felt to be the climax, and as such has become famous, a tiny motive keeps recurring, consisting in four strongly accented notes leading up to a full close, which not only closes the first part of this prayer, but afterwards mounts upwards in the passionate accents of the song and of the orchestral tissue woven about it till we almost imagine that we can see despairing arms uplifted and the wringing of hands.   Moreover, this miniature motive forms the central, or else the final phrase of nearly all the melodies assigned to the character of Tosca, and is like the impress of her seal upon them all.

All this is music, which, if not august in its nobility, none the less comes from the very well-spring of that inventive faculty which is a gift from on high, and cannot be drawn upon either at will or by the greatest constructive virtuosity.   I think it was Rossini who once, while listening to the work of a contemporary about which there was considerable controversy, suddenly pricked up his ears and said, 'Questo è inventore! (This man is a discoverer!)'; for in his eyes this was the one decisive criterion as to whether a musician had had the grace of inspiration vouch-safed to him, in comparison with which the most skilful thematic development was of secondary importance. There can be no doubt that he would have conferred the honourable title of *inventore* upon Puccini too. It must be admitted, though, that genuine inspiration can be conceded only to the preponderating part of *Tosca,* for much of the rest falls short of it. Puccini's action in accompanying some parts of the revoltingly horrible torture-scene by music that is mere noise is perhaps venial: there are stage situations of such overwhelming im-pressiveness—whether in the good or the bad sense of the word—that it is almost a matter of indifference with what music they are accompanied, for everything in them contributes toward the effect, as we have experienced at the cinema, of which we are unpleasantly reminded in this particular scene. All that is required is to provide a suitable musical atmosphere, in order still further to heighten the tense atmosphere accom-panying the deeds of horror. The same purpose is served by the gavotte, with its silvery charm, and the cantata, in which, during Cavaradossi's examination, Tosca's voice is heard in the 'luogo di lagrime (place of tears)', as Scarpia calls it—a point at which Puccini had originally intended to introduce a piece by Paisiello. But the final duet between the lovers, again, is stiff, almost laboured, and too superficial, while the part of Scarpia is weakly conceived, as is, indeed, understandable, for the expression of the stark insensibility, cold, sinister resolu-tion, and smiling elegance of this unhuman creature with his diabolical threats of torture, unmitigated by a single moment of warmer feeling, was not suited to Puccini's nature, though even here it is remarkable what colour he has succeeded in achieving at certain moments.

But a further element is also present, which is more plainly to be felt in this opera than in any of the Master's earlier ones.

PUCCINI WITH THE LIBRETTISTS OF *Turandot*

CARICATURE OF CARUSO BY PUCCINI

I do not mean the hidden sadness which casts a slight shadow over every one of these melodies, even those of a lyrical tranquillity and brightness, but rather the nameless dread that quivers in this music, the presentiment of something terrible, the insuperable feeling that some lurking evil is slowly approaching, that permeates everything in turn, and grips the listener by the throat from the very first bar. The association of ideas suggested by what we see on the stage undoubtedly does much to contribute towards this oppressive feeling of a horror that cannot be averted. From the moment when Angelotti, who has just escaped from the prisons of the Castle of Sant' Angelo, enters the church with timid haste, imagining all the time that he can hear police spies close on his trail, the music at once begins to suggest a depressing atmosphere of menacing danger, of something sinister and crushing, which never ceases to haunt us. Indeed, it had been present even before this: the very first three chords, the common chords of B flat, A flat, and E, crashing out on the orchestra one after the other without warning, and presenting, as it were, a portrait in miniature of Scarpia and his arbitrary power, seem to throttle one; and when the second Scarpia motive, equally terse and incisive, with its four diatonically descending notes in the sharp timbre of the piercing wood-wind, poignantly reinforced by the brass and the shrill tone of the violins, loses itself in a series of chords descending step by step and dying away into nothingness, we almost feel as though the invisible, gigantic hands of torturers were reaching out after the fugitive. The same sense of oppressive expectation overshadows even the tender love-duet between Tosca and Mario that follows, during which a storm-cloud seems to hover over the unsuspecting lovers. Even the comical merriment of the scene with the sacristan and choirboys, and the lilting rhythm of their glee, is somehow tainted with fear, and their gladness fails to communicate itself to the hearer. The dread that steals into the church on Scarpia's entrance is the direct outcome of his personality and of the presence of his prying myrmidons; but the same dread quivers in the music and robs

M

it of all colour. It swells to gigantic proportions in the second act, from the opening bars, formed by the diminished Scarpia theme, onward. Anything more bodingly sinister than the grim, grave, funereal motive heard on Cavaradossi's entrance and accompanying his removal to the torture-chamber, anything more agonizing than the apparently unconcerned phrase, none the less betraying a sense of oppression, that accompanies Tosca's words, 'Sgomento alcun non ho (Nor do I feel alarmed)', anything more diabolically sadic than the accompaniment to Scarpia's 'che ad ogni niego sprizza sangue senza mercè (from which a jet of blood spirts out at every denial)', which seems to pierce our nerves like the stabs of the instrument of torture, can hardly be conceived in music. The infinitely poignant, soft melody on the strings while the monster is writing the safe-conduct already implies the knowledge that Mario, whom it purports to save, will really die; and when it is repeated after the murder of Scarpia, it not only suggests a lament over his justifiable murder, which we hear with a catch of the breath, but further suggests the death of both Tosca and Cavaradossi. The words at the close of this act are unbearably theatrical: the scene in which the murderess leaves her victim solemnly lying in state, after placing candles on each side of him, laying a crucifix on his breast, and kneeling with superstitious piety by his side, is a great deal worse than a mere psychological impossibility; it is a piece of rank falsity to nature committed for the sake of a crude stage effect. But, abominable though this effect is, it is none the less produced by unerring means. Yet I would not for anything dispense with even this crude piece of stage effectiveness: for at this point Puccini has one of his moments of inspired intuition. First we hear the succession of notes that accompanied Scarpia's hypocritically insinuating and lustful advances, the feigned sorrow expressed in which, however, at the same time betrays the fact that the painter's death is at hand, and that Scarpia is cheating the singer of his life. But now all this seems to die away in a conventional figure, the suave motive of the first duet of the lovers recurs for

a moment like a gleam of light, recalling Tosca's love; and then
the dread chords symbolic of Scarpia seem to expire in deep,
ghostly notes on the strings, echoed in a triad sounded by the
flutes and harp, and followed by an almost inaudible drum-
beat, and the vague, shuddering sound of the gong.   The effect
is shadowy and vaporous, as though the dead man's last sighs
still floated along the walls, while, in the distance, the roll of
the drums that escort the condemned man to his death is heard
faintly, yet with ghastly distinctness.   The effect is such that
even now, after hearing the work so often, it gives me a cold
shudder, and perhaps it is the most powerful in the whole of
Puccini's works; while at the same time it is a triumph of the
eternal truth of music over the falsity of a calculating theatrical
imagination.

There is a letter extant from the Maestro to Ricordi, his
fatherly friend and publisher, who had felt doubts about the
third act of the opera, not entirely without reason, which even
the music could not altogether allay.   Puccini defended himself
and his music earnestly and with a fine dignity.   Hitherto he
had written about his work ironically, and at times even a little
plaintively, but always in a jesting tone, cracking jokes about
his 'Neronian instincts (istinti neroniane)', and making fun of
himself as the 'maestro cuccumeggiante (composer of "Harlots'
Operas")', as his fellow-townsmen of Lucca called it in their
local dialect.   Only when he had to wring some concession
from his librettists did his brow appear to contract in a frown
—for instance, in connexion with the phrase 'e muoio disperato
(and now I die despairing)', one of those which he had himself
introduced into Mario's farewell to life, for the purpose of
indicating the predominant atmosphere which he required for
the whole scene, in place of the lifeless apostrophe to art.   But
now, when he had to defend the completed work, he used a
tone of self-respect, mingled with a proud modesty, that is
curiously impressive: 'Nor is [my confidence in the merits of
Act III of *Tosca*] due to pride, but to my conviction that the
colour I have given to the drama with which I had to deal is the

best of which I am capable'.[1]   He pleads like an advocate for
the final love-duet, which he had, by the way, salvaged from the
fourth act that had been cut out of *Edgar*.   'As for its fragmentary character, that is intentional; this cannot be a uniform
and tranquil situation like that in other love-duets.'   He, too,
felt certain doubts, and complained of the obstinacy of his
literary collaborators in writing many passages not at all as he
wanted them; but he hoped that the faults would disappear in
performance, and firmly believed that he would yet convince
his '*caro papa Giulio*'.

Nor was he mistaken.   Never before had he worked with
such artistic insight as during those nights when he composed
till dawn ('I sleep during the daytime,' he says, 'and work all
through the night'); and his unerring eye for stage effect proved
itself more than ever in *Tosca*.   The nice calculation by which
he avoided all that was tedious, while still obtaining the utmost
effect of suspense, the way in which he used the device of
repeating motives with a menacing monotony, only to relieve
the tension at the right moment by a siren-like melody, which
at the same time provided relaxation from all the horrors, is
such a remarkable feat in the purely dramatic use of music that
every young composer should study it and learn from it.   The
young operatic composers of to-day, however, absolutely refuse
to hear of learning from others, least of all from the despised
Puccini, whose success is quite enough to condemn him.   They
prefer to fail by their own unaided efforts.

Possibly, however, they use different language among themselves.   I can state as an absolute fact that a distinguished
French composer, one of the chief of the purists who were
opposed to Puccini, was once sitting next a critic at a performance
of *La Bohème*, when he suddenly exclaimed: 'The devil! People
may say what they like, but that is fine stuff; it is competent

[1] TRANSLATOR'S NOTE.—Puccini's actual words, as printed in the *Epistolario*
(12 October 1899 to Ricordi), were: 'Non è orgoglio mio, no.   È la convinzione
di aver colorito come meglio non potevo il dramma che mi stava dinanzi. . . .
Quanto alla frammentarietà, è cosa voluta da me; non può essere una situazione
uniforme e tranquilla come in altri duetti d'amore'.

work, everything is just right! Only listen to that! He is indeed a formidable fellow (*un rude lapin*)—only one must not say so'. And the critic added: 'There may be things in it that are exaggerated, but such has been my opinion for a long time—only I durst not say so openly'.

And even to-day there are many who have not the courage to say so. Even at the banquet after the Berlin performance of *The Girl of the Golden West*, the German composers were still unrepresented. They know perfectly well what Puccini stands for, but they 'may not say so'—or perhaps they do not want to.

It is a curious thing that, in spite of many signs of immaturity, and the fact that his own personality was not yet quite clearly revealed in them, Puccini's first operas were received not only without opposition, but, if anything, more warmly and flatteringly than they deserved; whereas his works of mature artistry met with an almost bewildered reception, if not with positive hostility. Even *Tosca*, when performed for the first time at the Teatro Costanzi, Rome, on 14th January 1900, was given rather a poor welcome, though some of the separate numbers were greeted with great applause, the author was called before the curtain five or six times at the end of each act, and the whole finale of the last act was repeated in response to the audience's eagerly expressed desire. It is possible that these works, which seem to us almost too tame and obvious, were then felt to be too novel and audacious; that their melody seemed vague and blurred, and more like glorified declamation, without any clear-cut vocal line; and that their pungent and full-flavoured harmony was regarded as wilfully bizarre. This must, indeed, have been so. I remember what a curious shock, not to say consternation, was caused by the consecutive fifths in *La Bohème* and the piquant effect of the chromatic chords, and what a long time elapsed before Mimi and Rodolfo's tender, timid melodies were sung as such, and not declaimed tentatively by the singers as though they were passages interpolated into a recitative, instead of being attacked with conviction as what they really were. But this very hesitation and, still more, the reserve that was shown in accepting the new musical idiom, only bear witness to the living merits of the music, which are confirmed by the lasting vitality of the operas.

Moreover, the fact that, at its first performance, *Tosca* met with a reception which cannot be called more than barely polite was due to a reason having nothing to do with the work itself or the effects of terror in it, that were almost too much for weak nerves, for the public was out of temper and restive from the outset. This was partly because a certain clique had spread the report that the critics were going to be more severe this time, and would show rather less indulgence than usual for the undeniable defects in Puccini's music—in fact, that they meant to make the Maestro expiate his undeserved successes. But besides this, all sorts of rumours were going the round, and were calculated to produce an uneasy atmosphere in the house. It was even stated that a bomb outrage might be expected. In short, the birds of ill-omen were hissing and croaking, and, though nobody knew exactly what was the matter, the atmosphere was charged with electricity. Small wonder that on this occasion Leopoldo Mugnone, who, to quote the Master, was 'as nervous as he was sure of his effects', was on this occasion far more nervous than sure of his effects, and was even more timorous and reluctant to start the performance than he had been at the original production of *La Bohème*; for during an operatic performance at Barcelona he had actually witnessed a bomb outrage, which had mutilated a number of people. He could therefore remember the terrible scene, and his state of mind was not improved when a friendly police official impressed upon him that, if anything of the kind were to happen, he was at once to strike up the Royal March or the Italian National Anthem. But nothing did happen, except that people began shouting and making a disturbance at the very beginning of the first scene, though merely as a protest against late arrivals. The curtain had to be lowered, but rose again ten minutes later, and after this the performance proceeded without any further untoward incidents.   The tenor De Marchi's first aria was greeted with loud and instantaneous applause, five numbers had to be repeated, and Madame Darclée, who took the part of Tosca, was applauded to the echo when she appeared at the Maestro's side.   In spite of all this, its success was on the whole dubious.   At the end of the last act the audience, including Mascagni—who was present at the production, as he had been at that of *La Bohème*, like the loyal old friend that he was— Cilea, Marchetti, and other Italian operatic composers, together with the ministers and senators, who had all put in an appearance for the purpose of acclaiming a fresh victory on the part of the recognized leader among modern Italian operatic composers, hardly knew whether to congratulate Puccini or condole with him.

It would be a mere piece of gratuitous repetition to waste any more irony at the expense of the critics, and show how wrong they were.   On this occasion, moreover, they were anything but unanimous.   Scarcely one of them observed what bravura Puccini had displayed in mastering a subject which was to a large extent ill adapted for musical treatment.   None the less, certain of them were conscious of the disparity, not to say discordance, between the stage action and the music: 'La Tosca is not suited to Puccini's temperament,' said one; while another remarked: 'It is to be deplored that he should have ventured upon an experiment the fruitlessness of which cannot have escaped him'; and a third characterized the music as 'elegant', though less varied, incisive, and light than usual, and considered that the weakness of the work lay in the heaviness with which the colour was laid on, and the defective psychology of the drama, which had hampered Puccini's imagination.   But voices were also raised in enthusiasm over the wonderful music, overflowing melody and elevated style, and a sure and successful future was prognosticated for the work, 'as soon as the anxiety and nervousness of the first performances have worn off'.

This future has, indeed, been realized.   Yet outside Italy, at least, *Tosca* has made its way more slowly than Puccini's

other operas.   This may be due partly to the brutality of the
dramatic action; but the translations of the libretto cannot be
exonerated from a share in the guilt.[1] . . . In Germany, at
any rate, the opposition with which *Tosca* has met is certainly
due quite as much to the very cavalier treatment with which the
libretto associated with such pregnant music has been subjected
as to the crudities of Sardou's sensational drama.   As the
sacristan says: 'Già sono impenitenti tutti quanti'—translators
are incorrigible, the whole lot of them!

[1] TRANSLATOR'S NOTE.—A short passage dealing with the German translation
of the *Tosca* libretto has been omitted at this point.

CHAPTER X

By a curious phenomenon, which is, however, easily comprehensible, so soon as an artist's life comes under the influence of the fixed sign of fame and universal recognition, which can no longer be shaken even by isolated failures, his 'biography', in the true sense of the word, comes to an end. The artist no longer lives his own life; it is lived for him. His fame dictates how his day is to be employed, monopolizes his time, and loads him with responsibilities and burdens that he cannot refuse without prejudicing the outward success and resounding fame of his work. It causes him to be pestered by people—directors, managers, singers, conductors, journalists, interviewers, autograph-hunters, and sincere admirers, for whom he must always be in readiness, and who serve the purpose of megaphones for his artistic exploits, and often, unfortunately, for his own private personality. Supervision of the rehearsals of his works, journeys abroad in connexion with their production, negotiations with librettists, the receipt of official honours, as well as attendance at ceremonial receptions and banquets, become his duty, whether he find them welcome or not. For a large part of the year, at least, his existence has to be regulated like a machine, and the time-table that governs it is no longer arranged by himself. All this is not without its practical importance; but it provides no subjects of interest for him whose business it is to examine the artist's character and work. During periods when the externals of life follow a uniform course, it is superfluous to record them in detail; all that need engage the critic's attention with any particularity is the fate of some particular work, or some out-of-the-way experience of the author, and by the time he has reached this stage of his career, nothing important of this sort occurs very frequently.   Apart from these exceptional incidents only one thing is of importance to him—the artist's attitude towards these things, which are often detrimental to his character, and the acceptance or rejection of which provides a key to his qualities as a man.   Some are ruined by success and deteriorate through vanity; others enter into this round of busy occupations in a common-sense spirit, whether willingly or reluctantly, with a superior smile or in despairing resignation, but without losing or belying their true selves.   And there are a very few who manage to maintain their isolation, calmly shutting out all these accompaniments of fame, whether cheerful or exasperating, disregarding its very echoes, and ignoring the demands of their professional career, or else leaving their friends to do such things as appear to be absolutely necessary; for they are themselves indifferent to success and outward effect, and hold nothing of importance but their work.

Puccini belonged to the second class; but he was one of the despairing, not the resigned type.   His letters from foreign capitals are one long jeremiad.   A dinner or luncheon invitation made him 'ill for a week', the banquets arranged in his honour were an absolute agony to him, and once in Paris he flew into a perfect rage and wrote: 'I hate palaces!   I hate capitals!   I hate styles! . . . I hate horses, cats, and pedigree dogs!   I hate steamers, tall hats, and evening dress!'[1]   He rebelled furiously against the restraints of society: 'All persuasion is useless: I was not born for the life of drawing-rooms and receptions!   Why should I risk playing the part of an idiot and an imbecile?'[2]   Yet in the end he gave in, however much he might invoke the example of Verdi, who always behaved

---

[1] TRANSLATOR'S NOTE.—Puccini's actual words, as printed in the *Epistolaric*, were: '. . . Odio i palazzi!   Odio i capitelli!   Odio i stili!   Amo lo bello stile del pioppo, dell' abete. . . . Odio il cavallo, il gatto . . . il cane di lusso!   Odio il vapore, il cappello a cilindro, il *frak*'.

[2] Letter of 15 May 1898 to Ricordi in the *Epistolario*: 'A me un invito a pranzo mi fa star male una settimana . . . non sono nato per far la vita dei salotti e dei ricevimenti!   A che prò espormi a far la figura del cretino e dell' imbecile?'

as he found most convenient to himself, yet none the less had a 'bit of a career (quel po' po' di carriera)'.

But he devoted all his energy to following the great old master's example as far as was in his power. When he was abroad he made no attempt to win people's good graces by his amiability. His friend Carlo Clausetti says that he preferred to remain silent during all conversations, in large parties at least, though he could be charming in a *tête-à-tête*. During those pauses in his work that he dreaded, he took refuge in his retreat on the shores of the lake as often as he could. At these times, it is true, and especially when he could not go shooting, he did not particularly enjoy life. When he had not at least a prospect of finding a new libretto, he was moody, and, most astonishing symptom of all, when he felt unable to write a note, he was bored to death: 'Io mi noio a morte, non avendo nulla da fare (I am bored to death, for I have nothing to do)', he wrote shortly after completing *Tosca*. It is hardly conceivable, but this composer with such a wealth of inspiration never read a book, with the exception of those in which he hoped to find a subject for an opera, and never looked at any music, old or new, that was not already familiar to him; and nature had little to say to him when he had not a gun over his shoulder. It is astonishing, too, that he could never be induced to take up the baton, even as a pure pastime, and give his own interpretation of one of his operas, quite apart from the value that such an authoritative rendering would have had in founding correct traditions of style. It is all the more remarkable, since there were few conductors with whom he entirely agreed and scarcely any singers with whose performance he was quite satisfied; but he never conducted a single one of his own works. It is as though he confidently left in the hands of God the processes of his development and growing maturity, and the enrichment of his inner life.

Again, it seems extremely odd that during the last twenty years of his life, when worldly prosperity was being showered upon him, Puccini never took advantage of any of those pauses in his work that were imposed upon him by fate to travel round the world, or at least visit those exotic lands whose music had yielded him such fruitful results in three of his works: Japan, China, and California; not to speak of those from which he might have brought back fresh booty. It is evident that he could not bear to be far away while his librettists were at work. He was the most important partner in the combination, a tyrannical dictator who could not be absent without endangering his intentions. Yet surely this would not have applied to those periods when he had no subject to engage his attention. We can think of only two explanations: either he was always over-flowing with music to such an extent that it, as it were, fermented within him, producing a sort of spiritual fever, until he could succeed in extricating it from this internal chaos by means of a new libretto and clothing it in form; or else, after the creative effort of writing an opera and the years of high tension that this involved, he felt, as it were, exhausted and incapable of taking in any impressions save those of the life to which he was accustomed, and remained absolutely impervious even to intellectual and artistic impressions.

During the later years of his life, however, he had become less unmanageable during his phases of enforced leisure. As frequently happens with musicians—a significant fact!—the Master had from an early age had an almost childlike predilection for mechanical devices, and taken a great interest in everything connected with machines, and all sorts of technical inventions. He had also become an ardent motorist, making short, and sometimes considerable excursions from Viareggio. On one occasion he even made a week's trip through Nuremberg, Würzburg, and Cologne into Holland, during which he felt as happy as a boy at wandering through foreign countries for sheer pleasure, and not merely for professional reasons, and, above all, in so far as that was possible, incognito. He was accompanied by his son and one of his friends, who enjoyed his radiant good-humour and the myriad tokens of love and respect shown him everywhere, which gave him a double pleasure when he had not been recognized. The memory of this journey has been preserved in a chronicle, written in very jovial verse and embellished with delightful caricatures, now in the keeping of Tonio Puccini, and, conscious that I am but anticipating further revelations, I here reproduce two incidents from it, one which, though merely trivial in appearance, may possibly have had tragic after-effects, and another which, insignificant though it may be in itself, is none the less a symptom of the almost legendary popularity of Puccini's music, for his melodies were sung both in the Polar regions and in the Australian bush, just as they were in the heart of Europe. The motor had already travelled many miles, when a halt was called at Ingolstadt for luncheon. Puccini ordered his favourite dish, roast goose, of which he partook with the best of appetites, taking the bone in his fingers in his usual unconventional fashion in order to pick it thoroughly. A splinter of it remained in his mouth, however, stuck in his throat, and simply refused to move. A doctor had to be sent for, and removed the little bone with his forceps. It is more than probable that this little accident was responsible for the fact that the chronic laryngitis from which Puccini had suffered for a long time degenerated into the malignant and fatal affection that had probably been latent in him for long past, and came to a head shortly afterwards; for only two years later the end had come. Of course he had no idea of this at the time; but it is significant of the superstition which the Master shared with so many of his fellow-musicians that he took the place and its name as symbolic, and held them responsible for the unpleasant incident. 'Ingolstadt,' he would say, 'means *in-gola-stat*—it sticks in one's throat.'

They arrived in Cologne late at night, and could not find a lodging anywhere. They rang at the door of six hotels in succession, but everywhere received the answer: 'I am sorry, we are full up'. On arriving at the seventh, and meeting with the same response, Puccini persisted in his demands, being hungry and exhausted after his long journey, but he was still unsuccessful, the porter politely repeating that there were no rooms disengaged. He was just about to shut the door, when the Master seized him by the coat-sleeve, and asked him in a very humble voice: 'Do you know *La Bohème*?' The man was taken aback at first, and then indignant at the sudden and unexpected question: 'Of course I do! How could I fail to know it? I have heard it often and often at the theatre!' 'Ah,' said Puccini, 'do sing us something out of it!' The good man was still more amazed, but none the less flattered, and sang them something simply abominably, both the diction and the melody being very dubious, but just recognizable by those who knew the opera thoroughly; after which he added proudly, 'I know *Tosca* and *Butterfly* too, and . . .' 'Very well,' interrupted the Maestro very modestly, 'I am Puccini.' 'Ah, if you are Puccini!' he shouted joyfully—and rooms were found for them. Had not Puccini left again early the next morning, he would have had to let the hotel porter sing him every single one of his operas.

Twenty-five years earlier, however, he was not yet so famous, and was far more impatient when his work languished. The worst time of all was after the first production of *Tosca*, when he simply could not find a new libretto. His thoughts kept returning to the idea of a Dante trilogy, consisting of three one-act pieces: an *Inferno*, a *Purgatorio*, and a *Paradiso*, each of which was to be a separate little drama, whether drawn from the *Divine Comedy* or invented independently. He was full of enthusiasm for this plan, and described it to his friends till he observed, to his astonishment, that the thought of the tedium of Paradise aroused positively purgatorial feelings in him, so that he ultimately dismissed the idea—to the infernal regions. Next, since he received no answer from the 'infernal American' who had written such a genuine and touching tragedy about a little Japanese girl, he desired to compose music for Oscar Wilde's *Florentine Tragedy*, out of which Alexander von Zemlinsky afterwards made such a successful opera. But he soon abandoned this idea too, and chafed with fury at the inaction of his librettists. 'Things cannot go on like this,' he once exclaimed in exasperation when he had heard nothing from Giacosa for ten whole days—Imagine! Ten whole days!—and his threats of dying became sinister in their frequency. Things had got to change; 'se no, presto sarò cadavere (if not, I shall soon be a corpse)'. Next, d'Annunzio had to be approached on the subject of a drama with the title of *L'Alchimista*, in which the central figure was to be Cecco d'Ascoli; but this, too, proved to be unsuited to his purposes. In the meantime the Maestro kept reverting enthusiastically to *Madame Butterfly*, an American tragedy of a geisha by David Belasco, the author of which, he wrote, had still failed to send any answer, confound him! While awaiting his reply Puccini had settled the plan of the piece in his own mind: he might have two acts, one in North America, the other in Japan. Illica would certainly supply what was required afterwards, out of the novel. If only the original text would arrive! 'I am in despair,' he wrote, 'and my mind is in a state of torment . . . if only I could get an answer from New York! The more I think of "Butterfly" the more passionately excited I am about it. Ah! if only I had it before me here, so that I could set to work on it!' [1] At last Belasco's consent arrived, and Puccini threw himself into the work in an unspeakably blissful mood, such as he had never felt before. For the first time he had a book with which he was thoroughly satisfied, apart from a few trifling objections. He 'plunged deep into it' with the greatest joy, and took more pains over the work than ever. He endeavoured to make Mr. F. B. Pinkerton (rendered in the German translation as Linkerton, evidently in order to avoid confusion with the famous detective of the same name) sing 'in as American a fashion as possible', and to this end had

[1] TRANSLATOR'S NOTE.—Puccini's actual words, as printed in the *Epistolario* (letter of 20 Nov. 1900 to Ricordi) were: 'Io dispero e mi torturo l'anima . . . almeno arrivasse la risposta da New York!

'Quanto più penso alla Butterfly, sempre più mi ci appassiono. Ah! l'avessi qui con me per lavorarmela! Penso che invece di un atto se me potrebbero fare due e belli lunghi. Il primo nel Nord America—e il secondo al Giappone. Illica dal romanzo poi troverebbe certamente quanto occorre'.

recourse to the somewhat naïve device of weaving into his music here and there as a motive the successive notes of the common chord with which the American national anthem opens. On the advice of Illica he paid a visit to Milan for the purpose of seeing the great Japanese tragic actress Sada Yacco, with her strange, twittering voice, which was none the less so profoundly stirring, in order that the memory of its timbre might enable him to infuse a more genuine racial colour into his own music. He took infinite trouble over trifling details, such, for instance, as the names. 'Yamadori' sounded too womanish for the name of a prince, and there were others that puzzled him; so he made up his mind to call upon the Japanese ambassador's wife at Viareggio, and hear what she would have to tell him about all these names, such as Sarundapiko, Izaghi, or Sganami.[1] Next he abruptly decided to jettison a whole act, the scene of which was to have been laid in the Consulate. He hesitated, however, to divide what remained into three acts again, and insisted upon having two only, for otherwise, he said, a fiasco was to be expected without fail. In this, however, he committed the only dramatic error in his life. He was thoroughly fired with his subject, and hardly troubled about his physical condition. Not even an indisposition was allowed to keep him from his work, though he suffered constantly from a slight throat trouble, frequently accompanied by a curious huskiness and loss of resonance in his voice; but it never occurred to the doctors to suspect any more serious trouble. Symptoms of a diabetic tendency also appeared, and he often felt a slight weakness due to a touch of fever. But none of this was able to check his creative frenzy, and when the results were successful, he was radiant with joy.

But now the worst thing that could possibly have happened to him took place: he was forced to suspend his work for nearly

[1] TRANSLATOR'S NOTE.—But the actual words of Puccini's letter, as printed in the *Epistolario* (18 Sept. 1902 to Ricordi), were: 'Ho avuto adesso la visita della signora Ohyama, Ambasciatrice del Giappone. . . . Non ha trovato giusto il nome di Yamadori, poiché è femminile, e poi, non appropriato, perché là danno dei nomi suggestivi e consoni al tipo e al carattere nei loro drammi'.

THE LAST PORTRAIT

eight months, which reduced him to a state of the blackest depression. The Maestro, accompanied by his wife and son, had spent the evening of 25th February 1903 in his native town, but, with his usual obstinacy, he could not be dissuaded from returning home after nightfall, even though he meant to pay a visit to the dentist at Lucca on the following day. The chauffeur failed to notice a sharp curve, with the result that the motor crashed into a tree and overturned. Donna Elvira and Tonio were thrown out, but, by a miracle, remained uninjured, while the chauffeur lay writhing in the ditch with a broken leg, shrieking with pain. Puccini, however, was nowhere to be seen, and their agonized shouts died away without any response —not unnaturally, for he was lying unconscious under the motor with a broken leg, almost smothered by the fumes of benzol. Fortunately the accident had taken place close to the house of a doctor, who administered first-aid on the spot. Puccini had to have his leg put in plaster, and was not allowed to leave his bed for months. He was happy when he at last recovered enough to be pushed along the lake-shore in an invalid chair, and even more so when he was able to hobble a few steps every day by himself, first on crutches, and then by the aid of two sticks. But even before this he had already resumed the work for which he had been longing so vehemently. Who knows, indeed, whether the music of *Madame Butterfly*, with its tender but compelling power of suggestion, may not have accumulated an even more concentrated force as a result of this long confinement, yielding up its very quintessence, as it were, through the evaporation of all that was superfluous. Puccini himself had once more fallen thoroughly under the spell of his dreams, with their sad sweetness and exotic illusions, and from time to time a letter to Ricordi would report: 'Work is going on well. I am pleased with it,' without the old hesitating, doubtful 'Chi lo sa? (Who knows?)' of former days. And he had every right to be pleased with it.

Setting aside all reference to the music for the moment, we may lay it down once and for all that *Manon Lescaut* is still a

N

mere puppet play, *Tosca* and *The Girl of the Golden West* have scenes worthy of a chamber of horrors and theatrical in the bad sense of the word, while *Il Tabarro* is theatrical in the good sense, *Suor Angelica* suggests an altar-piece transferred to the stage, and *Gianni Schicchi* is directly derived from the best traditions of the Italian *commedia dell' arte*, being a burlesque of such bewilderingly exuberant humour that we hardly trouble about its 'verisimilitude'—besides which, it does not strain probability too far. *Le Villi* and *Edgar* need not be taken into consideration, but as regards both style and language, in *Turandot* we are in the land of faery enhanced by poetry, for, thanks to the distinguished patronage of Schiller, the subject was already immune from all taint of the matter-of-fact; while both *La Bohème* and *Butterfly*, apart from the end of the Japanese tragedy, which is painful for two reasons, undoubtedly possess a poetic quality, and are tersely dramatic and logically constructed, while their characters have genuinely human traits, and not merely those of lifeless masks and automata, and their destiny appeals to our sympathies, making us their brethren through pity. There are but few operatic libretti of which as much can be said. Is it just, then, to castigate Puccini as 'the negation of an artist (*Unkünstler*)', aiming at nothing but sensational effectiveness, simply because he has not shrunk from strong, and at times brutal effects, sometimes worthy of the cinema, it is true, though it is obvious that he is never completely possessed by his work, and cannot put his whole soul into it, except when he has a real poet to second him, and when the naïve emotions of a sincere heart give free course to his inspiration. Let us be honest: what is *Don Giovanni* but a play of puppets? Does not *Der Freischütz*, for all its woodland freshness and glorious folk spirit, verge upon the melodramas familiar to us in the travelling theatres at a fair? Are the characters in *Fidelio* made of real flesh and blood, or are they not rather mere masks, representative of fidelity, longing for freedom, middle-class good nature and crafty despotism; and is Pizarro so very different from Scarpia? Or again, does not the bloody head of Jochanaan, which introduces such an equivocal note into the magnificent final scene of *Salome*, that splendid work of genius, remind us of the chamber of horrors at a waxwork show? For the hundredth time I repeat that I know perfectly well what Mozart, Beethoven, Weber, and Richard Strauss are, on the one hand, and what Puccini is, on the other; I know that comparisons are never quite valid, especially when we are considering artists on such a different intellectual plane. But we are not here concerned with ethical problems, nor even with music, but simply with artistic intentions; and if a master such as Puccini is abused year in and year out for his choice of subjects, the least we ought to do is surely to ask ourselves whether there exist any operatic libretti in other languages than Italian, either before or after Wagner, that possess greater artistic merit than those of the Italian composer, and in which are to be found characters more touching and true to life than all these dainty little women with their capacity for love—poor, consumptive Mimi, or even the girlish figure of the geisha Cho-Cho-San, with her infinite patience and trustfulness, her humble love, and her quiet, heart-rending self-immolation. There are advanced musical thinkers of our day who have no idea how sterile musical radicalism really is in the long run, and who preach the gospel according to Schönberg while secretly enjoying the intoxication of Puccini, whose 'unchaste' style they would be glad enough to imitate if only they had sufficient powers of invention; but they really ought to consider for a while the question of where the more honest artistic ideals are to be found—in the much-abused Puccini, or in the many present-day musicians who are either merely playing tricks (*Unfug verüben*) with music or else suffering from the malady of a 'progressive philosophy of life'.

I have already described more than once how Puccini was as much in love with nearly all the feminine characters in his operas as with any living woman; but for none of them did he feel such a whole-hearted love, which positively haunted his dreams, as for this dainty Madame Butterfly, who has contracted a marriage with a smart, thoughtless naval lieutenant merely by declaration, according to the usage of her country, but is under the illusion that she is loved by the frivolous American and is permanently and legally his wife. She waits for him for two years in hunger and want, steadfastly rejecting all the advances of rich men, and when he returns with a wife, and wishes to adopt the child born during his absence, she makes this supreme sacrifice to him, together with that of her poor little broken heart. None of his heroines has he clothed in such precious music: among all that Puccini wrote during his whole life this music stands almost alone in the sheen of its musical colour, like mother-of-pearl, in the opalescent, shimmering tone, the filigree-like melody, as soft as a breath and as fine as a cobweb, which is more perfectly sublimated, less corporeal and more gossamer-like than ever in this opera. Not till *Turandot* did he once more achieve art with such economy, such elusive colour, such unusual and exotic qualities. But before turning to a detailed consideration of the individual beauties of this exquisite music, woven, as it were, out of moonbeams, and as unsubstantial as the little bamboo houses of Japan, I will first describe the fate meted out to it by the composer's fellow-countrymen, for very different interpretations can be put upon this.

On the day of this performance, after the general rehearsal, Puccini wrote the following cordial and confident letter to Rosina Storchio, the eminent artist who was to sing the part of his Butterfly:

DEAR ROSINA,

It is superfluous for me to wish you success. Your great art is so true, so delicate, so impressive that it is sure to subjugate the public. And I hope that, through you, I shall hasten on to victory. Till this evening, then, with a confident mind and with so much love, dearest,

G. P.

We see how thoroughly convinced he was this time of the unfailing success of his work, and every one had been quite carried away by it at the rehearsals, from the performers to the triangle-player, and the very stage-carpenters and workmen, who would tiptoe off the stage with tears in their eyes and come back day after day to listen. Even these simple people had been moved to the depths of their hearts by both the action and the music of the opera. The Master took this as symptomatic, and was so absolutely sure of success that, for the first time, he ventured to invite his brothers and sisters to the first performance of *Butterfly* at the Scala, Milan, though he had never asked them to that of any of his other operas. But he had cause to regret his action, for the evening of 17th February 1904 had a black ending, and *Madame Butterfly* was hissed.

At first the same atmosphere of tense expectation and friendly welcome prevailed, tinged with a certain love of sensation, as is usually felt when the public is about to hear a new work by a popular composer. But suddenly the atmosphere changed, and went to the opposite extreme, presumably because a phrase of the melody that accompanies the entrance of Butterfly in her wedding attire reminded the public of one from *La Bohème* and roused their opposition. At the end of the first act the applause had to compete with audible hissing, and not even the sight of the Maestro, who limped on to the stage leaning upon his stick, to acknowledge the applause of his faithful friends, led by Mascagni, imposed sufficient respect to check the irrepressible uproar. Puccini withdrew with a gloomy, hurt expression on his face, and could not be induced to appear before the curtain again. He sat in the wings watching the uproar increasing, first in perplexity, but afterwards with growing anger, biting his nails savagely, while from time to time words of fierce irony broke from his compressed lips in his most expressive Tuscan: 'Splendid!—Louder still, you beasts!—Shriek, yell, jeer at me!—But it is I who am right, I!—You shall see!—Ruin it all for me!—It is I who am right!—It is the finest opera I have ever written! . . .' Before very long most people were of the same opinion; but next morning Puccini had to listen to the hoarse voices of the newsboys shouting 'Maestro Puccini's fiasco!' outside his windows, that looked on the street.

What had happened? It was one of those rowdy nights whose real causes remain for ever a puzzle. A sort of indefinable hostility seems to float in the very air; somebody shrugs his shoulders at a fine passage, and makes his neighbour feel uncertain; a spiteful remark is launched and flies like lightning round the theatre; the first hiss is heard—and a tumult breaks out that can no longer be checked. After this all sense of measure is generally lost; the most insignificant accident causes it to break out afresh. On this occasion a draught distended Madame Storchio's robe for a moment, and this provoked shrill whistling and laughter. It is possible that a cabal of envious and malevolent persons was at work on that evening, who were bent upon bringing about the failure of this new opera by their much-fêted colleague; but we are loath to believe this. No doubt the plan of *Madame Butterfly* might in itself have provoked an unfavourable reception from a public that had arrived with the joyous intention of applauding their favourite operatic composer, but certainly not such an insulting one as this. In this original version of the work the second act lasted more than an hour and a half, and that is too much for any Italian audience. Moreover, the fact that the tenor disappears after the first act, and does not reappear till the third, and even then only as an episodic figure, is open to objection, and not to the taste of the ordinary La Scala audience. But people could not have known either of these things during the first act, when this low scene already started; and it was afterwards seconded by the critics in a spirit that makes us disinclined to do them the honour of quoting them. The sole exception was Giovanni Pozza, who recommended the public to be calm, and to wait and see. It really looked as though the dastardly and the unintelligent had banded themselves together against the Master, with the object of making his work a failure. The reflection that conspiracies of this sort meet with nothing but contempt from posterity, and can never succeed in the long run, when genuine merit is in question, does not alter the facts.

But Puccini was well aware of this. Ten days after this

stormy evening he wrote to his friend Don Pietro Panichelli in Rome:

DEAR PADRE (*Caro Prete*),
  You must have been dismayed at the vile remarks of an envious press. But never fear! *Butterfly* is full of life and truth, and soon she will rise from the dead. I say it and stick to it with unwavering conviction. You will see, and that in a few months' time, though I cannot at present tell you where.[1]

He retired to Torre del Lago, where his soul never failed to find healing for its wounds. A bitter taste still lingered in his mouth, but, as he said in a letter to another friend: 'I hope that this bitterness will be transferred to other mouths as soon as possible, but in a somewhat more poisonous form'. By agreement with Ricordi he withdrew the opera after the very first evening, refunding the enormous sum of 20,000 lire which he had received from the management for his royalties. He next proceeded with perfect equanimity to revise it. He could not have failed to see that he had been wrong in stubbornly insisting upon dividing it into two acts; and he now added an orchestral intermezzo separating the second act, which was too long, into two parts, introduced into the latter of these a new canzone for the tenor, full of genuine feeling and poignant grief, eliminated the superfluous episode of the drunken uncle in the first act, added a few touches to certain passages so as to produce a more intimate glow of colour, and on 28th May of the same year had the work produced at the Teatro Grande, Brescia, with Campanini of the Scala as conductor and Salomea Krucenisca and Zenatello in the principal roles. It was an unmixed success. The point to which the public of the Scala had taken exception—that is, the fact that the music was 'genuine Puccini' —aroused absolute rapture here, number after number had to

---

[1] TRANSLATOR'S NOTE.—The actual words of Puccini's letter, as printed in the *Epistolario*, were: 'Caro Prete, tu sarai spaventato dalle vili parole dell' invida stampa. Niente paura! La Butterfly è viva, vera, e presto risorgerà. Lo dico e lo sostengo con fede incrollabile—vedrai—e sarà fra un paio di mesi; non posso dirti dove, per ora'.

be repeated, and Puccini, now dispensing with his stick—a fact which seems almost symbolic—had to respond to innumerable and enthusiastic calls. From this point onwards the opera made its way all round the globe, as though on the wings of the wind, and down to the present day it has vied with *La Bohème* as first favourite among his works.

They vied with one another in Puccini's own estimation, too, for he remarked on one occasion: 'I never listen to my operas with pleasure, with the exception, perhaps, of the last act of *La Bohème*. But *Butterfly*, yes; the whole thing both entertains and interests me. I am conscious that in it I have written the most modern of my operas'. The most modern? It is hard to see in what respects *Butterfly* is to be considered more modern than its predecessors. It is possible that Puccini was referring to the national element, the use of Japanese folk-songs, of which hundreds of gramophone records were sent him from Tokio, though only infinitesimal doses of this music found a way into his work. Perhaps, too, he was thinking of certain exotic sequences of notes, whole-tone scales, Debussy-like touches in his harmonies and the iridescent colour, like a butterfly's wing, of his incomparable instrumentation. All these devices may, indeed, be 'modern' in the sense in which this word is popularly used to-day, and undoubtedly have their own positive value. But after all, the composer has surrounded each one of his works with a characteristic musical atmosphere of its own, providing it with the colour best suited to it, and the perfume, so to speak, of its setting, and he has done no more than this in his Japanese romance. It is not its modernity that lends this music its power of suggestion and its attractiveness, but its specific aroma, its combination of a foreign atmosphere with the universal human emotions that are the same everywhere, for, however much they may vary in temperature, they have remained the same in every quarter of the globe since the first days of creation, whether at the North Pole or in the tropics. There is a marked contrast between the characteristically Japanese robe of rustling silk, with its heavy embroideries, and the woman's heart beneath it, eternally the same as it throbs with apprehension, hope, rapture, and despondency. It seems to me that the secret of this opera's triumph, perhaps the secret of the triumph of all Puccini's music, lies in this contrast—or, if we prefer to put it so, in this blend of what is peculiar to some special place with the primitive emotions that are independent of place or time.

Or it would be more correct to say that this is one of the secrets. The second is to be found, here as ever, in the sweetness and tenderness of the love-breathing melody, which is, however, free from weakness and sickliness, and, in this work in particular, has a shimmering lustre and thrills with soul as it had hardly ever done before. The atmosphere pervading it suggests the smile of Monna Lisa, and lends it something of that melting softness known to the Italians as *sfumato*, the term applied by Leonardo to that which has a clear, yet not a sharp outline, to the soft gradation of colours that pass insensibly into one another instead of being placed side by side in hard masses. But there is a peculiar fascination not only in these melodies, which often seem, as it were, to tremble and flutter like shivering, frightened little birds that have strayed from some realm of fantasy, but also in the way in which they develop from vague beginnings, tiny fragmentary motives and thematic germs, which begin gradually to glimmer through the vocal part as it enters in an indeterminate form, and finally blaze up as in radiant sheaves of gold. It is as though we could watch the whole thing growing up under our eyes; and this music may be described as being in a constantly nascent state. What is more, Puccini's art has by now attained full maturity and mastery in expressing with the utmost truth that which is still half tacit, the intimate music of the heart, and emotions that are, as it were, muted and timidly repressed—an effect which he achieves by means of *fioriture* which, though fleeting, have none the less great intensity and melodic pregnancy; and in striking exactly the right note in a conversation under whose surface there quivers an aching pain, at first hinted at quite timidly, and as though with polite unobtrusiveness, but afterwards working up into an unrestrained outburst, or at times, again, into one of those palpitating vocal melodies, throbbing with ardour, that are felt by some people to be his supreme achievement in this opera. But I must admit that, in my opinion, what lingers longest in the memory and penetrates the heart more deeply than the brilliant vocal numbers known and loved by everybody, is precisely what may be called the latent melody that develops from the germ of some pregnant phrase, the way in which unseen emotions grope their way into the music—for instance, the stifled tears and questions full of longing in such scenes as that between the Consul and Butterfly in the second act, or the half-smothered words in which she resigns herself to death in the third, when she insists upon knowing the truth and hearing her doom, and is already preparing to bear the blow.

But since everybody knows the opera so well, I do not propose to enter into details. As Rembrandt said: 'You need not poke your noses right into my pictures. Paint is bad for your health (An meinen Bildern dürft ihr nicht schnüffeln—die Farben sind ungesund)'. Yet in spite of all, I cannot quite restrain myself from drawing attention to some of the more precious among the heavily-perfumed blooms of this garden full of cherry-blossoms, bamboos, and orchids: for instance, to the vigorous energy of the opening *fugato* passage, which reappears by way of thematic allusion in connexion with so many situations, clearly illustrating Puccini's method of bringing out the varying significance of a motive, and also his use of monotony as an artistic device, of iteration as a means of producing suspense, and his skill in breaking it off at the right moment. I would also single out the frivolous, jaunty insouciance of the tenor aria,[1] at the end of which the two male voices join in proclaiming 'America for ever!' till we feel as though we could see the flutter of the Stars and Stripes. Or

[1] TRANSLATOR'S NOTE.—Pinkerton's first aria, 'Dovunque al mondo (The whole world over)'.

again, the way in which, as Butterfly approaches, the love-
motive is heard, vaguely adumbrated through the great sweeping
augmented triads of the harps, which suggest a shower of sparks.
This motive, and the one that forms an accompaniment to the
wedding ceremony—a melody which reminds me of the old
German lullaby, *Wenn wir Kinder schlafen geh'n*, though here
it produces such an exotic effect—first reach their full development in the ecstatically flowing love nocturne with which the
act closes, and swell into a harmony of two hearts that wells up
ardently, full of a childlike purity, and softly pervaded by the
murmur of waters and by voices that echo clearly through the
night.   This melody, which first remains in close relation to
the tonic and next descends a fourth, afterwards mounting
higher and higher diatonically, is one of the finest ever produced in Puccini's hours of most lavish inspiration.   Possibly
the aria in G flat major in the second act—'Un bel dì (One
fine day)'—has been sung so much that we are almost tired of
it, and is therefore too hackneyed to produce its full impression
any longer; but its line has been traced by the exquisite hand
of a master, originating, as it were, in a 'thread of smoke (*fil
di fumo*)', then growing like a flower out of a germ consisting
in the four-note orchestral figure in the second bar, and gaining
a contour which is firmer for all its rhapsodic quality.   How
fascinating, too, is the way in which the melody is now carried
on in the orchestra only, being interrupted in the vocal part by
an eager, excited passage in a conversational tone.   Besides
this, we should note the way in which, like others of his melodies,
it seems, on reappearing, to be transformed by some quite slight
changes of rhythm, just as a little Japanese paper house is
transformed by sliding back a wall.

From this second act onwards the opera really develops into
a great monologue on the part of little Cho-Cho-San, only here
and there supplemented by another vocal part, the most gracious
example of this being in the duet between Butterfly and Suzuki,
with its riot of flowers, which seems to be flooded with sunshine, and to sway with the movement of a spring breeze as the

two women adorn the room with sprays of blossom for the expected lover; from the tenderly dithyrambic passage in common time in G flat major, on through the light, swinging six-eight movement in A flat major, till it arrives at the graceful melody, like a twining garland, of 'Tutta la primavera (Balmy breath of spring)', rising to a perfect fervour of exultation, while the orchestra seems to shower down blossoms upon it, it is like some peerless illumination, the song of a much-tried woman's heart, delivered at last from dejection and grief, and throbbing at the approach of the new love and happiness that are to be the recompense of her long waiting.   And now comes a stroke of genius: the neatly-rounded theme, like some design delicately traced upon rice-paper, which had already been sounded while the Consul was reading out the letter from the faithless Pinkerton, now becomes the predominating motive in a miniature symphony of patient waiting.   It accompanies the scene in which the women and the child spend the whole night looking out through the holes in the thin wall for him who never comes. The sustained notes on the harps and clarinets, the distant chorus of voices humming, and the light, dripping notes of the flutes and pizzicato strings, with their monotonous rising and falling motive consisting in the successive notes of the triad, and rounded off at intervals by a hesitating little ornament formed of a two-quaver figure twice repeated, all go to make up a scene exactly like some little Japanese print.   It is infinitely touching in its childlike simplicity, its patient waiting and hopeless trust, and the Japanese quality finds expression as much in the picturesque stage setting as in the slight touch of exoticism in the music, which is harmonically constructed upon five degrees of the scale.   Rarely has Puccini drawn such fruitful results from his characteristic discovery—that of a musical monotony and insistent iteration of motives that excite the nerves and stir the blood, that lacerate the feelings or else lull them to sleep.   It is almost like that Chinese torture that consists in a drop of water constantly falling upon the brow in the same place; but this musical torment is full of sweetness.   This

passage has such a compelling charm that it is hard for anything
of what follows to come up to it, whether it be the intermezzo,
with its harrowing grief and exaltation and its passionate progressions of chords with a Wagnerian suggestion, as of some
Tristan disguised as a modern naval lieutenant; or the noble
lines of the trio, or the mingled elegance and poignancy of the
tenor's remorseful song. Somehow none of it seems quite
suitable to the occasion. Moreover, the painfulness of the
dramatic events undoubtedly prevents us from fully surrendering ourselves to the music, noble, sincere, and full of inspiration
though it continues to be, and cleverly and ingeniously though
Puccini makes use of reminiscences of former motives. But
one need not be a sentimental weakling to feel indignant at the
reappearance of Pinkerton—who, though he is too cowardly to
meet the woman whom he has abandoned, is brutal enough to
bring his 'legal' wife with him and demand the child through
her agency; or to be revolted when Butterfly commits *hara-kiri*.
This is an example of the excess which dulls the hearer's respon-
siveness and sympathy, relaxes his fevered interest, and reacts
upon the nerves of the stomach rather than the compassionate
heart.

The economy of resources by which Puccini succeeds in producing a foreign impression, and a Japanese atmosphere in
particular, is amazing. He has, indeed, made but little positive
use of those phonographic records of Japanese music for which
he sent to Tokio, and which served him rather as a preliminary
means of acquainting himself with the musical character of that
strange land than as material for supplying him with motives.
He has used very few of these original melodies, and even when
he does use them, has translated them entirely into his own
Puccinian idiom. What is more, he has adopted few modes
of expression, either tonal or harmonic, from the musical idiom
of Japan in general. Successions of whole tones, and augmented or diminished chords had already been a distinctive
mark of his music before this; and there is but little trace to be
found in *Butterfly* of the pentatonic scale, the simultaneous

intervals of heterophony, or the primitive heptatonic scales which are typical features of Japanese music, or of the minor progressions derived from the use of the Doric, Phrygian, Aeolian, and hypo-Phrygian modes. Even the last chord of the work, the unsatisfying close on a chord of the sixth, is a Europeanized version of the Japanese conventions for treating the close of a melody, according to which the last note is not always to be regarded as a tonic, but often as a sixth or a seventh, a fifth or a second, and is determined by the line of the melody. The 'pedal-point music' of the Japanese must have been in accord with Puccini's own most personal predilections. The close of the second act, constructed out of the most simple elements, to which we have referred before, owes its wonderful effect to the use of this device. The Japanese flute, the clear sonority of whose note approximates to that of the African ocarina, is as little used by Puccini as is the thirteen-stringed *koto* (the place of which is taken by the harp), or any other instrument from that land beyond the seas. In spite of this, the European flute and the ordinary resources of orchestration sufficed for him to produce an overwhelming impression of something un-European, of a music from the land of Samurai and geishas, of bonzes and the frequenters of the tea-house. How he did so is his own secret, and we may suspect that even he himself would have been unable to give any other explanation of it than that his whole soul had gone out to this land and so discovered its real essence.

We cannot but admit that his technique in this work has much that has become stereotyped: that in all these operas, in *La Bohème*, *Tosca*, and *Butterfly*, and even as early as *Manon Lescaut*, his predominating mode of work is a sort of musical mosaic, an often abrupt and rhapsodic alternation of constantly recurring motives, in which fragmentary melodies start, only to break off again before they reach their final development, though without any consistent system of symbolic reminiscence of the Wagnerian type. It is a striking fact that in almost all Puccini's operas, immediately after the preliminaries that serve as a prelude, there comes a tenor aria, which does not seem absolutely indispensable to the dramatic action, but serves to captivate the listener at once. It is equally striking to note that the climax is invariably marked by a vocal number for one of the feminine characters, starting without any prelude: we may instance Musette's waltz song, Tosca's prayer, or Butterfly's aria in G flat, all of which produce a great effect by artistic devices that are quite slight. The question is whether Puccini really made use of these consciously. We hardly think so; but there is a certain fascination in peeping into the secrets of this unerring master of dramatic effect.

In *Butterfly*, subject and music have combined to produce a rare power of suggestion. In it, moreover, we have a well-tried subject associated with music that is novel in both form and invention. The proof of the vitality of the few fundamental ideas on which the opera is based is that they are constantly recurring elsewhere. Julius Korngold has pointed this out somewhere in his clever criticism of Puccini's works: 'Butterfly has a grandmother named Selika [1] and a cousin named Lakmé'. A few years afterwards he might also have claimed a grandchild for her in Rezniček's Satuala, the Indian girl who has to try and tempt an English naval lieutenant to play the traitor, but is forced, like him, and, for the rest, like all her predecessors, to die as the result of her love for him. Nor can we very well ignore the fact that the ancestor of them all is Othello, the Moor of Venice.

Among all these figures in the ethnographical museum of opera, some of which are already a little damaged, and stand in need of some kind of preservative, little Madame Butterfly may well prove to have the greatest vitality, for she is simple, moving and true to life, and consequently, not in the least operatic.

This may seem strange praise for an opera, but the future of this category of music would seem to lie in its ceasing to exist as a separate category.

[1] TRANSLATOR'S NOTE.—In Meyerbeer's *L'Africaine*.

CHAPTER XI

UNCLE GIACOMO'S CABIN ('THE GIRL OF THE GOLDEN WEST')

Das Wirkliche ohne sittlichen Bezug nennen wir gemein.—GOETHE.[1]

OUTSIDE the Metropolitan Opera-house, New York, there was a press of carriages, extending as far as the eye could see. The crowd was dense, and had to be pushed back by the police over and over again. For hours on end motor after motor drew up beneath the canopy that protects the main entrance. The chauffeurs lost patience, and those behind shouted and swore, for every time a carriage drove up some minutes elapsed before the next could approach. The reason why the process took so long was that not one of those alighting from a carriage was admitted till he had proved by signing his name that he was genuinely the holder and purchaser of the tickets that had to be produced. The handwriting was then compared with the signature that he had given on buying the tickets at the box-office, and then, and not till then, could the next person come up. The object of these precautions was to prevent speculation in the tickets; yet in spite of all, it reached positively fantastic proportions on this occasion, and even now speculators were hanging about those who were arriving on foot, sizing them up at a glance, and then, in a prudent whisper, offering them seats at ten, twenty, or thirty times the box-office price, though for the most part without success. Inside the opera-house only half the lights were turned on at first; yet even so the effect was more brilliant than usual, for the men's white shirt-fronts and waistcoats and the necks and shoulders of the countless lovely dollar princesses diffused a shimmer of light, not to speak of the pearls and diamonds displayed for the occasion, the

[1] Concrete reality apart from all ethical bearings we regard as vulgar.

192

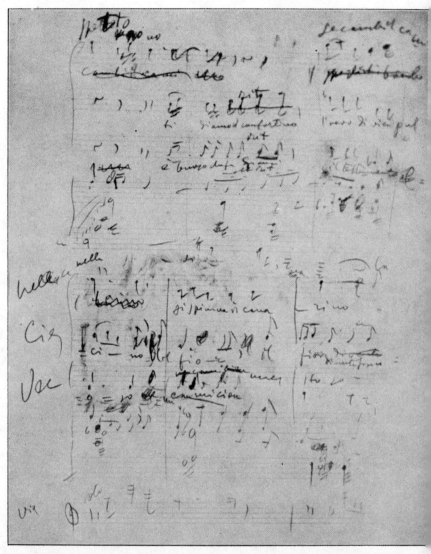

PART OF A PAGE FROM THE ROUGH DRAFT OF *Gianni Schicchi* (reduced facsimile)

splendour of which was like the fantastic dreams of the Thousand
and One Nights come true. If the precious stones that were
filling the great theatre with flashes of white, red, sea-blue, and
mystic green could have been sold, the proceeds would have
been sufficient to heal the sufferings of central Europe at the
present day—if, indeed, it is possible to heal these by material
means. The upper two thousand out of the upper ten thousand
of New York were all present, and proud to be there, for they
had almost had to engage in personal combat in order to succeed
in attending this long-expected performance, which promised
to be the greatest event of the year. It was as though the
whole credit of Broadway depended upon their being there, and
those who had succeeded in getting there might well give themselves airs, for the very fact of their presence meant an increase
in their prestige, and presupposed a bank account running to
at least ten figures in dollars.

Yet this sensational event, which had mobilized the whole of
New York, as well as half the artistic world, was neither a
presidential election, nor a trust war, nor the departure of an
airship: it was merely the first performance of an opera. But
it was one that had been anticipated with greater suspense than
any other since the Grail had been filched from Bayreuth and
Parsifal produced in America in contravention of all morality
and justice. The opera was Puccini's *La Fanciulla del West*
(The Girl of the Golden West), which was being performed for
the first time at the Metropolitan Opera-house, with Toscanini
as conductor and Caruso and Destinn in the principal roles,
and, what is more, in the presence of the Master himself.

He had, indeed, visited the American continent before then.
Ten years previously, *Manon* and *Edgar* had been performed
at Buenos Aires, and in the year 1906 he had visited New York
too, in order to be present at the final rehearsals of *Manon*.
But by the time he arrived, these were already over, and he was
rushed straight from the ship to the opera-house, so that he
might at least be in time for the first performance. He managed
to arrive just in time for Caruso and Scotti, the baritone, to

o

receive him and lead him before the curtain, where he acknowledged the frantic applause of the public at the end of the first
act. He had therefore had a foretaste of American ways, of
interviews, press photographers, and advertisers eager to use
him for the purpose of puffing their wares, or to attach his
name to their soaps, hats, or liver-pills. But in spite of this,
everything on this occasion was new to him, for any claims that
had been made on him before, and any functions arranged in
his honour, had been child's play in comparison with what now
awaited the Master who had in the meantime become world-
famous. His voyage in the royal suite of a luxury liner, the
band of which had reduced him to an amiable frenzy by their
well-meaning but incessant performance of fragments from his
operas, and the homage of the passengers, each of whom had
tried to snatch a word or an autograph from him, had already
brought his international renown fully home to him for the
first time; but all this had passed by like a dream, though not
always like a dream of delight. America had produced an
imposing impression upon him. He had liked the fresh vigour
of the people and the grandiose proportions of the cities and
their life, and had been most eager to return there, but he would
have liked to do so incognito. Yet here he was, being treated
like a sovereign. When he looked out of the window of his
room on the tenth story, he was seized with giddiness; and it
grew worse when he caught sight of the enormous piles of
invitations that arrived daily, all of which, however, he declined,
with the sole exception of a dinner at the Vanderbilt mansion.
His son Tonio, who, in spite of the comically despairing pressure
put upon him by Puccini, refused to forge his father's signature,
willingly acted as his secretary, and had quite enough to do in
answering all inquiries, in addition to comforting his father,
who was suffering from homesickness and the nerve-racking
turmoil of New York; for an artist of Puccini's type could
hardly be expected to keep up with the pace of American life.
There was one millionaire and Puccini enthusiast who offered
five hundred dollars for a line from the Master's hand, calling

daily, only to receive a daily refusal, and finally attained his
object for the sole reason that Puccini fell in love with a motor-
boat and became the owner of it for the precise sum offered by
this man in return for the opening bars of Musetta's waltz,
written out by Puccini's own hand. He was only typical of
a hundred such persons who made life a burden to the Maestro
in that land of unlimited possibilities, for the very reason that
it offered him too many limitations and impossibilities.

But for all this, the very pace and rush of American life, and
its excess in all things, provided the right atmosphere for the
production and success of *The Girl of the Golden West*, and no
better start could have been desired for it. Its very success
was marked by a typically American exaggeration, and was
renewed a few days later at Chicago, immediately afterwards in
Boston, and a little while later in the composer's own native
land, at the Teatro Costanzi, Rome, where *La Fanciulla* was
produced at the opening of the Exhibition of 1911, with the
much-admired scenery from Boston, consisting of trees modelled
in plaster and foliage cut out of leather, and likewise under the
masterly conductorship of Toscanini. A secondary symptom
of this extravagance was the sum paid the author in royalties on
the first New York performance, which exceeded the figure of
120,000 lire. From that time onward Puccini never had
another failure. In future every one of his new compositions,
even the anaemic *La Rondine*, with its rather feeble inspiration,
was immediately received with unstinted and unanimous
applause. The first performance of *Butterfly* was his last unpleasant experience. But it is curious that it was precisely
those operas of Puccini's that were at first received with hesitation, or even with hostility, that have gained a triumph on every
operatic stage in the world, and maintained their position till
the present day; whereas those that were received with wild
acclamations, such as *Le Villi*, *La Fanciulla*, *La Rondine*, and
the *Trittico*, have either ceased to be performed at all, or are
put on in a few places only, and even there very seldom. Once
again it has been demonstrated that the fate of a piece is decided

not by the success of the first performance, but only by the intrinsic vitality of the piece itself.   If this does not seem to hold good for *Gianni Schicchi*, the third of the 'Triptych' of one-act operas, and, what is more, a gem of operatic gaiety, this is due to the fact that, in spite of their fine qualities, the other two pieces, *Il Tabarro* and *Suor Angelica*, have hitherto failed to win sufficient favour with the public to be kept afloat by the sparkling gaiety of *Schicchi*, for people feel others of their favourite Puccini's works to be more spontaneous; while, on the other hand, this comic opera, as an isolated piece, has suffered the fate of all one-act operas, which are difficult to fit into the programme, and especially into that of an opera-house, in which few of these short pieces have shown any lasting vitality.   In Vienna, where Puccini's masterly little comedy is often chosen to follow Peter Cornelius's enchanting *Barbier von Bagdad*, which is itself maintained in the repertory only with the utmost difficulty, the performance is always a treat, though it is significant that it never draws a full house.   But a whole chapter could be devoted to the question why, in spite of the undeniable need of humanity for laughter and high spirits, the life of *opéra comique* as a class, not to speak of such delightfully refreshing isolated examples of it as *Falstaff*, *Der Widerspenstigen Zähmung* (The Taming of the Shrew), *Feuersnot*, *Der Barbier von Bagdad*, or such charming one-act operas as Leo Blech's *Versiegelt* and Erich Korngold's *Der Ring des Polykrates* can be prolonged only by great circumspection, and why their wit and gaiety so often have to succumb to the public's tragic lack of discrimination; or again, why *opéra bouffe*, or the atmosphere of light and witty comedy, even when inspired by genius, seem to have less power of attraction than mediocrity, even when this is 'serious'.   But no answer has yet been found to this question, which applies to *Gianni Schicchi* as well.

For the present, at any rate, *The Girl of the Golden West* has been equally unsuccessful in achieving a triumphant career. This may be partly due to the fact that the principal female role demands not only a singer of considerable ability, but also an actress of the highest order, with more varied qualities than are required for the impersonation of Tosca or Butterfly. She should possess not only charm, tenderness, and ardour, but both innocence and energy, elemental passion and a fresh, unspoilt naturalness. Wherever such an actress exists, as for instance in Vienna and New York, where Madame Jeritza both acts and sings magnificently in the part of Minnie, and above all, wherever the heroine finds adequate supporters in the roles of the noble bandit Ramerrez and the dissolute sheriff Rance, an effect will be attained that will not be impaired even by the romantic setting of bandits and gold-miners, the unwholesome fascination of the threatened Indian tortures, and the circus effects demanded by the book, which is, however, by no means devoid of merit apart from these points. But the public estimate of the opera has been modified since its initial success. People now feel a little ashamed of their vulgar instincts, which were so easily subjugated by the theatrical crudities and false pathos of the stage action, and are possibly more unjust to the work than they should be. They inveigh against the libretto for its false sentiment and sheer melodrama. They consider that the music shows unmistakable signs of a certain flagging; that, thanks to the enhanced refinement of the workmanship, nothing is left but a weak dilution of the earlier type of Puccini's once so popular melody; and that the whole is rather a *réchauffé*, consisting of music that has been, as it were, artificially galvanized into life, and is, moreover, worthy of the cinema. But here I will call a halt. I search my conscience, and know that I am free from all prejudice in favour of Puccini, and for that very reason I hold that we ought not to keep on asking ourselves what seems to be wanting in this opera by comparison with former ones, but should rather consider whether on this occasion he did not intend to do something different from what he had done before, and to what extent he has succeeded in realizing his intentions. And the answer must certainly be that he did, in fact, mean to do something different, and that in places, though not everywhere, he has succeeded.

One thing must unquestionably be conceded to Puccini:
that he had clearer ideas than most people about himself and
the quality of his talent, and was well aware of its limitations.
But he would not have been an artist had he not longed at times
to broaden its scope, or at least to cultivate some department of
it that was as yet unexploited.   It is quite easy to understand
that there were hours in which the 'little things' that he loved
seemed too small and circumscribed, so that he felt a strong
desire to venture outside this over-cultivated pleasure-garden,
and for once in a while to exchange the perfume of luxury for
the smell of fresh earth and the sweat of toiling men, to abandon
the haunts of civilization for the wilds, and the men of unbridled instincts, lusting for gold and adventure, who people
them, and grapple direct with life.   It is significant to note
how often the expression-mark *ruvido* (harsh) occurs in the score
of *The Girl of the Golden West*; he meant the music to be rough
and even brutal in tone, instead of *amoroso, teneramente,* or *con
dolcezza,* as before.   It is significant, too, that while he was
still working at his American opera, his mind was running upon
one on the subject of Marie Antoinette, the idea of which he
had never quite dropped, and for which Illica, who shortly
afterwards followed his friend Giacosa to the grave, had even
sketched the plan of a first act; but in the long run the conditions of his life left him no liberty to carry out his project.   It
throws a flood of light on his character that he should have
been pleased with Belasco's play about gold-miners, which had
the advantage, shared by all Puccini's libretti, of being comprehensible even to a deaf man.   Nature in all her grandeur yields
up her music here, and he could not have failed to see great
possibilities in this motley crowd of men, all living outside the
restraints of morality, free, horny-handed, and only too prompt
to take up the knife or the revolver.   But though every vice is
to be found among them, it is accompanied by much good-
nature, tender-heartedness, and even gentleness, though the
deeds of blood that they have committed do not weigh over-
heavily upon their consciences, and they are always ready to

appeal to lynch law in self-protection. Equally promising is
the principal female character, Minnie, the brave, high-spirited
girl, who teaches Scripture to the whole gang, and is on friendly
terms with every single one of these wild young men, whom
she knows how to control and keep at a due distance. Every
one of them loves her, and therefore protects her from the
lusts of the others, and we feel it to be perfectly suitable, and
even to have a sort of wild, primitive psychological logic, that
her heart should be drawn towards the bandit Ramerrez,
with whom she has come in contact in the character of the
harmless Johnson; that she should receive him in her hut, only
to drive him away again indignantly on obtaining proof of his
identity with the great bandit, who has been betrayed by his
mistress and is being pursued by the sheriff; that her love should
blaze up uncontrollably when the hunted man has been wounded
by the bullet of one of the gold-miners before her threshold,
where he threatens to bleed to death; and that she should try
to hide him, and finally, by putting forth all her spirited elo-
quence, save him from the gallows and go off with him. But
if anybody had told Puccini that it is not to be endured that the
sheriff should openly attempt to do violence to Minnie on the
stage, that the presence of Ramerrez should be betrayed by
the drip of his blood, that Minnie's honour and the bandit's
head should be the stakes in a game which the brave girl can
win only by flagrant cheating, and that the last act should
degenerate into a revolting man-hunt, in which the stake is set
up and the noose is already round the neck of the unfortunate
wretch, who has fallen into the hands of a lynching party—the
Master would probably have opened his eyes wide in astonishment and said that, however this may be, these are none the less
the scenes that produce the surest effect, and for the sake of
which the public puts up with the episodic character of the
rest; and he would have added with some pride that the whole
of this third act, in which some eight or twelve horses and a
howling, blood-thirsty mob of desperadoes literally tread the
boards, was his very own invention, thanks to the drastic

alterations that he insisted upon making in Belasco's last act. And we should have been silenced and disarmed by the naïve insouciance of this theatrically-minded composer, and felt quite diffident as we expressed the decided opinion that blood on the stage is anything but a noble fluid, but, on the contrary, a wretched one that immediately destroys all illusion, for, after all, it is nothing but red paint; while a death that takes place on the stage is open to precisely the same objection. Our imagination is prepared for anything. What happens behind the scenes kindles our most impassioned sympathies; and that is why the torture-scene in *Tosca* causes us the most shuddering horror. But all this disappears the moment the actor is carried in, all daubed with red paint. Nobody can possibly imagine any longer that the tenor drawing an enormous salary has really suffered serious pain, and even the rope which, in the third act of *La Fanciulla*, is intended to bring about his shameful death, fails to produce a particularly terrifying effect. This is equally true even of the blinding scene in *King Lear*, and of all such horrors that take place before our eyes. The impression produced is rather that of a crude stage effect, like those familiar to us in films or pantomimes, or at best in an English melodrama. But the Maestro would certainly not have been convinced by these arguments.

It is hardly necessary to point out that none but these scenes that contain a violent explosion of feeling admit of vocal and orchestral numbers of a broadly comprehensive and fairly well-defined order, while the brightly diversified and episodic character of the rest, though the details are often picturesque and full of life, too, offers a good opportunity for Puccini's method of piecing together motives and, as it were, fitting them into a mosaic of tiny pieces, and for his use of little melodies that only gradually develop their complete form. But on the other hand, we should point out that these more homogeneous *cantilena* passages bear the stamp of Puccini's melodic individuality less distinctly than usual. The most distinctively Puccinian of them is the melting aria, full of sorrowful

earnestness and manly composure, sung by the tenor beneath
the gallows, once more in Puccini's favourite key of G flat; but
Cavaradossi's farewell grips the emotions with greater power.
It is as though the gloom of the wild Californian mountain landscape did not offer a fruitful soil in which music could flourish,
and men certainly cannot sing with such finish or such supple
voices in the primeval forest as in civilized regions; the rough,
jagged, untamed quality of the natural surroundings imparts
itself to the melodies too. Yet though Puccini failed to discover a whole mine of song, he at least found a nice pocket of
small nuggets, and he has not polished them to such an extent
that none of their native soil can still manage to adhere to them.
The whole piece is full of characteristic local colour. At times
it is as though the composer were trying to say: 'Do not settle
down calmly in a land where people sing like this'. But the
songs sung by these people, who, though turbulent, are not
wicked, resemble them in character, being confused, lacking
in sonority, and at times uncouth or astonishingly sentimental.
Puccini used only one of the many Indian melodies for which
he sent on this occasion, too, in order to enable him to enter
into the atmosphere of what was, to him, quite a new world:
the minstrel's song of longing for his home, so quietly plaintive
and moving in the very hopelessness of its monotony. The
rest merely served to determine the colour of the music, with
its chromatic intervals, and the mourning that can often be felt
even in the harsh or sentimental motives on which are based the
songs of these men, who, though outwardly rough and strong,
are melancholy at heart; and we have already seen in what a
masterly way Puccini manages to express the noisy joviality that
does not come from the heart. These are little motives, jotted
down fragmentarily, music that is still in process of emerging
into form—in fact, true backwoodsmen's melodies. The vocal
parts that accompany the sheriff's game have the sombre colour
of Scarpia's music; yet in spite of the dexterous suggestion of
cruelty, the tender-hearted master does not really quite succeed
in producing an impression of something evil, for, if associated

with other words, these *arioso* phrases might equally well express the annoyance of a respectable citizen or the advances of an energetic pastor.   The pastoral and Old Testament atmosphere of the Bible-reading scene is very charming in its idyllic serious-ness; very charming, too, is the little waltz, which comes into being, as it were, before our eyes to the rhythm of hand-clapping, with its childlike tune hummed by the crowd, as though impro-vised on the spot, until it acquires a symbolic significance, and develops in the two love-scenes into a soaring melody.   An unusually strong atmosphere hovers over the close of this first act, which, from the musical point of view, is undoubtedly the most varied in colour and rich in inspiration of the three.   The motive associated with Minnie is softly accompanied by fifteen tenor voices 'with closed lips', which lends it a peculiarly deli-cate instrumental colour.   Since his use of this device in *Butterfly* Puccini had had a predilection for such passages hummed in chorus, and using the timbre of the human voice in a purely instrumental fashion.   In *Turandot* this indeterminate sound, playing round the purely orchestral tone of the instruments, again produces a magical and shimmering effect.   But in Act I of *La Fanciulla*, the peculiar harmonization of the final chord of C major, with the unresolved double suspension on the seventh and second, might claim Debussy as its godfather.

In the second act the suggestion of the snowy atmosphere of the Sierra Nevada is more penetrating than that of the *Barrière d'enfer* in *La Bohème*.   But the music, too, is more tempestuous in character, especially in the love-scene, when the door flies open and the howl of the winter storms intrudes upon the springtide of the heart.   The Indian lullaby is lent interest and genuineness of colour by its harmonization with secondary chords; the monotonous melody on three notes, with its hurdy-gurdy effect, is merely its primitive rudiment—a mere scalp of a melody.   This act does not yield any very rich results: the headlong speed of the action, reminding us of a film, offers little opportunity for lingering over lyrical passages.   It may be noted that, in these expansive scenes of emotional outpouring, the climax is not marked, as in the earlier operas, by a vocal number full of intense emotion sung by the anguished and over-wrought heroine.   Minnie's spiritual agony knows no law pre-scribing, as a matter of course, an emotional *arioso*; she has no 'prayer' to sing for the purpose of softening the heart of this Scarpia of the Wild West—though it is true that she could hardly say 'Vissi d'arte', but rather 'Vissi delle carte'.   In the poker scene the composer displays his supreme power of creating a fitting musical background for grim events: the motives of love and jealousy fade away, the music ceases, and the hasty, disjointed words of the gamblers are accompanied only by the shadowy murmur, nerve-racking in its monotony, formed by the sinister passage in semiquavers on the lower strings, till Minnie bursts into hysterical laughter as she wins the game. Then at last the orchestra bursts forth, expressing the raging storm within her soul.   The whole passage is simply masterly, and the old circus trick by which the music suddenly stops at the moment when the acrobat is making his most dangerous dive, thus raising the tension to an almost unbearable pitch of suspense, appears here as a powerfully theatrical device that makes us gasp for breath.   It would be simply crushing if it were really dramatic—that is, if the characters really enlisted our sympathies.   The same cause is responsible for the lack of real interest and the merely superficial excitement with which we watch the exciting events of the third act.   The bandit has to be executed: very good.   He is going to be used as a target: again, very good.   The girl who loves him is to hear nothing about his shameful end: that is quite as it should be.   Yet he is saved after all—and, so far as I am concerned, nothing could be less interesting.   There is altogether too much ado about nothing.   We sit unmoved, shrug our shoulders, and go home, and we should have been left absolutely indifferent had it not been that, at certain moments, the music speaks to the soul.   Nor, moreover, is the music that accompanies the hideous man-hunt mere noise, as has often been alleged; it is well constructed, and leads up characteristically to a sort of wild, tango-like movement well suited to the *tango feroce* which Ramerrez is threatened with having to dance.   Yet it falls flat; and even Ramerrez' song of farewell, though in itself broad and rising in a fine vocal line, comes too late, and so does the imploring melody of the last prayer.   The closing ensemble, however, which, trusting to the power of reminiscence, is throughout based on the motive associated with Minnie, produces a comforting impression after the girl's fervent and agitated appeal to the love of the man who has been saved, and lends the right appeasing note to the whole.   This is music that points the way out into the open country, a farewell song full of warm humanity.   But curiously enough, the happy ending of the opera does not give satisfaction even in America.   Possibly people feel that music charged with really heartfelt emotion leads us towards that which is not of this world, and is the prerogative of the lonely.

This work almost gives us the impression that Puccini was purposely checking the ample flow of his melodies, as though he desired to express the character of a human type that has returned to primitive conditions, escaped from the great world and gone back to Nature, and wished to choose some other vehicle for doing so than the cultivated and nervously over-subtilized type of vocal line that he had used in the earlier operas.   In this opera he has certainly displayed to a supreme degree his art of musical interjection, of highly intimate expression that is absolutely true to life, yet compressed into a few bars, and of associating the most everyday language with suitable, melodically simple phrases charged to the utmost with emotion.   Every one of these miniature dialogues has the very colour of spoken language; though his sensitive, feeling nature has often saved him from extremes of harshness, and from the concentrated power and abruptness necessary for depicting these rough men living outside all established order. Even in this Fenimore Cooper atmosphere he managed not to develop a sensationalism like that of the novelist Carl May, but remained himself, Giacomo Puccini.   I have frequently expressed the opinion that his characteristic and individual method of forming the typical melodic fragments, which, by means that are anything but ordinary, raise ordinary things to the plane of musical expression, gives a clue to his essential nature, which finds its most concentrated expression in this device.   If this be so, then the general verdict on *The Girl of the Golden West* will have to be revised a little.   It is certainly not Puccini's strongest work, but equally certainly it is not his weakest one. And perhaps it is his most personal one.

CHAPTER XII

As we have mentioned above, the Master's residence at his beloved Torre del Lago had now been spoilt for him. The local authorities had failed to prevent the building of a factory next his house—perhaps, indeed, it had been beyond their power to stop it—and the noise of machinery and the pestilential smells that came from it exasperated him beyond endurance and made his life a burden. He had to reconcile himself to the idea of leaving this spot, which had been a perfect paradise to him and which he loved above all others. But he did not feel that he was leaving it for ever, for he knew that from time to time he would still be drawn back to his beloved lake. But it was with a heavy heart that he gave up his permanent residence in this place, which had been the scene of his best work and of his happy home life. He now built himself a villa at Viareggio. I have already spoken of the red-brown house beneath the sombre green pine-trees, bent by the sea-wind, and have called it a sort of bungalow. It is an irregularly planned, straggling building, with a wooden veranda running round the outside of it, following the line of the façade as it projects in some parts and recedes in others; the light, gently sloping roof of one wing rises above the roofs of the rest of the building, and is supported upon gaily coloured pillars, producing an almost Malay effect. The whole house gives the impression of having been wafted to the spot from India or Farther India by some kindly spirit of the air. On one of the outer walls Puccini had a portrait relief of himself put up, which is remarkably like him; the other has been adorned by the citizens of Viareggio with a marble memorial tablet bearing a grateful and sorrowing inscription in memory of the departed Master. Here, in his study on the ground-floor, which was directly connected with his bedroom by an inside flight of stairs, Puccini often worked and dreamed at the splendid Steinway grand piano presented him by the firm, wearing his hat on his head in his usual fashion, and with a pencil in his mouth, looking out into the wind-swept garden over the top of his eye-glasses when he had to think over an idea longer than usual. Yet it seems as though he never felt himself anything but a sojourner there. He was not at home anywhere but by his Lake of Massaciuccoli, and when he was forced to leave it he felt that now indeed, for the first time, his youth was at an end.

Perhaps this feeling was increased by the fact that he had lost certain of his friends, who had seemed so closely bound up with his period of formation that he felt them to be part of it. The first to die was Giacosa, the kindly, easy-going poet, who had felt no trouble too much, so long as it was taken for Puccini. In 1919 Giacosa was followed by the choleric, turbulent, and imaginative Illica, with whom the composer had, however, long been out of touch. But much earlier than this, shortly after the first performance of *The Girl of the Golden West* in New York, the dearest of them all had been torn from him—Giulio Ricordi, his untiring collaborator, best adviser, patron and friend, who had been a second father to him. The bonds that connected him with Tito Ricordi, Giulio's son and heir, who now became the head of the publishing firm, were far from being as intimate as those which had existed between him and the patrician old man, from whose death it took him a long time to recover. In spite of various differences of opinion, their relations remained excellent on the surface, but lacked real warmth, in spite of all assurances of mutual regard.

But he had to look to the future. 'Without work my life has no meaning,' he would sigh over and over again. 'What a useless thing art is; yet people like us cannot exist without it.' He felt full of creative power; but he had long since passed the age of fifty, and wanted to say all that he had left to say. 'Yes,

we are popular—but old', he wrote from Paris, while near at
hand the hotel orchestra was playing tunes from *La Bohème*.
Even while still engaged in orchestrating his opera of the Wild
West, he had already resumed the search for suitable subjects
for a libretto. Once again he applied to Maeterlinck. He
would have liked to compose music for *Pelleas and Melisande*,
but that play of sombre fantasy had already been assigned to
Debussy. D'Annunzio sent him a proposal for an opera on
the Children's Crusade, and he was enthusiastic over the idea,
but his enthusiasm did not last long enough to be put into
action. He had thoughts of Victor Hugo's *Notre-Dame de
Paris*. The subject would certainly have offered him great
scope, and it is a pity that he gave up the idea, if only for the
reason that we should then most likely have been spared the
luxuriantly melodious, but flimsy opera on it composed by the
Viennese, Franz Schmidt. For a long time his mind ran upon
a play entitled *Genio alegre* (The Cheerful Mind), with which
the authors, the brothers Alvarez Quintero, had created quite a
sensation. The libretto had already been planned and versified,
when he suddenly dropped it again; for unless he could keep
up a keen interest in a subject, he would drop it without mercy,
and he was quite right to do so. 'In general,' he said on one
occasion, 'I am quite calm. But if I am to be any calmer,
I ought not to have become an artist. That, too, is a serious
malady.' But it was a malady of which he never showed any
desire to be cured.

After the death of his two trusty collaborators, he next had to
look for new librettists. The title-page of *The Girl of the
Golden West* had already ceased to bear the familiar names of
Luigi Illica and Giuseppe Giacosa. Puccini was not ill-satisfied
with the book written for it by Guelfo Civinini and Carlo Zanga-
rini, but it appears that he did not want them as regular
collaborators. At any rate, he went on looking for the right
man, and found him in Giuseppe Adami, whose first piece of
work for him was to draw up the scenario and versify the
libretto for *Anima allegra* (based on *Genio alegre*), and whom we

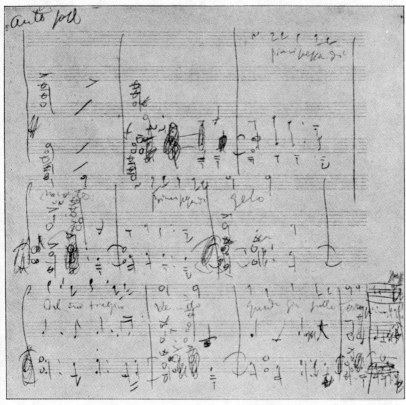

PART OF A PAGE FROM THE ROUGH DRAFT OF *Turandot* (reduced facsimile)

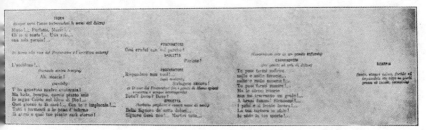

A PASSAGE FROM THE FIRST VERSION OF THE LIBRETTO OF *Tosca* (reduced facsimile)

THEME FROM *I Crisantemi*

have to thank not only for the admirable libretti of *Il Tabarro* and *Turandot*, and the less happy one of *La Rondine*, but also for the *Epistolario*, the collection of Puccini's letters published by him. He now became an intimate friend of the Master, who called him his 'caro Adamino'.

With the assistance of Adami he hoped at last to carry into effect a long-cherished plan of his: that of a cycle of one-act operas, forming a whole evening's entertainment, in which a tragic, a lyric and a burlesque piece should be combined to form a varied whole. But subjects were still not easy to find. The Dante theme, consisting of an *Inferno*, a *Purgatorio*, and a *Paradiso*, was once more considered, only to be rejected. It is curious that, after all, a fragment of it should have survived in *Gianni Schicchi*. But now he at any rate chanced upon an idea for a one-act opera. An old French lady had talked to the Master about a piece which had met with some success in Paris, entitled *La Houppelande*, by Didier Gold. Possibly Puccini was more attracted by the atmosphere of Paris by night and the unspoilt emotions of the proletarian characters in it than by the subject itself; and he requested Adami to proceed with the composition of a libretto without entering into any contract for the present. The whole libretto was completed within a week, and the composer at once set to work, though there was still a risk that the two remaining one-act pieces required to fill the bill might not be found; but he had to put an end to his recent period of inaction, if he was not to fall into a state of incurable melancholy. Maxim Gorki, Matilda Serao, and his old collaborator David Belasco had been as little able to help him as any of the other poets from whom he had tried to obtain a libretto. He therefore concentrated his fresh creative faculty, which for too long past had remained in a state of dull stagnation, upon *Il Tabarro*, and trusted to God for the rest. He had soon completed this little operatic tragedy, and would probably have subsided into despair again, owing to the temporary lack of the two pieces required to supplement it, had he not been temporarily distracted from his idea of a triptych by the unfortunate

P

incident, not to say catastrophe, that took place in connexion with *La Rondine* (The Swallow).

The preliminaries to this unsatisfactory affair had taken place in Vienna. Puccini was on a visit to the Austrian capital for the production of *The Girl of the Golden West*, and was delighted with the rehearsals, in which Madame Jeritza was taking part, and with the unusually fine mounting and scenery, the credit for which was due to Hans Gregor, the then director of the Court Opera-house (*Hofoper*). In addition to this, he took advantage of his evenings to see what was going on at the other theatres. Among others he attended a performance of an operetta at the Carltheater, the two directors of which, Eibenschütz and Berté, tried to tempt the Master to write an operetta for their theatre by the promise of an unusually high extra fee in addition to the usual royalties. At first Puccini laughingly but quite firmly declined, and prolonged conversations failed to induce him to enter into any contract. But on returning home, he began to think the matter over. He had no objection, in principle, to attempting something quite light and graceful, and, what is more, the sum of 200,000 Kronen to be paid on account was by no means to be despised. A little misunderstanding between him and Tito Ricordi may also have had some influence upon his decision, and he informed the directors of the Viennese theatre that he was prepared to enter into negotiations. By the following day they had arrived in Milan, and the contract was signed. The Master was to write an operetta for the Carltheater, the libretto for which, or at any rate the plan of it, would be sent him from Vienna. Had Puccini only known that type of man better, he would have realized that the libretto would not be entrusted to any writer of the eminence of Arthur Schnitzler, for instance, in whose plays we are often conscious of an atmosphere somewhat akin to that of Puccini's music, but to the smartest and most dexterous commercial librettists in the world of Viennese operetta; and he would promptly have declined with thanks. These gentlemen of the Carltheater considered that they were doing all that could be expected of them if they allowed the Maestro to be served by the best local firm, that is, by von Willner and Reichert, who were much sought after as purveyors of subjects for popular cabaret entertainments. They were always prepared to deliver their goods promptly, and now produced a piece of the first quality from the supplies they already had in stock. It was about a girl with an assortment of lovers, among them rather a shop-soiled and threadbare specimen of a provincial Don Juan trying to be Parisian, together with the inevitable mother who writes letters; nor did they spare him a final renunciation-scene of the most sickly and oleaginous banality. The whole thing was a sophisticated blend of the nobility of *La Traviata* with the light-heartedness of *La Bohème*, together with a large admixture of hackneyed sentimentality; and they felt sure that Puccini would be delighted with it. But Puccini was not delighted; he was aghast. He began to see what he had embarked upon, to feel that no money in the world would induce him to associate such rubbish with his music, and to determine that he neither could nor would write an operetta at all—in fact, he wondered how he had ever been able to entertain such an idea. The Viennese theatrical directors were naturally reluctant to release the composer from the obligations to which he had pledged himself, but they were ready to come to some other form of agreement; and the matter was ultimately settled in this way. Giuseppe Adami was requested to expurgate and rewrite the text; but it was understood that the work was to be a grand opera, and not an operetta. The fabricators of the original book were now to act merely as the translators of the new version, and the original production was reserved, as before, to the Carltheater, Vienna. Yet even Adami's version failed to satisfy Puccini, and yet another one had to be written. He then set to work, but still with a lingering dissatisfaction. He would have liked to be rid of the work, and wished, moreover, to acquire the performing rights over *La Rondine* for the whole world, for he had originally reserved them for Italy and South America only. What he would have preferred most of all would have been to cancel the contract and regain his freedom. The Viennese directors naturally refused to agree to this, and for the first time in his life Puccini had to pledge himself, reluctantly and with many sighs, to deliver his work at a stated time. But now the war broke out, rendering all contracts null and void. The Master was anxious, however, not to do anything irregular. Sonzogno, who had wished to acquire the work, volunteered to come to terms with Vienna, to smooth all difficulties from his path and to arrive at a settlement of all the obligations into which he had entered, so that in future the composer would have to deal direct with him alone, and need not trouble about anybody else. Puccini accepted the proposal with a sigh of relief. He completed the opera, for which he suddenly began to feel a particular affection, and had it produced for the first time at Monte Carlo. But now attacks began to rain down upon him; the Italian newspapers accused him of lack of patriotism for having composed music to an Austrian, that is, an alien libretto, and Léon Daudet next started a campaign against the Master in *L'Action française*, reproaching him with not having abandoned a work which brought him into relation with countries at war with the Entente. For the only time in his life, Puccini resolved to make a public statement. He quite justifiably insisted upon his patriotism and love of Italy, whose cause he had always actively served, both professionally and as a private person; and he wound up with the emphatic words: 'Monsieur Daudet's accusation accordingly resolves itself into this: that I have withdrawn from our enemies something that was their property and entrusted my work to an Italian publisher. If that is my crime, I have a right to be proud of it'. This last statement is, however, open to some question. In the eyes of reasonable men, his action might, after all, be regarded as a breach of contract, and it may well be asked whether he would have availed himself of the pretext of the war in this way, instead of simply waiting till the madness that had descended upon the world was over, had he been sent a libretto that was worthy of him, instead of the inferior production of Herren Willner and Reichert. Yet, apart from all this, he might have had just cause to be proud if the opera had only been a little better. I have always had a feeling that the reason why he embarked upon the whole business, and above all, upon the agreement with Sonzogno, was merely in order that he might annoy Tito Ricordi and show his independence of him; and no real work of art has ever arisen out of such motives. *La Rondine* is feeble from beginning to end. Hardly ever has Puccini been less happily inspired. Not that the music is unworthy of his name: his light touch, his careful workmanship, and the trace of his individuality, can still be recognized in it. But the impression it produces is that of an imitation of himself; there is not a single bar in it that does not echo something he has said before, not a phrase that can possibly be regarded as an enrichment of his personal idiom. Everything is colourless and, as it were, washed-out. There is no need to attach much importance to this unfortunate mistake. Puccini was particularly attached to this opera, for which he felt the affection, mingled with a sense of secret guilt, that parents feel for backward children. But in spite of all his efforts, he never contrived to obtain any but sporadic successes with it. This 'Swallow' could never be encouraged to make a very long flight.

By way of compensation for this, the Master had in the meantime succeeded in finding subjects for two more one-act pieces. These were original compositions written by Giovacchino Forzano, and had the double distinction of being terse and effective dramatic anecdotes and at the same time presenting a brilliant contrast to each other. Each of the pieces was so entirely different from the other in setting, content, and historical colour, that, when combined with *Il Tabarro*, they form the most promising cycle, well suited to fill the bill at an opera-house. Puccini grouped them together under the title of *Il Trittico* (The Triptych), and this Triptych turned out to be one of his masterpieces. Possibly it does not possess the same youthful freshness of invention as the earlier ones, or teem with spontaneous musical creativeness as richly as usual; but, on the other hand, it has a noble elevation and an art that compel our sincere admiration. Every touch of colour is in the right place, and there are no thin passages, while a supreme sense of style preserves the unity of the whole, yet at the same time lends each of the three pieces its own individual musical idiom. It is true that all three of these miniature dramas have a setting that easily lends itself to music, whether it suggest the sombre night sky, a background of pure gold, or the bright sunshine of old Florence. Again, we have in one of these pieces the sultry, oppressive atmosphere of guilty love and an elderly man's jealousy, in another the gentle, pious faith of the penitent nun, and in the third the atmosphere of sly hypocrisy, cunning, and jovial mockery characterizing a rogue in the age of Dante. Or again, we have in one the joyless, oppressive atmosphere of the proletarian quarters of Paris on the banks of the Seine, in the second the sweet piety and suavity of the convent, and in the third the typically Tuscan atmosphere of hearty laughter, which belongs to no age, for the period costumes are mere externals. All these provide opportunities at which any composer would have grasped with rapture, and Puccini has succeeded in turning them to advantage with positive *bravura*.

Il Tabarro (The Cloak) is the closing scene of a matrimonial drama. Marcel, an elderly barge-owner, is jealous of his wife and of Henri, a stevedore on his barge;[1] for their parents had been neighbours, and they have now fallen in love with each other. By accident he gives the signal agreed upon between them for their assignation by night, surprises the young man, forces from him a confession of his adulterous love, and strangles him. He hides the corpse in his cloak, and when his wife, uneasy and conscious of her guilt, comes up to him and tries to cajole him with feigned submissiveness, as though touched by his reminder of how often, before her child died, she had been wrapped in his cloak after the heat of the day was over,

[1] TRANSLATOR'S NOTE.—The names in the vocal score published by Messrs. G. Ricordi and Co. are Michele and Luigi.

he throws it open and lets the dead lover's body fall at her feet as she collapses in a faint.   Suor Angelica is a young nun of noble birth, who has spent the last seven years expiating a sinful earthly love.   Her aunt the princess, a woman of austere severity, comes to visit her with the object of persuading her to renounce her property in favour of her younger sister, who has just become betrothed.   On learning from her aunt that her son, the fruit of her forbidden passion, has died, she plucks poisonous herbs in the convent garden with the intention of killing herself; but the Madonna herself floats down to her in a glory of dazzling light, bends over her graciously, and gives her the child that is sitting on her lap.   We are left in doubt, however, whether it is Angelica's child, or the infant Jesus.   In *Gianni Schicchi* the legacy-hunting relatives sit weeping crocodile's tears at the bedside of Buoso Donati, who has just died.   But all the time they are really worrying lest the old bigot may have left his large fortune to the Church and the monks—a presentiment which soon receives confirmation.   They now send for the cunning Gianni Schicchi, at whom this arrogant set of people has hitherto looked askance, and whose daughter is loved by one of the young heirs.   He has the dead man carried into the next room, and lies down on the bed himself, with a pre-liminary warning to the crowd of would-be heirs that the Florentine law condemns the forger of a will to have his arm chopped off by the executioner, and then be sent into exile. He next impersonates the dead man, dictates a new will to the notary, in which he throws a sop to each of them, but reserves the lion's share of the property to himself, and finally drives the whole pack of them out of the house, while his daughter and young Rinuccio are locked in an embrace.   This delightfully burlesque version of a very human comedy was suggested by three or four verses from the *Divine Comedy*.   But we may note that, even in these three impeccable short operas, he cannot dispense with the stinging savour of cruelty.   In the first we have a man strangled to death, in the second a suicide through taking poison, and in another a corpse that is put to a dishonest use, involving a threat of mutilation by the public executioner. We see, then, that Puccini has remained true to his character.

But these tersely constructed dramatic situations have provided him with opportunities for great musical achievements. In *Il Tabarro* we are surprised from the outset to note a harshness of tone, a virile solidity, such as had not hitherto been noticeable in Puccini's rather feminine, subtly sensitive melodies; and this music evokes a powerful atmosphere far more intense in its effect than the not very original tragedy in itself. The very opening bars, with their languid, swaying motive and delicately piquant harmony, in which suspensions and their resolutions are sounded simultaneously, convey a most suggestive impressionist picture of evening hours on the Seine, and, thanks to Puccini's unfailing secret of bringing out the varied possibilities of all his symbolic themes, this dominates the whole of the first half of the drama, rendering the impression of monotony as the bustle of day gradually subsides, the pleasing, yet unsatisfied languor that accompanies the sunset hour, and the indifference of the dark river as it flows by, heedless of the sorrows of man. But it further suggests with unsurpassed power the sullen sense of bitterness felt by weary men dulled by the heavy servitude of hopeless toil. How vigorous, fresh, and original is the brisk measure of the drinking song, how dainty and naïve is the *chanson* sung by the hawker of songs (Il Venditore), with its delicious allusion to *La Bohème* in the refrain 'È la storia di Mimì ('Twas the story of Mimì)'; how delightful is the simple waltz played out of tune by the barrel-organ, with the amusingly discordant sevenths of the abominable hurdygurdy, almost suggesting an allusion to Stravinsky, whose work Puccini always followed with curiosity and eager attention, if not with very great sympathy. The rag-picker, known as 'La Frugola (The Busybody)', longs, like Tosca, for a *casetta*—a little house of her own; but we have only to compare her curiously hurried little song, clinging with stupid persistence to the same note, and constantly reverting to it in a way that exactly symbolizes her narrow, unassuming existence, with the dreamy harmonies and sensuous warmth of the beautiful Floria's melodies, to perceive how much more sharply Puccini now characterizes his figures. The love theme in B flat major, too, yearning upwards with a frank, free movement, and saved from all banality by sometimes abbreviating and sometimes extending the rhythm, in such a way as to lend it abundant variety, is well suited to a pair of young and healthy working-class lovers; whereas the catastrophe itself is conceived with greater musical economy, though Michele's sombre monologue, with its re-strained yet spasmodic rhythm and its brooding, almost funereal theme, afterwards acquires a fearful, rushing impetus in the murder-scene, which produces a stirring and powerful effect. It suggests the inexorable river with its unchanging flow, and, further, the unchanging flow of time as well. If only the plot of the piece and its characters were less repellent and uninterest-ing! It is they that are responsible for the fact that this one-act piece, with its masterly concentration and uncommonly powerful atmosphere, has so rapidly declined in popular estimation by comparison with the other two; though, as we have already said, even these find it hard to maintain their position in the repertory. Even singers, who usually compete eagerly for Puccini roles, are not fond of singing in this little piece, and they are to some extent justified in this; for the fact remains that it contains no effective roles. . . .

Yet it should not be allowed to fall into oblivion, if only for the sake of the magnificent contrast that is produced when the first notes of the bells, blended with the tone of the organ, are heard immediately after it, in *Suor Angelica*. Here we have harmonies recalling the colour in Murillo's paintings, pure celestial blue and silver. Not a single male voice is heard; nothing but the clear women's sopranos and the deep, velvety tones of the contraltos, an exquisite harmony that warms the heart—though perhaps it is all a little too clear, soft, and ex-quisitely sweet. But the chanting nuns in the convent have such pure tones of sheer innocence and gentle devotion, childlike

gladness and charming seriousness, that they reconcile us to
a good deal of sameness; while the whole is shaped by a careful
and meticulous hand. We can see how Puccini's ecclesiastical
music had developed since his days in Lucca. There are some
perfectly delicious episodes in the piece, the chatter of the nuns
is full of fascinating touches of inspiration, we are given little
thumbnail sketches, such as that of the sister who is stung by
a wasp, and the melody of Angelica's first song has a note of
absolute submission and abnegation of all personal will. Only
the orchestra betrays the flame that still smoulders unquenched
at her heart. But in the long run the whole effect would be
monotonous in colour, if it were not for the stirring scene
between Angelica and the Princess, a scene drawn by a master's
hand, which forms the central point of the whole. Here are
tones devoid, as it were, of all soul, that stab like icy, piercing
needles, expressing nothing but senile heartlessness and pitiless
arrogance, till Angelica's passionate outburst of grief breaks
into the midst like a lava-stream into a withered garden. Unfortunately the final scene, in which the miracle takes place, is
only a stage miracle, finding no counterpart in the music; the
heavenly hosts sing noble, but not particularly expressive hymns,
and the real apotheosis is that which takes place in the orchestra,
with its harp effects and bright suavity of tone, accompanied
by the strains of the organ. The composer was still a thoroughly
mundane one, and may have seen the Church opening before
him, but never the heavens.

The part of Suor Angelica has been sung by a number of great
singers, but most finely of all by Lotte Lehmann in Vienna, and
every time it has touched the heart of the public. But rarely
can it have had such an intimate appeal as at a performance of
it of which there is no record on any play-bill, and in which the
figures of the legend formed, as it were, their own public. As
we have already related, Puccini's elder sister Romelde, whom
he loved with all his heart, had gone into a convent. Her
brother visited her as often as he could, and we can hardly be
mistaken in supposing that her life, and perhaps her destiny

too, were what really inspired him with this delicate piece of operatic pastel. When it was completed, his sister longed eagerly to hear it; but this was forbidden, for her order was strictly enclosed. Giacomo accordingly went to the convent, and played and sang the opera to her and the other nuns. They sat there with wide eyes, transfixed with ecstasy and full of a secret agitation, and each of them found in this music something of her own experience. They crowded round the Master, asking him to tell them the story of the unhappy Angelica, and were stirred to the depths of their hearts by the sorrows of their suffering sister, till at the end they all knelt down and prayed for the salvation of the nun who had committed suicide, imploring the Blessed Virgin to intercede for the penitent sinner. Certainly the work has often had a more intellectual audience, with a more cultivated artistic taste, but never a more pious one, with a more understanding heart.

Gianni Schicchi is the crown of the whole Triptych. In it all the good spirits of comedy do homage to Puccini, the master of farcical humour: they titter and mock, abuse and hoax one another till it is a joy to watch them. It is an odd thing, but here, too, Puccini can only smile; he cannot burst out laughing from a full heart and an easy mind. Even in this piece a very slight, subtle cloud seems to lie upon all this exuberant jollity; but perhaps this is a charm the more. It is impossible to enter into details; the work is entirely made up of 'details', all captivating in their traditional roguery, from the very beginning, with the furtive, droning, hypocritical whine of the praying mourners, to the short, roguish epilogue, on the last chord of which the knave seems to leap down from the stage. The few lyrical passages in it are not Puccini at his very best, but, occurring where they do, they produce a fresh effect that cheers the heart; for instance in the lilting, hymn-like song in praise of Florence, the maidenly fervour of Lauretta's prayer, or the soaring melody of the *duettino* between the lovers; while side by side with all this we have a giddy whirl of scenes, representing the comic fury of the avaricious heirs, the pompous absurdity of the death-bed, the pathetic buffoonery of the notary and the defrauded heirs, cackling like geese and braying like asses, while the orchestra turns everything to ridicule, whether it is babbling out all their most intimate secrets and supplying a malicious commentary upon what is going on, or suddenly turning dignified, or joining in the hypocritical mourning.   It is a joy from the first bar to the last.

The *Trittico*, which was performed at the Teatro Costanzi, Rome, for the first time on 11th January 1919, amid tremendous applause from the public and the royal family, and was recognized as a masterpiece even by the critics, has none the less failed to find a permanent home in opera-houses outside Italy.   Gianni Schicchi alone continues to pursue his knaveries here and there, when a two-act opera has to be performed and something is required to fill the bill, a purpose for which it is very well adapted, though the piece is too good to be treated like this.   The work as a whole was conceived as a unity, and ought more often to be presented as such to the public, which swallows rapturously so much that is mediocre. Little by little the public would be sure to get fond of it. Directors of opera-houses ought to have more courage, and so ought the critics.

I have reserved for the present occasion the few words I have to say about the attitude adopted towards Puccini by critics outside Italy, and I may take that of the German critics as typical—I mean, of course, those of them who are serious judges, and not the irritating type who are presumptuous enough to set themselves up as self-appointed judges of art, and in their ignorance take up a superior standpoint towards everything. Possibly things have changed by now, but during his lifetime Puccini was thoroughly lectured even by the 'real' critics in Germany; and every time a new opera was produced, the newspapers castigated him as though he had been a criminal.   They found fault with him for lacking depth, and he certainly is not deep; he never felt himself to be the victim of some dread fate, and never posed as such.   But he was also stigmatized as a 'drawing-room musician (*Salonmusiker*)', and his music dismissed as insipid and fit only for hotel orchestras; which seems to me rank injustice. Even his unique talent for the theatre was cast in his teeth, and on the wrong grounds, too, for the critics alleged that, though he possessed a sense of the theatre, there was none in his music. It is symptomatic of a serious confusion of ideas that musicians lacking in all sense of the theatre are being for ever extolled to the skies, and positively having it imputed to them as a merit that they cannot succeed in gripping the public. It would appear as though Richard Wagner's lofty and imperishable work of art has done much to confuse people's ideas. His idea of a *Festspiel* is one that aims at an experience standing apart from ordinary existence, and reserved for those consecrated hours in which we are rapt away from everyday life and the necessities of existence: and any one who succeeds in following his example by composing works capable of achieving the same thing deserves that we should abase ourselves to the dust before him. But it is rather difficult to understand why we should therefore throw mud at a composer who raises everyday things to a higher plane, though he is not capable of lifting us out of them, who enchants us with 'the small things', and, in spite of all his weaknesses, which nobody would think of defending, none the less delights us by a really rare wealth of genuine music, full of southern warmth and overflowing with inspired melody; or why we should necessarily be expected to prefer to him either stilted boredom or those whose motto is 'experiment at any price'. It is almost as though Germans did not consider music worth anything unless it bored them, and as though they had an uneasy conscience at listening to any other; and if they can actually take a subscription ticket for the purpose of being bored, they are sure that what they hear must be immortal. As a matter of course they feel it their duty to regard anything pleasing and charming as vulgarly banal. But their children listen to it with secret pleasure, and, when they are given the choice between the *Matthew Passion* and *Parsifal*—they go to *Madame Butterfly*.

Must I repeat, for the hundredth time, that Wagner is a spiritual possession and enriches the whole content of our life, while Puccini is 'only' a sensuous pleasure? We ought not to compare things between which no ground of comparison exists, but in the same way, we ought not to try to measure one of them by the standards of the other. In *Il Tabarro* the signal that the lover may approach unmolested is given by striking a match. But let us then recall the torch in *Tristan*, which serves the same purpose and likewise leads towards death. The difference between the two expresses what I am trying to imply. The torch and the match are symbolic at once of the two composers, their art, and the relation between them.

CHAPTER XIII

A DREAM OF THE EAST ('TURANDOT')

By this time Puccini had fresh cause for melancholy: his age. Not that he could detect in himself the slightest sign of physical decay. He was as supple and strong as ever, and took an undiminished pleasure in motoring, motor-boats, and shooting, as well as in the fickle hearts of women; and the fact that he occasionally had trouble with his larynx, and that certain symptoms of diabetes had appeared as the inevitable accompaniment of his time of life—for he was by now in his sixties—failed to cause him any excessive irritation. But he was conscious of youth's most important implication, which is that a man still has time before him; and he realized that, for his own part, he no longer had any too much. 'Only consider how many years I carry on my back,' was the constant plea with which he appealed to his librettists; for he wanted them to be on the look out for subjects night and day, and they could never submit enough ideas to him, particularly at this period, when he once again desired to write a work of some length, after the concentrated tragedies of the *Trittico*, with which he had associated music having the terse brevity of the Morse code. Over and over again we find the old complaint: 'I am full of a feverish desire to work, but I have no libretto, and am in a state of misery'. We are strangely moved every time by the spectacle of his almost morbid suffering during the pauses in his creative work, his incapacity for filling his time with intellectual pursuits, and, most of all, the difficulty he experienced in producing anything, however richly his brain might teem with music, so long as he had no libretto to work upon. In order to set free the exuberant flow of his music his imagination had to be stirred by some dramatic situation, scene, or gesture. He had to enter

223

into the experiences of his characters, for his own personal experience failed to open the flood-gates of the music stored up within him. It is remarkable to find such dependence upon some extraneous drama in words on the part of one who has shown in so many of the orchestral interludes of his operas what a wealth of emotion he had to express in the wordless language of the instruments. We cannot help wondering whether he really lacked the faculty of pouring forth in orchestral compositions all that stirred his innermost feelings, and was always bound to hang it upon lay figures. In spite of his considerable technical ability, he is certainly not a symphonic composer; even when he occasionally departs from his mosaic-like thematic method, and composes a complete movement in the form of an intermezzo, his only mode of achieving unity is through the melodic curve that holds the whole together. He lacks the faculty of construction and articulation, the power of developing motives and placing them in relation to one another, which in opera, as in other types of music, possesses virtue to generate values of a higher order and shed an inner light upon the dramatic action. Moreover, that which constitutes the greatness of the true symphonic composer—that is, a meta-physical quality transcending concrete reality—is foreign to him. He does not look upwards to the stars, but always remains upon earth, imprisoned in what is material. But the fact that, in spite of all, he is unable to make any subjective confession in his music, or to pour forth his soul in it directly, but requires the medium of imaginary characters, not created by himself, remains to some extent an enigma.

During these periods of paralysis he seemed as though ship-wrecked on the reefs of boredom, and remained restlessly on the look-out for any ship that might save him, with Giuseppe Adami as the captain who should steer him back to the shores of those regions of art in which he was at home. Meanwhile he would lie in his boat, now and then shooting a few wild-duck, or go for drives in his motor, or occupy himself with technical devices. He always took a childlike delight in original

PUCCINI'S LAST LETTER (facsimile)

Wednesday evening.

Dear Adamino,

For the present the treatment is not too bad—external applications—but God knows what they are going to do to me on Monday—so as to get at the inside, below the epiglottis! They assure me that I shall not suffer pain—and they even say that I shall get well. I am now beginning to hope—some days ago I had lost all hope of a cure. What days and what hours [we have passed]! I am prepared for everything. Write to me sometimes. Affectionately, your devoted friend, Giacomo.

mechanisms for everyday use, such as gigantic cigar-lighters, specially constructed pocket torches, pencils of abnormal size, and all such mechanical trifles, a tendency which has, moreover, been inherited by his son Tonio. He would amuse himself by inventing such things himself; but they did not as a rule prove very practicable—on the contrary—and, what is more, they were hardly ever put to practical use. One of his inventions really was carried into effect, however, and he was prouder of it than of all his operas put together: he made himself master of the rain, by constructing a system of pierced pipes for watering his garden during periods of drought, and having it carried up to the height of a tree. The water was pumped up, and it was only necessary to press a lever to set it playing. It was his delight to drench the thirsting shrubs, and, above all, his un-suspecting guests, cooling them with an abundant shower of rain if they complained of the unbearable heat. In every way, indeed, he remained like a great child.

Yet for all this, can he have been one of those 'necessitous masters (*hochbedürftige Meister*)' to whom Hans Sachs refers in *Die Meistersinger*? He often complained of the troubles of life, it is true, and at times bitterly: 'I have always lived remote from men,' he once said to his friend Pagni; 'my life has been filled with work and passed amid modest circumstances. Who can say what others might have done in my place? I was always cut off from the world, like a shepherd on the Campagna. I have never got in anybody else's way, and have helped people, according to my powers, as far as I have been able—and my only reward has been an abundance of malice. Why can this have been?'

To this question there is no answer, least of all where Puccini is concerned, for he was the very opposite of Goethe, and it would have been impossible to apply to him the latter's words: 'Ich schreibe nicht, euch zu gefallen—ihr sollt was lernen (I do not write to please you; you have got to learn a lesson)'. The public is always restive under the hand of him who subju-gates it, even when it loves him, as a wild beast is with its

Q

tamer. But though his primitive existence could boast every modern comfort, he, too, could find no way of escape from the afflictions of his own unstable soul, so easily clouded by shadows, save by creating an image, a 'memorial, clear and stable', in which could be summed up all his youth and the feminine tenderness that had been lavished upon him. And this is why he was beside himself when he had to lay his colours and brushes aside for a time untouched.

Yet, much as he loved his retirement, he found pleasure in every token of his steadily increasing renown, as well as in the showers of gold that poured down upon him year after year in growing profusion. Puccini was one of those rare people whose heart does not become metamorphosed into gold, for wealth never made him hard, and he made no change in his way of living, with its few wants. Moreover, he still remembered the days when he had had to go hungry and stay his stomach with bean soup in order to still its pangs. He was always ready to assist anybody in need, and did so in absolute secrecy and on the most generous scale: every month he would give away with lavish hand from two to three thousand lire in charity, without inquiring too closely whether, in the long run, his good nature was abused or not. One day he heard someone singing outside his window. It was a man's voice of incredible beauty, and so full of soul that it stirred him to the depths. He looked out: it was a convict who had been told off for road-mending, and still had his feet in irons, for he had been sent to the galleys for attempted murder. But Puccini could not conceive that any one who sang in such a voice and with such feeling could really be a criminal. He therefore invoked the intercession of the Queen of Italy, and did, in fact, obtain a pardon for the condemned man, who was now allowed to return to his wife and child, and remained devoted to the Master with a dog-like affection for the rest of his life. Perhaps the best proof of his devotion was that he did not become an opera-singer.

Puccini's relations with the royal family were a source of delight to him. He was anything but a courtier, and associated with the king and queen and the princesses as though he had been their equal. But what he welcomed was the genuine and enlightened interest taken in him by all the members of the royal house, which they showed in many more ways than merely by attending the first performances of his operas. He thought far less of the marks of distinction conferred upon him, in the shape of orders, than of the interest taken in both himself and his work by the queen and the Princess Mafalda in particular. When they went into residence for the summer at San Rossore, the Master was invited to luncheon in their most intimate circle, whenever this was possible. He had to report to them how the opera upon which he was engaged was getting on, and was quite unembarrassed, except when he was asked to play something; for he was a very poor pianist, and his habitual timidity rendered his defective piano technique even worse, so that it was only by a supreme effort that he could overcome his paralysing shyness enough to respond to the wishes of his beloved Queen Elena and the little princesses, and give anything approaching an adequate rendering of his own music, whether from memory or with the notes before him; for he felt absolutely stupefied and confused all the while, and had a loud buzzing in his ears, as though he were still the clumsy, bungling student from the Conservatorio at Milan. Yet this was not due to excess of respect for the high rank of his listeners, with whom, in spite of all his convinced monarchism, he felt himself to be quite on an equality, in virtue of his own artistic ancestry; but to his invincible timidity, which afflicted him in society of all sorts alike and often made him perfectly wretched. For the rest, the cordial and informal tone that prevailed between him and these royal ladies was so thoroughly friendly and frank that his original embarrassment soon disappeared, and only reappeared when he had to strum on the piano. The artist in him made him loathe playing such a sorry role, and he always did all he could to evade these commands. This was not always easy; for the Princess Mafalda, an ardent music-lover and an enthusiast for Puccini's music, interested herself with all the intense eagerness of youth in *Turandot*, which was being composed at that time; though she hardly liked to express her ardent and secretly cherished desire that Puccini should dedicate the new work to her.   But the Master's subtle ear divined her wish, and he was happy, as well as rather proud, to dedicate his opera to this beautiful king's daughter with a passion for art.   It had been his intention to word the dedication as follows: 'My Princess—to a Princess'; but before he could inscribe the words on the score, death had struck the pen from his hand. But the noble young creature guessed how uncomfortable he felt when he was forced to play before them, and noticed the 'povera faccia', the 'suffering face', as his children called it, with which he sat down to the piano when even remotely threatened with anything of the sort.   So she quietly helped him to evade the queen's repeated wishes without offending against etiquette, though Her Majesty, too, was naturally anxious to hear this work at once.   For this reason alone, if for no other, he resolved to dedicate *Turandot* to the Princess Mafalda.   But there was another reason too: for all unconsciously she had assisted him in his work.   She was now betrothed, and it was the happiness he saw glowing in her eyes that suggested to him the idea of the moment in which 'Turandot principessa crudelissima diviene Turandot principessa innamorata'—the moment, that is, in which, by a departure from Gozzi's original, Turandot, 'the most cruel of all princesses', becomes Turandot, 'the princess in love'.   The scene in which Turandot becomes a woman with a feeling heart, thanks to the unknown prince's kiss, is due to a personal inspiration of Puccini's own.

At last he had found the subject that was to crown his lifework.   The search had lasted even longer than usual, and had been an agonizing one.   Puccini had even applied to the amusing Tristan Bernard, in the vain hope of being stimulated by this witty writer of comedies to compose a gay comic opera. But the anecdote of the black man who had been exhibited in Europe in a 'negro village', and, on returning home with a few white men whom he had captured, treated them in the same way, charging a fee for exhibiting them, till such time as they should be eaten, somehow seemed a little too 'original' to suit the composer of *La Bohème*. Nor was Adami very successful in making anything out of *Molly*, an English piece based upon Dickens. The librettist now proposed to call in the writer Renato Simoni as a collaborator. The Maestro consented, but then waited and waited with a more and more piteous face, while his literary treasure-hunters continued to give no sign. At last he abruptly made up his mind, went to Milan to see them, and put a pistol to their heads by saying that he would not go home till they had settled upon a subject. But this was a difficult problem, and everything they proposed was rejected by Puccini. Adami describes the whole scene in most lively fashion in his illuminating introduction to Puccini's letters. The composer was already packing his bag in desperation at having to depart empty-handed, when, just as one of them was handing him his dressing-case and the other his pyjamas, the name of Carlo Gozzi was thrown out in passing, with the suggestion that it might not be a bad thing to look through his fantastic comedies. Puccini straightened himself with a jerk, saying that he quite agreed, but it must not be any particular piece, only the essence of them all, a sort of epitome of his themes. Adami and Simoni ran through a few titles, but at each of them they all three shook their heads. All of a sudden, just as Puccini was about to tuck his slippers into the trunk, he exclaimed: 'How would *Turandot* do? I saw the thing produced by Reinhardt in Berlin, and it quite impressed me'. No sooner had he mentioned the name, than all three of them took fire simultaneously. A translation of Schiller's version was sent for, and the Maestro took it with him on his journey; but his first remark was: 'If I compose a *Turandot*, it must be different from Gozzi's version and from Schiller's too; I have no use for the bloodthirsty woman, but only for one who is capable of love'. And he knew the reason why, which was that he was incapable of composing any music suited to creatures whose love finds expression in cutting off heads, and who have their wooers put to death out of mere caprice.　There must be a substratum of humanity, offering the possibility of a change of heart, if Turandot is to be more than a mere purveyor of victims for the executioner, who arouses universal repulsion, and is, in point of fact, no more than a puppet moved by insensate cruelty, rather than a being of flesh and blood.　'Put Gozzi aside for a little while,' he kept on admonishing them, 'and work with a little logic and imagination'; and his exhortations were successful.　An idea was found that would explain Turandot's character: she was not to act out of merely sadic motives every time a suitor appeared, as though she were only a capricious creature in a fairy tale; but she was to be haunted by the fate of an ancestress, who has been betrayed and reduced to poverty by her husband, so that Turandot intended to test every suitor, and revenge herself upon the whole male sex by the death of the rejected ones.　She had failed to find a single real man among them all, or, at any rate, one worthy of her love, but hated and despised all men in memory of the wrong done to her ancestress, which she had never forgotten.　The explanation is a tolerable one, in the world of fairy-tales, at least, where so much is taken for granted; though, once the premises are accepted, the consequences work out logically and consistently.

Thanks to this idea a fine libretto was produced, full of poetic feeling, fantastic dreams and Chinese colour, a sort of combined masque and drama of sex hostility, in scenes as elaborately ornate as coiling dragons embroidered in heavy gold, as daintily grotesque as lacquered designs, or as Chinese porcelain with greens and reds on a white ground, yet humanly convincing and full of fire and passion; and Puccini took the greatest interest in composing the music for it. He was untiring in his suggestions for giving greater animation and dramatic impressiveness to the work, and his suggestions always bore fruit and were entirely to the point.　He probably knew Voltaire's saying: 'What is too silly to be said may be sung in opera', and he was very careful not to let any absurdities slip into it.   The fairy-tale atmosphere was intended to raise everything to the plane of fantasy, lending all that happened the atmosphere and changing hues of dream; but it could not be permitted to justify anything utterly irrational.   He insisted upon having his way, too, much to the advantage of the work, which, though the music may sometimes produce the effect of Puccini at second hand, is his maturest and most weighty production, masterly in its colour, which is that of the Chinese world of bizarre fantasy, as well as in its intricate ornament and restless splendour, which, however, merely serve as the background for a drama of fierce passion and sacrifice.

Yet for all this, the composer seems still to have felt something lacking, and I can quite imagine what it was.   This Turandot is a woman who propounds three riddles to each of the princes suing for her hand—such difficult and obscure ones that they fail to guess any of them—and then has all those who have failed beheaded, while she herself remains quite unmoved. Next she is subjugated by Calaf, who elucidates the riddle, but, in his frenzy of love, gives himself into her power once more, and would have had to die too, had she not been overcome by her feelings, and fallen in love in turn.   But this woman is still too abstract, too much like the unknown quantity in an algebraical equation—an unknown princess, in fact, corresponding to the unknown prince who appears to woo her.   It was necessary to reveal her as being something more than a spoilt, self-willed creature, full of vanity, who insists upon exhibiting her brilliant intellect at the cost of the lives of the young men whom she destroys, handing them over to execution in obedience to an ancient law, even though this causes suffering to her as well.   She had, moreover, to be shown as one who hates her own baleful beauty, and longs to be loved not only for the sake of her enchanting mask, but for her own sake alone, in spite of her apparently insatiable cruelty.   She deliberately desires to make herself hideous; but since she cannot bring herself to destroy the beauty of her face, she means to choose this way of testing even the suitor of her choice, in order that she may know that it is not her body only that he desires, but her soul too; herself, and not only her bewitching exterior. Even her riddles have to betray something of that which her pride will not allow her to express otherwise, and are intended to reveal her true nature to her suitor. And the curious thing is that, every time I hear *Turandot*, I feel as though the music were telling us all this, and that Puccini has expressed in his music a Turandot whom his librettists failed to create.

It is a remarkable and compelling work, full of sombre splendour, hieratically rigid, yet the next moment darkly turbid with the music of an anguished soul and the tormenting fever-fits of a passionate love. In it we find intricate heraldic forms and musical automata side by side with human and suffering figures. Porcelain figures give forth music, processions of mandarins and eunuchs go past with mechanical pomp, bells tinkle, the gong booms, the bony clatter of the xylophone suggests the skeletons in a dance of death, the celesta and cymbals add their silvern glitter and flash of gold, strange drums are heard that rattle and roll, and through it all rings the sobbing outcry of a heart laid bare. All this allows no opening for mosaic-like minuteness of detail, but offers an un-mistakable invitation to broader forms and well-rounded-off numbers, each complete in itself. We look in vain here for the musical feuilletonist, the melodramatic composer. Yet Puccini has not changed. Every bar bears the trace of his hand; but his style has become different, and his orchestral palette has been enriched to a hardly conceivable degree.

Once again we find an opening motive like a personal signa-ture—that of Turandot, which next, in a diminished form, crashes out piercingly in the explosive chords that announce the mandarin's entry, after which it is developed thematically throughout the howls of the bloodthirsty crowd. A striking feature is the singing melody in the orchestra, broad, exalted, and panting, which does not seem quite in keeping with the shouts and murmurs of the frightened crowd. It is obviously the musical emblem of the princess, the banefully lovely cause of all the horror, who is at that moment mercilessly dispatching the Prince of Persia to his death, and the sight of whom has collected a crowd of people, hardened to bloodshed. Next comes the horrible ensemble of the execution scene. The sword of the executioner is sharpened with hideous assiduity, the grindstone turns and turns without ceasing, the fifteen attendants with their bass voices are given a brisk, sly, monotonous motive, suggestive of their grinning faces, which seems to revolve simultaneously with the grindstone, and shouts of 'Al supplizio! Muoia! (To the scaffold! Slay him!)' mingle piercingly with the whole, producing a grim sense of oppression. Immediately following this comes the magically tender night music, evoking a picture of the rising moon, in sustained, veiled notes, with a pedal note held for several bars, and lulling sextolets on the cello suggestive of dark waters, across which quiver the pale rays of a vague, almost formless melody; then comes a shower of figures on the harps and flutes, like a passing flash, and all is over. Next we have the procession to the place of execution, like an elegy over the victim's untimely death with its plaintive minor thirds, in the nobly mournful rhythm of an unheroic dead march, ushered in by a graceful, solemn folk-tune, an autumn song with a melancholy charm. Boys' voices are heard singing, accompanied softly by distant saxophones; the humming chorus and the faint boom of the gong mingle with the slight, delicate tones of the orchestra and the clear bird-notes of the flutes—and, again, all is over, leaving us, however, with an impression of the whole landscape. The spell cast over Calaf by the sight of Turandot, the fervent adjurations of Liu, the loving slave, and the bobbing figures in masks, with the changing measure of their droll song of warning, varying between two-four and three-four time, all provide a telling and not too pregnant contrast, and an effect of over-wrought ecstasy; though there is an incomparably stronger force of suggestion in the few bars of the sweet, sad, ghostly chorus formed by the shadows of the dead suitors, still singing of their love even in death, that accompanied the preceding scene of the execution of the Persian prince. And here we may note a defect in the scheme of the piece; for immediately after this the second act, too, opens with yet another interlude in the form of a masquerade. This is a delicious passage, and though it is perhaps the only really superfluous number in the whole of Puccini's work, none the less we would not be without it, though it ought certainly to be suppressed without further ado were it not that it adds an important touch of colour and, at the same time, a necessary contrast with the stately ceremonial that follows. The scene in which the three comic masks of the Chancellor, the Lord High Steward (*Gran Provveditore*), and the Master of the Kitchen (*Gran Cuciniere*) express with farcical dignity and ill-humour their disgust with their offices about the Court and the reign of terror that prevails, and their longing for a quiet life in the country, has suggested to Puccini the idea of a deliciously comical *scherzo*, with restless, hurrying, neat little motives, daintily ranged in sequence and interwoven with one another, like delicate trifles turned in ebony, carved in wood, or spun out of stiff silk, while between them come others that seem to glimmer like coloured paper lanterns. The measure is constantly changing, for the most part tripping in two-four time, but afterwards passing into the more idyllic three-four time as they think of their idyllic existence beside 'the lake of blue (*laghetto blù*), all surrounded by bamboo', but reverting every time to the shorter two-four bar, with a few reminiscences of the boys' autumn song. Add to this the slightness of the orchestral colour, as faint as a breath, like the paintings on Chinese tea-cups; and the whole thing is simply delicious, there is no other word for it. The great scene in the Imperial Palace is weaker in substance, in spite of the splendour of the music, which depicts the ineffable glory of the Son of Heaven with a fresh virtuosity and the most amazing detail. The court procession is based upon original Chinese motives, which are picturesque enough in their pentatonic effects. Turandot's address is rhetorical and ceremonious rather than really inspired, and in the riddle scene we are struck by the fact that not only the three riddles, but also the answers to them, are all based upon the same theme. It might have been expected, particularly of a composer with such an innate sense of the theatre as Puccini, that he would have given some pictorial expression in the music to the different subjects of the riddles and their answers, thus heightening the suspense, and, at the same time, achieving a far more striking musical crescendo, instead of this stately monotony, which ends by exasperating the nerves. The fact that he did not do this is a fourth enigma to add to the other three. Calaf's song in the third act, 'Nessun dorma (None shall sleep to-night)', does not rise to the heights of the arias sung by his predecessors, Cavaradossi, Pinkerton, and Ramerrez, but it has a noble melodic line of the authentic Puccinian type, and swells to a fine intensity in the chorus of women which takes up the tranquil, exalted theme. In the scene of the torture and death of little Liu the same excited, interjectional, spoken style is used to accompany her agony as in the corresponding moments of *Tosca* and *La Fanciulla*; but Liu's appeal to Turandot, her confession of love, her death, and the chorus of men and women who bear away her frail body, are among the gems of this score, and cause our very heart-strings to vibrate in sympathy with her. Here we are no longer in China, with its ornate cult and foreign type of music; this is simply a human creature in all her pain and weakness. Liu's last song in particular, with its melody still based on a five-note figure, but afterwards soaring freely upwards, accompanied by the poignantly mellow timbre of the accompanying wood-wind, the sparkling tone of the celesta, the muted violins, and the pizzicato violas, is one of the most exquisite passages that Puccini has ever consecrated to any of his feminine characters. And then, after this——

But nothing came after. At this point the pencil fell from the Master's hand; it was not granted to him to finish the work. It was Franco Alfano who wrote the concluding passage of the opera, with the aid of the thirty-six pages of the rough draft which the Master had taken with him on the journey to his sick-room in a distant land, in the passionate hope that he might still be able to orchestrate them. Alfano performed his task as a labour of love, entirely suppressing his own personality, and carefully preserving the Master's style; yet we are conscious of the break. The very aspect of the page is different; everything is harder, clearer, less atmospheric and more rigid, and the final scene, compressed till it contains only what is absolutely essential, seems superficial and violent. There are works in which a continuation written after the composer's death has been so successful that it is scarcely possible to discern where the composer left off and the adapter began. Such are Mozart's *Requiem*, the recitative scenes in *Carmen*, and Weber's *Die Drei Pintos* in Gustav Mahler's masterly arrangement. But, to quote Hebbel, 'it is as impossible to continue a poem where another man has left off as it is to continue somebody else's dream'.[1] And this is equally true of Puccini's last work.

It was an unspeakably moving moment when, during the first performance of *Turandot* at the Scala on 25th April 1926, Toscanini laid down his baton at this point, during the lament over the body of Liu, and said in a trembling voice: 'Here ends the Master's work'. On that occasion the performance ceased at this point. It was not till next time that the whole opera was performed, as completed by Alfano. There could have been no more worthy way of doing homage to the dead man's memory.

---

[1] 'Man kann ebensowenig weiterdichten, wo ein anderer aufgehört hat, als man weiterträumen kann, was ein anderer geträumt hat.'

CHAPTER XIV

THE MASK OF SUFFERING

FOR four whole years Puccini worked at *Turandot* with absolute self-surrender, putting forth his highest faculties, and with a meticulous conscientiousness such as scarcely any of his previous works had cost him, but at the same time with a secret uneasiness, a faint dread that he might be unable to complete it. He shuddered when he thought of his age, but this only proved a further incentive. 'Onward without fear or anxiety!' was his motto. He harassed his librettists as he had never done before, nagging, cajoling, finding fault, and urging them onwards. 'Perchè, perchè non m'ami più? Perchè? (Ah, why can you not love me still? Ah, why?)',[1] he wrote; 'I ought not to be treated like this. It seems to me that your willingness to collaborate with me is flagging. . . . You should not hide your head under your wing. You must spread your wings and hold your heads high: we shall triumph!'[2] Such were the appeals that rained down upon them every two or three days. He was pleased with his work; yet the doubts that haunt an artist sometimes raised their heads. 'Who knows,' he would sigh again and again, 'whether I am not deceiving myself?' Most of the time he was cheerful, but these periods of self-confidence would be followed by times of the deepest depression. 'My dear Adamino,' he wrote in March 1923, 'I am a poor, most wretched man, without confidence, old, discouraged, null. What am I to do? I do not know, I shall go to bed, then I shall not think

[1] A quotation of Michele's words to Giorgetta in his duet with her in *Il Tabarro*, No. 74 in Ricordi's vocal score.

[2] TRANSLATOR'S NOTE.—Puccini's actual words in his letter of 11 Nov. 1921 to Adami, in the *Epistolario*, were: 'Mi pare che in voi diminuisca ogni volontà di lavorare con me'. And in his letter of 8 Nov.: 'Non è così che io debbo essere trattato. . . . Se avete tante volte espresso fiducia in me . . . dovreste ascoltarmi e non mettervi nella posizione di testa sotto le ali. Le ali devono essere spiegate, e la testa alta—vinceremo'.

or fret myself.'[1] He often felt a physical languor, and was more irritable than he had been in earlier days. He was also out of humour by reason of his strained relations with Tito Ricordi; he would have preferred above all things to reimburse the sums he had received from him, and so regain his liberty.

But these barometric depressions of his vitality were as a rule followed shortly afterwards by a rise, and the farther he advanced with *Turandot*, the more firmly confident he became. If his progress suffered a check at times, the variety of business that claimed his attention, added to his various distractions, saved him from relapsing too far into his old melancholy. On one occasion, as a member of the jury in connexion with a prize competition, he had to examine no less than twenty-five operatic scores, but what he saw in these works by the youngest generation of Italians gave him no cause to burn his own work in discouragement. He had no need to feel fossilized and behind the times yet. He by no means under-estimated his contemporaries, however, and there were a few of them outside Italy in whom he always showed the keenest interest, besides which they had a fertilizing effect upon his own harmonic resources and command of musical colour. Among them was Igor Stravinsky, the Cossack wildness and barbaric quality of whose rhythms fascinated him, though he could not listen to his music without a slight shock. He quite shuddered at *Le Sacre du Printemps*, though that is a comparatively mild work. 'Ridiculous choreography!' was his verdict. 'The music is cacophony pushed to its utmost limits. Curious, yet written with a certain talent. But, taking it all in all, stuff worthy of lunatics.'[2] In spite of these words, there are some who think

---

[1] TRANSLATOR'S NOTE.—Puccini's actual words, in his letter of 6 March 1923, printed in the *Epistolario*, were: 'Sono un povero uomo tristissimo, sfiduciato, vecchio, nullo, avvilito. Che fare? Non lo so. Vado a letto. Così non penso e non mi torturo'.

[2] TRANSLATOR'S NOTE.—Puccini's words, in his letter of 27 Nov. 1907 to Tito Ricordi, printed in the *Epistolario*, were: 'Coreografia ridicola. La musica una cacofonia all' estremo. Curiosa, però è fatta con un certo talento. Ma nell' insieme, roba da matti'.

they can see signs that Puccini was not entirely unaffected by the provocative audacities of the headstrong Russian. The chorus of executioners in the first act of *Turandot* would scarcely work on the nerves with such a stinging effect, or produce so inexorable an impression by the monotonous violence of its movement, had it not been for Stravinsky's example. But a far stronger effect was that produced upon Puccini by Claude Debussy. Though he had himself desired to compose music for *Pelleas and Melisande*, he felt an extraordinary admiration for his rival's work, which, he says, is uncommon and individual, and uniform in style and tone, music with the value of a rarity, though as monotonous as a Franciscan's frock.[1]   But there can be no mistaking the fact that in *Butterfly*, and still more in *Turandot*, we may find echoes of Debussy's characteristic haze of sound, of his blurred, iridescent mixtures of tone, his whole-tone scales, and the preciosity of the blended harmonies, like some subtle opiate, that characterize this music, with its proud aloofness; and Puccini undoubtedly used these qualities as an element in his most characteristic melodies.   On the other hand, unlike most contemporary composers, he was not in the least influenced by Richard Strauss. He esteemed him, but his esteem was vigilant, rather than affectionate, and he hardly felt the fascination of *Salome* at all, though the overwhelming effect of this work of genius gave him much food for thought. He thought far more highly of Strauss's symphonic poems than he did of his dramatic compositions. He was greatly impressed by *Till Eulenspiegel*, while *Don Juan* and *Tod und Verklärung* seemed to him (though wrongly so) to contain the Bavarian master's most magical inspiration. But he took an even keener interest in Arnold Schönberg. On one occasion he even made a special journey to Venice for the purpose of hearing *Pierrot lunaire*. The impression it produced upon him

---

[1] The passage on *Pelléas et Mélisande* in Puccini's letter of 15 Nov. 1906 in the *Epistolario* says: 'Ha qualità straordinarie di armonie e sensazioni diafane strumentate. È veramente interessante, malgrado il suo colore *sombre*, uniforme come un abito francescano'.

was one of disquieting strangeness; this music, with its nihilistic
and solvent quality, combined with strict form, remained as
utterly incomprehensible to him as a Sanskrit poem, and he
could listen to it only with a calm shake of the head. For all
that, he did not consider it at all impossible that this might
prove to be the music of the future, though he was not in the
least anxious to live on into a future of this sort. But he did
not allow the thought of it to depress him.

When he did not spend his evenings working, he would
occasionally take part in the highly un-Socratic pranks of the
Gianni Schicchi Club that had recently been formed of his
friends, and in comparison with which the La Bohème Club
had been a perfect School of Athens. Or else he would sit in
his arm-chair meditating, lost in a cloud of cigarette-smoke.
At such times as this he was fond of tuning in his wireless
receiver with some place where one of his operas was being
performed; and the search was never a long one. As a rule he
could hear fragments of all his operas within the same hour,
for they dominated the operatic stage. It gave him a queer,
but magnificent feeling to sit in his quiet room listening to the
voices of the singers who were at that moment performing his
music in London, Paris, or Vienna, observing how the orchestra
sounded, forming an opinion on the artists or the conductor,
and noticing the hearty, incessant applause that came flowing
into the room as though in warm waves, and made his heart
overflow with gratitude and love. The audiences seated in the
proud, brilliantly illuminated opera-houses had no idea that the
composer of their favourite operas was in their midst, enjoying
their audibly expressed admiration. And he would meditate
how fate had favoured him above many others, in that it
was vouchsafed to him to create beautiful, living works, to
speak to innumerable hearts, increasing the world's treasury of
happiness, and winning affection everywhere, whether in the
drawing-room or the seamstress's workroom, the factory or the
palace, in the tropics or on the shores of the Caspian Sea. Not
long before this time he had received a card from his friend

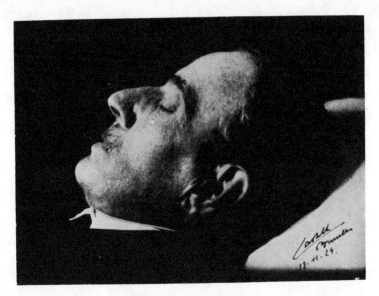

PUCCINI ON HIS DEATH-BED

THE DEAD MAN IS BROUGHT HOME

Fraccaroli, written from the Polar regions, describing how he had heard across the water the Laplanders singing tunes from *La Bohème*. In such moments as these a feeling of almost solemn peace came over him, and this 'luckless' man felt a deep inward tranquillity, and was almost happy. But then again a shadow would fall upon his spirits as he asked himself: 'Shall I be able to finish *Turandot*?'

For the last few years the trouble caused by his chronic laryngitis had increased to a really irksome extent. Puccini was constantly suffering from sore throats and sudden fits of hoarseness, which had begun to make their appearance quite twenty years before, without attracting any particular attention from either himself or his doctors. But the frequency with which they now occurred made them a perfect torment to him, and a moral, even more than a physical one. The impatient Maestro was irritated by the slightest indisposition, and his strong constitution had always offered a tough resistance to any bodily ailments. The little roughnesses that had appeared on his vocal chords had proved to be harmless, and from time to time he had had them removed by a caustic; but the unpleasant symptoms that had recently appeared were of a different character, and Puccini expressed a wish for a thorough examination. Since his own doctor could find nothing, the Master paid a visit to a specialist in Florence, and requested him not to spare his feelings, but to give him an absolutely frank opinion. When the laryngoscope failed to reveal anything serious, Puccini insisted upon a closer examination; he felt a sensitive spot lower down in the throat, and did not rest until the specialist had reached it with his sound. A tiny granulation was, in fact, discovered there, about the size of a pin's head; but this still gave no cause for anxiety. The doctor advised him to come back in three weeks' time, but forbade him to smoke, and this not only irritated his nerves and made him find less pleasure in life, but also made him profoundly uneasy. He felt that he simply must be sure what was the matter, so he visited Florence again in secret, and consulted a professor of medicine, from

R

whom he returned home in a state of utter depression; for the
doctor had noted the presence of a swelling, and expressed the
hope that it was not malignant in character. For the time
being, however, he could say no more. 'But what sort of a
swelling is it?' asked Tonio Puccini anxiously. The only reply
was a piteous gesture, and a sigh that was more like a groan.

Tonio Puccini could bear this uncertainty no longer. He
hurried to Florence to see the professor and asked him to tell
him the truth. The reply shattered all his hopes. A sentence
of death was passed upon his father, for Puccini was suffering
from an acute cancer of the throat, which had reached such an
advanced stage that all attempts to treat it were useless. All
that could still be done, in view of the pitilessly rapid progress
of the malady, was, as far as possible, to mitigate and alleviate
the evil, and leave the sick man in ignorance of his condition.
It was fruitless to argue whether it might have been possible to
diagnose the complaint earlier, and treat it with any prospect
of a cure, or at least of some alleviation; and whether the
ignorance and clumsiness of the doctors were to blame, or a
pitiless destiny which could not have been perceived earlier;
for now it was all too late. Tonio Puccini swallowed the
hideous certainty and kept it to himself; he had to conceal it
from everybody, and must not betray himself. His father had
to be lulled into security, his mother must not be allowed to
suspect anything, and even Donna Fosca Leonardi, Tonio's
sister, was not taken into his confidence till later. Moreover,
he kept wondering whether this fact, which it was almost beyond
his powers to realize, was really true, whether the doctor might
not, after all, have been mistaken, and whether there might
not still be some way of saving him. A consultation took place,
and once more hope revived. The upshot was that an operation was judged to be urgently necessary, but Professor Grade-
nigo recommended that it should take place at Brussels, in Dr.
Leroux's clinic, where a special radium treatment had been
successfully carried out for patients suffering from this particular ailment; for Dr. Leroux was a brilliant ornament of his

profession, and was said more than once to have cured cases that seemed desperate. Haste was, however, essential. Puccini himself was eager to start, and particularly so because the pain had become extremely violent, whether owing to the irritation set up by his repeated examinations, or as a result of the rapid progress made by his treacherous complaint. Donna Elvira was confined to her bed by bronchitis, so that she did not notice very much of what was going on in the house, and was left under the impression that what was in view was a cure undertaken as a precautionary measure, which would necessitate a few weeks' separation. When her husband said goodbye to her, she had no idea that it was to be for ever.

But Puccini, too, had no idea of this. In spite of the increasing pangs in his throat he felt as though he had a new lease of life, and was full of faith in his imminent recovery. Only in isolated hours of gloom did he begin to hesitate again, looking up at those who approached him with the deepest dejection. Apart from this he was quiet and composed. If he himself was under no misapprehension about his real condition, and was only deceiving those around him, the Master's attitude during these days was stoical and worthy of all admiration. He continued to avail himself of every free moment before his departure for his work, and made all arrangements in connexion with it. On the day before his departure he sent for Toscanini, showed him the completed portions of *Turandot*, and arranged with him everything pertaining to the rehearsal and production of the piece at the Scala, which were to take place as soon as possible. Toscanini was quite fired with enthusiasm for the work, and uncommonly impressed by the music, and promised to advance its cause by every means in his power. Puccini was overjoyed. He was not used to hearing the great conductor, who was usually reserved and distant, and from whom he had, moreover, been estranged recently by certain little misunderstandings, speak in such exalted terms of anything, and it almost seems as though he applied the enthusiastic verdict of his best interpreter to his future physical progress as well, as

though it were a promising sign of his recovery.   But as Toscanini left the Master, whose face was now beaming with
delight, Tonio Puccini drew him aside, for he did not wish to
bear the responsibility of setting in motion the whole vast
machinery of preliminary preparation, or starting the study of
the work, till he knew that it would be possible for it to be
finished.   He therefore told Toscanini the grim truth, which
filled him with consternation.

On 4th November they started for Brussels.   Tonio Puccini
travelled with his father, who was sick unto death, and they
were also joined by the faithful Carlo Clausetti.   The Master
bore a talisman with him in his bag, in the shape of thirty-six
pages containing the draft version of the finale of *Turandot*,
which had still to be orchestrated.   He was supported in all
times of depression by a feeling that he could not be summoned
hence before he had completed the work to which he had devoted
himself so whole-heartedly, and of whose success he was at last
convinced.   He was calm and cheerful as he stepped into the
train, for he felt that the sheets of manuscript made him proof
against all harm.   His travelling-companions had great difficulty in restraining their tears, but they assumed smiling faces
for fear of shaking his confidence and disturbing his quietly
sanguine mood.   Yet who knows?   Perhaps he too was playing
a part, which cost him as much as it did his son and his friend,
who sat beside him with lacerated feelings, and took care of
him without allowing him to notice that the attentions they
gave him were such as are required by one seriously ill.   But
suddenly a sense of hopeless gloom descended upon them all;
for violent bleeding started from his nose and mouth, and made
the whole of that long journey a misery to him, so that it seemed
endless.   He arrived in Brussels weary and apathetic.

It was neither anxiety nor physical pain that upset him to
this extent, but the very fact of being ill caused him moral
suffering as well.   He felt humiliated and unclean, and had a
sense of physical shame, as though his most intimate sensibilities
were outraged by his malady; and he was sensitive to it as

constituting a blemish.   Like so many thoroughly strong men, whose bodies have never given them any trouble before—like Johannes Brahms, for instance, with whom he had so little in common in other ways—he felt as though his malady had left a brand of shame upon him, which he tried to conceal by every possible means.   They went first to a hotel, and Puccini felt painfully embarrassed at the thought that the servants might find his blood-stained handkerchiefs, and draw conclusions with regard to his illness.   In order to set his mind at rest, Tonio washed the handkerchiefs in the bath, where they reminded him in the most heart-rending way of Mimi coughing blood in the last act of *La Bohème*, and now became symbolic in his eyes of another last act.

Father and son were next accommodated in two communicating rooms in the Institut de la Couronne, kept by Dr. Leroux, Clausetti remaining at the hotel.   Dr. Leroux subjected the Master to a thorough examination, lasting for an hour and a half, after which he examined under the microscope a piece of tissue taken from the lump in the sick man's larynx, and confirmed the Florentine doctor's diagnosis, the correctness of which could now no longer be doubted.   The alarming virulence with which the disease was gaining ground next prompted the doctor to try an experiment with the object of ascertaining whether it was still any use to have recourse to an operation; the local application of radium would show how far the swelling might react to this external action.   The effect produced was almost startling: the bleeding stopped, and during the next few days Puccini felt a sense of relief.   He was delighted at once more being allowed to light the cigarettes that were a necessity to him, and smoked with the zest of a schoolboy secretly enjoying cigarette-ends that he has picked up.   He went out, had his meals with Tonio and Clausetti at the hotel, and recovered his former appetite, while many evenings were spent at the cinema, for which he had always had a great taste, as German critics were never tired of pointing out.   He was in good spirits, and now felt a positive conviction that he would return to Viareggio and resume his work. Only at the Sanatorium did he still have moments of gloom, during which he would take his poor pages of manuscript out of his portfolio, gaze at them with a sigh, making the gesture of resignation with which, at those times when he felt a sense of his defencelessness, he signified his submission to fate.

When the radium cure had gone on for twelve days, an operation was decided upon, for it offered, if not a guarantee, at least a prospect of preserving this precious life for a few years longer, and of mitigating the Master's physical suffering; whereas without it a painful death was certain, and that before very long. Puccini had long since made up his mind to it. The family gave their consent, and on 24th November the surgeons set to work. On the night before the operation Puccini slept for ten hours, more softly and peacefully than he had done for months past. In the morning he was given an injection of morphia in order to minimize the pain and put him at least into a somnolent state. They could not venture upon complete anaesthesia, on account of his weak heart, but only upon a local anaesthetic, in so far as this was possible. He had to be bound, and for three hours and a half on end endured the torture inflicted upon him with heroic composure, experiencing in his own person the torture-scene from *Tosca*. He still summoned up enough energy, however, to rise from the stretcher and put himself to bed without assistance.

Tonio, with Clausetti and his sister Fosca, who had just arrived, spent what seemed an eternity in the corridor waiting for the operation to be over, and could with difficulty restrain a cry, for Puccini was as white as chalk, and his throat reminded them of St. Sebastian, with the seven radium needles inserted in it instead of arrows, while above the Adam's apple was a silver tube, through which his breath whistled as he drew it in and out. The next two days were a perfect martyrdom. He could take nothing to sustain his strength but liquid nourishment and champagne, administered through the nose. He was not allowed to speak, but had to write down all that he wanted.

On the very first sheet of paper was written a greeting to Donna Elvira, perhaps the last she ever received from him.

By the third day the miracle had been effected. He was stronger, the fever was abating, he could get up, walk about his room and read the papers, and declined all assistance. The doctor was delighted, and held out prospects of complete recovery. He could now hand over the syringe for administering nourishment to Tonio Puccini, and was no longer required himself; but the radium treatment had to be continued for another five or six days, after which they might perhaps think of returning home quite soon. Fosca and Tonio were radiant with joy, and telegraphed to their mother that she might now come to Brussels too, while Clausetti wrote a jubilant letter to Giuseppe Adami, that ran as follows: 'Things are going on in a way that exceeds all our hopes. They could not be better. The doctors now say without the least hesitation that Puccini will quite definitely be saved. You will understand that no doctor would speak in this way unless he were absolutely certain that he was not in error. Moreover, Dr. Leroux is by no means inclined towards optimism, being rather a severe and reserved person'. There had been no complications of any sort, the heart was in perfectly good order, the lungs and bronchial tubes were working absolutely normally, and the miracle was to be ascribed to the effects of radium. Had it not been for the splendid Brussels doctors, their famous, but suffering friend would have been left with no hope of recovery. Great was their jubilation.

But their joy was premature. On the evening of this day which had seemed so full of promise, the catastrophe occurred. The Master collapsed while sitting in his arm-chair. Dr. Leroux at once removed the radium needles in order to relieve the furious throbbing of his heart. But it was too late.

Carlo Clausetti described these last hours to me with as much emotion as though he had gone through them only a day before, instead of seven years. When he came to visit the sick man in the evening, the doctor drew him out of the room and told him that there was no hope, for heart failure had ensued. Nobody could have foreseen that the healing radium, which had given undoubted relief to the malady itself, would so suddenly have proved dangerous to the vital organ. The patient had spent a restless night. His consciousness of the inevitable could be read in his eyes. His breath came in gasps; he tossed incessantly on his bed, and lost patience when his anxious son refused to go to bed: while his hands were constantly moving, as though beating something. The end was at hand.

Early on the morning of 29th November Monsignor Micara, the papal nuncio, arrived at the Master's bedside, accompanied by the Italian ambassador, on the pretext of visiting the sick, and the priest pronounced the last benediction, after which the death-agony began.

Donna Fosca Leonardi has described to me how her father lay there quietly, with eyes that no longer noticed any material things, and a perfectly tranquil, peaceful expression. Once he raised his hand as though to salute his son and daughter, after which his fingers ran over the coverlet, as though they were playing chords and melodies, while his half-closed lips seemed to be humming an accompaniment. There can be no doubt that, even as his consciousness was ebbing away, he was thinking of *Turandot*, and that his music was still hovering round him when, after he had drawn two deep, peaceful breaths, his pale, handsome head fell on its side. Giacomo Puccini was no more.

His death was felt as a national disaster. The newspapers appeared with black edges, and for days on end were full of reminiscences of the Master, accounts of his life, and estimates of his work, in which even his opponents lowered their blades and muffled them in crape. His body was brought home. It was received at every station with solemn tokens of respect, and the greatest in the land followed the procession at his provisional funeral in Torre del Lago. It was as though one great wail of lamentation went up from the whole of Italy.

A few months later Giacomo Puccini really came home to the spot which had been dearest to him upon earth and where

THE MORTUARY CHAPEL

he had known happiness. Between the Master's study and his
bedroom is a space that was now arranged as a chapel. Adolfo
de Carolis, Antonio Maraini, and Professor Pilotti—painter,
architect, and sculptor—all worked together to carry out the
idea conceived by Puccini's bereaved son. Through a round-
topped stained-glass window the sunshine falls upon the floor,
inlaid with marble slabs, and on the fresh flowers arranged
round it. On the left-hand side is a broad ledge of greyish-
white marble, supported on a bracket, upon which the composer's name is carved in heavy lettering. Over it hangs an
enormous crucifix of gleaming white stone, and in the wall
behind it is a small arched recess in which stand the two coffins.
Here rests Giacomo Puccini, close to the little old piano from
which he charmed all his harmonies, and whose strings vibrated
with strains that spoke only of love. By his side, since the
summer of 1930, has lain Elvira, his life's companion, who
followed him to the grave at the age of seventy, six years after
his death.

But another mausoleum—a spiritual one—has been raised
in his honour by the filial piety of his son in the villa at Torre
del Lago, in the shape of a little museum and a collection of
archives, both of which are set out in Puccini's study, where
nothing has been altered since he left it. Everything is still
lying in the same place as it was then, and it is as though the
Master had only gone out of the room a moment or two ago,
leaving his cigarette-end lying on his writing-table. In the
glass cases are manuscripts and photographs, and among them
is still to be seen the letter written by Ponchielli to 'Mamma
Albina', telling her that Giacomo was his best pupil, and that
he simply must have another year's study—lines evidently
intended for the eye of the munificent great-uncle. The complete rough drafts of all Puccini's operas are preserved here,
together with bundles of newspaper cuttings, containing a whole
arsenal of malevolent stupidity, narrow conceit, and impudent
presumption, with but little kindness, good will, or friendly
sympathy. Besides all this there is another curious thing, in

the shape of rolls of films, upon which the Master has been photographed walking, gesticulating in conversation, or sitting gossiping with his friends, and gramophone records on which his voice is preserved. But Tonio Puccini cannot yet bring himself to open this little case. He could not bear to see his father living again in pictures only, or to hear his voice coming forth from the unseen world; and everybody will understand this and respect his feelings. But it is a strange reflection that in this little case a part of Giacomo Puccini's life is still preserved, and that in it he has been, as it were, immured for the second time.

I look back over his life and work, and am strangely moved by many things in them both. How can it have been that a man and artist who ought to have been the happiest of all men should have been consumed during his whole life with melancholy and a sense of inadequacy, both in his life and in his art? He won fame at an early age. In spite of all his critics and opponents, his rise was phenomenally rapid and unobstructed. While still quite a young composer he had the most splendid of publishers at his side, who guaranteed him security of existence from the very beginning, and afterwards showered boundless wealth upon his house. He had both wife and children, and loved them all; he was independent and spent his life exactly as he desired. What can have been the cause of the melancholy that made his life, and often that of those about him too, a hard one—a melancholy for which his spasmodic fits of gaiety and love of fun were no real compensation? In many ways his life was indeed a failure. Did he only play with his melancholy, too, or did he really feel it to be insuperable? Eighteen months before his death he wrote a poem which was found among his papers. We quote it here because it is almost inconceivable that its author should have been the same Giacomo Puccini who was the object of unbounded love and admiration, and who, apart from those little annoyances that every man has to endure, and especially those who lead a public life, really had no cause to bewail his fate.

Non ho un amico,
mi sento solo,
anche la musica
triste mi fa.
Quando la morte
verrà a trovarmi
sarò felice di riposarmi.
Oh com' è dura
la vita mia!
eppur a molti
sembro felice!
Ma i miei successi?
Passano . . . e resta
ben poca cosa.
Son cose effimere:
la vita corre,
va verso il baratro.
Chi vive giovane
se gode il mondo,
ma chi s'accorge
di tutto questo?
Passa veloce
la giovinezza
e l'occhio scruta
l'eternità.[1]

(I have not a friend, I feel myself to be alone. Even music
makes me sad. When death shall come to seek me, I shall be
happy to find rest. Ah, how hard is my life! And yet to
many I seem happy. But my successes? They pass, and what
remains is of little worth. They are ephemeral things. Life
hastens past and descends towards the abyss. He who lives
and is young enjoys the pleasure of the world. But who is
aware of all this? Youth passes swiftly by, and the eye scans
eternity with a questioning gaze.)

If life really appeared to him in this light, he was to be
pitied; for if this were so, then all that life lavished so richly
upon him—friendship, fame, and the love of beautiful women
—must have been valueless in his eyes, while even his art, if it
really caused him nothing but sadness, cannot have brought

[1] TRANSLATOR'S NOTE.—The full text of these verses is taken from Arnaldo
Fraccaroli, *Vita di Giacomo Puccini*, p. 223.

him release, a refuge within himself, and a palliative for all the sorrows of existence. But he certainly did not see it under this aspect—or at least, not always. Such verses as those quoted above, which he jotted down, ought not to be taken as a key to his nature. People of mobile character, such as he was, easily flying from one extreme to another, often perpetuate in words some hour of bitterness and solitude in a way that such a momentary mood hardly merits. Moreover, had he been able really to express himself in words, he would certainly have written his own operatic libretti too, and would not have had to endure incessant annoyance from his collaborators. No, he was a musician, and therefore expressed his true nature in his music only. His character was undoubtedly such as his music reveals him to us; and in this sincerity lies its secret, and at the same time its vitality. Perhaps it is really only the 'little things' that are able to enchant us. The great ones elevate, ravish, and metamorphose us, but it is the little ones in which we rejoice. The very fact that Puccini's eye does not 'scan eternity with a questioning gaze' but looks upon the blooming earth as well, that it is drawn towards all that is young, loving, ardently sensuous and athirst for life, is what has won such affection both for himself and for his music, in which men love him in another guise. In this wealth of human feeling that throbs in them, this confession of the intimate secrets of the heart, lie their magic spell and the warrant of their survival. And for this reason a long career still awaits them.

Or did Giacomo Puccini fail to answer the last riddle of Turandot, and was he therefore bound to depart from life before she had surrendered herself to him fully? Was he forced to remain the unknown prince from the realms of music, who was no longer able to force a real confession of love from her, so that he had to leave the supreme word unspoken?

But this is an idle question, to which the grave can make no reply.

INDEX

ADAMI, Giuseppe, 20, 208, 209, 211, 229, 237, 247
Aïda (Verdi), 29, 34, 37, 43
Alfano, Franco, 235, 236
Avanti ! 96

Battistini, Mattia, 84
Bayreuth, 94
Bazzini, Antonio, 38, 42
Belasco, David, 154, 175, 198, 200, 209
Bells, use of, 34, 87, 142, 148, 158, 232
Berlioz, Hector, 88
Bernard, Tristan, 228
Bernhardt, Sarah, 153, 154
Bersezio, Carlo, 150
Berta (critic), 123, 151
Bizet, Georges, 69
Bohème : see *La Bohème*
Bohème, Scènes de la Vie de (Murger), 49, 50, 129, 130
Bohème, Vita di (Leoncavallo), 131
Boito, Arrigo, 43, 67, 98
Bonturi, Elvira: see Puccini, Elvira
Boston, Mass., 195
Brass instruments, use of, 49, 82, 146, 161
Brescia, 73, 183
Bruneau, Alfred, 127
Brussels, 242, 244
Buenos Aires, 85, 193
Burgmein, 74
Butterfly : see *Madama Butterfly*

Campanini, Cleofonte, 183
Capriccio sinfonico, 48, 49, 50, 137
Carltheater, Vienna, 210
Carolis, Adolfo de, 249
Caruso, Enrico, 115, 150, 152, 193
Cavalleria Rusticana (Mascagni), 79, 80
Celesta, use of, 232, 235
Cerù, Dr., 46
Chicago, 195
Chinese music, 234
Chorus, use of, 60, 76, 84, 102, 103, 107, 141, 232, 235
Chromatic effects, 105, 165, 201
Church music, 34, 36, 83, 158, 218
Cilea, Francesco, 167
Civinini, Guelfo, 208
Clarinet, use of, 137, 147, 188

Clausetti, Carlo, 153, 171, 244, 245, 246, 247
Concerted numbers, 102, 141, 143
Consecutive fifths, use of, 51, 135, 138, 142, 165
Cornet, use of, 51, 142
Cremonini (tenor), 121
Cymbals, use of, 51, 232

D'Albert, Eugen, 3
Dance rhythms, use of, 59, 60, 61, 101, 104, 105, 141, 142, 144, 147, 202, 203, 216
D'Andrade, Francesco, 67
D'Annunzio, Gabriele, 19, 126, 175, 208
Darclée, Madame, 167
Daudet, Alphonse, 19, 126
Daudet, Léon, 212
Debussy, Claude, 14, 202, 239
De Marchi (tenor), 167
Depanis, Giuseppe, 123
Destinn, Emmy, 193
Dialogue, musical, treatment of, 45, 103, 104, 136, 140, 204
Die Meistersinger von Nürnberg (Wagner), 126
Drums, use of, 49, 163, 232

Edgar, 55, 56, 75-7, 82-5, 96, 116, 164, 178, 193
Elena, Queen, 227
Epistolario, 18, 38, 96, 145 n, 158, 164, 170, 175, 176, 183, 209, 229, 236, 238, 239
Exoticism, 81, 84, 184, 188, 189, 190, 198, 201, 202, 234

Faccio, Franco, 48
Farrar, Geraldine, 115
Ferrani, Madame, 150
Fife, use of, 142
Filippi, Filippo, 48
Flute, use of, 87, 137, 142, 147, 163, 188, 190, 233
Folk music, use of, 53, 184
Fontana, Ferdinando, 43, 55, 56, 57, 67, 73
Forzano, Giovacchino, 213
Fraccaroli, Arnaldo, 12 n, 31, 32, 33, 48, 69 n, 85 n, 112, 128 n, 241

253